THE BABIES ON OUR BLOCK.

SONG AND CHORUS.

Words by **ED. HARRIGAN**.

Music by **DAVE BRAHAM**.

1. If you want for in-for-ma-tion, Or in need of mer-ri-ment, Come o-ver with me
2. Of a warm day in the sum-mer, When the breeze blows off the sea, A hundred thousand
3. It's good-morn-ing to you, landlord; Come, now how are you to-day? When Patrick Mur-phy,

so-cial-ly To Murphy's ten-e-ment; He owns a row of hous-es In the
chil-der-en Lay on the Bat-ter-y; They come from Murphy's build-ing,—Oh, their
Es-qui-re, Comes down the al-ley way, With his shi-ny silk-en beav-er, He's as

9779—3

(continued on inside back)

Ned Harrigan

From Corlear's Hook to Herald Square

Ned Harrigan

From Corlear's Hook to Herald Square

Richard Moody

Nelson-Hall ⌷nh⌷ Chicago

Books by Richard Moody
America Takes the Stage
The Astor Place Riot
Edwin Forrest, First Star of the American Stage
Dramas from the American Theatre, 1762–1909
Lillian Hellman, Playwright
The Revels History of Drama in English,
    Volume 8, *American Drama*
    (with Walter J. Meserve and Travis Bogard)

Library of Congress Cataloging in Publication Data

Moody, Richard, 1911–
                From Corlear's Hook to Herald Square.

    Bibliography: p.
    Includes index.
    1. Harrigan, Edward, 1845–1911.   2. Dramatists,
American—19th century—Biography.
PS1799.H73Z76   812′.4 [B]   80–221
ISBN 0–88229–674–4 (cloth)
ISBN 0–88229–755–4 (paper)

Manufactured in the United States of America

10   9   8   7   6   5   4   3   2   1

**For
Nedda**

Contents

Acknowledgments

Pursuing the Harrigan story would have been exciting under any circumstances. It would not have been so pleasant without the generosity of Nedda Harrigan Logan. She shared her memories, spread out her collection of scrapbooks, pictures, letters, programs, and miscellaneous memorabilia, and gave me a room where I could work at my own speed and where I could rest my eyes studying the traffic on the East River.

A Senior Fellowship from the National Endowment for the Humanities and a sabbatical leave from Indiana University freed me to live in the libraries in New York, Washington, Boston, Cambridge, Chicago, San Francisco, and Berkeley.

Other members of the Harrigan family helped along the way: Ann Connolly (Nedda's daughter), having herself scoured the libraries for information about her grandfather, graciously settled many questions for me. Mrs. Donald Muller (Adelaide's daughter) wrote about her mother. Mrs. Stuart Sheddy (Philip's daughter) shared her father's reminiscences about his father. And Anthony H. Harrigan (Anthony's son) gave me access to the papers he had deposited with the University of Wyoming Library.

Old friends and relatives lent a hand with research and preparation of the manuscript: Paul Myers, Louis Rachow, Marvin Seiger, Pamela Powers, Carol Moody, Charles Railsback, and Andrew Apter. They know what they did, know now I thank them more than I've said.

A small army of librarians and library assistants helped uncover fresh Harrigan news in many unlikely places. Among the libraries, the New York Public must head the list. Most of the Harrigan holograph and typed play scripts are in the Manuscripts and Archives Division; and the Theatre Collection of the Library and Museum of the Performing Arts has a wealth of Harrigan scrapbooks, clippings, letters, and programs. Harrigan-related materials were also available in the Music Collection at Lincoln Center and in the Genealogy and Local History section on Forty-second Street. The story would have been less complete without several other New York libraries: those of the Museum of the City of New York, the Players Club, and the New York Historical Society.

For several weeks I thrived on the resources of the Library of Congress, the Boston Public Library, the Theatre Collection of the Harvard Library, the Bancroft Library at the University of California in Berkeley, the San Francisco Historical Society Library, and the Chicago libraries: Newberry, Chicago Public, Chicago Historical Society, and the University of Chicago. And as usual I have depended on the Indiana University Library and particularly on the Lilly Rare Book Library, which has collected some 150 pieces of Harrigan-Braham sheet music through the enterprise of the late David Randall and the generosity of Mrs. Bernardo Mendel.

Other institutions responded quickly to my requests: the California State Library, the Syracuse Public Library, the Humanities and Research Center at the University of Texas, and the University of Wyoming Library.

1
Ned Harrigan Club

One bright Sunday morning in September 1914, the Patten Line's *Little Silver* steamed down the bay from the tip of Manhattan to the mouth of the Shrewsbury River for a Ned Harrigan Club clambake at Pleasure Bay, New Jersey. The picnic committee had clotheslined the deck with patches of green, anything that could pass for an Irish flag, and as usual Capt. Joe Humphreys was in command, ably assisted by Charlie White, the old-time prizefight referee. Both men had learned navigation in the boxing ring.[1]

Assemblyman Al Smith (later governor) had been the first club member aboard at the East Twenty-Fourth Street pier, followed by Assemblyman James J. Walker (later mayor), John Hanley, director of the Tombs, and Harry Bell, sergeant-at-arms of the United States Senate. With the faithful from that part of town securely on deck, Captain Humphreys had eased the excursion steamer into the East River and, after rounding Corlear's Hook, slipped into the Battery to take on the remaining passengers. The crew then broke out the breakfast beer, and, as the *Little Silver* plowed into open water, two hundred fifty lusty voices supported by Braham's band sang "Paddy Duffy's Cart." According to one reporter, the genial first deputy of the Tenement House Department led the chorus "with éclat—if a French word is permissible at an Irish racket." It was a grand and glorious day, and, when they sailed home by moonlight (the voices then well lubricated), the Harrigan repertoire had not been exhausted. The lyrics of the songs were by Harrigan, the music by Harrigan's father-in-law, David Braham.

Al Smith, the most illustrious Harriganite, served the club as commodore for three years. From childhood Smith knew the same Lower East Side that Harrigan had put on the stage, and like Harrigan he had raced with the firefighters. He loved the theatre, loved singing (even if his hoarse tenor sometimes distorted the tune), and, having memorized most of the Harrigan songs, he was singularly well qualified to be commodore. One friend recalled a train ride when the governor concertized with a Harrigan program all the way from New York to Albany.[2]

When Smith went to the San Francisco Democratic convention in 1920, he instructed his campaign managers that he wanted "Maggie Murphy's Home" as his theme song. They dutifully supplied the band with a stack of Harrigan-Braham tunes. But by some political misfortune, another piece of music had infiltrated the stands, and when Bourke Cockran announced to the convention, "We brought him here to you from the sidewalks of New York, and we offer him to you for the nomination of the presidency of the United States, and if you reject him, we will take him back and elect him governor again," the bandmaster, quickly riffling through his selections, spotted "The Sidewalks of New York."[3] Al Smith never escaped "Sidewalks of New York," but when he was called on for a song at the fiftieth anniversary of the opening of the Brooklyn Bridge in 1933, he sang Harrigan's "Danny by My Side."

When the Harrigan Club was organized in 1910 by the prize-fight referee Joe Humphreys, Harrigan was invited to the inaugural clambake, but he was too ill to attend. On his next birthday, October 26, 1911, four months after his death, some four hundred old New York boys met for beefsteak, beer, and dhudeens (clay pipes) at the Teutonia Rooms on Third Avenue. Every guest sported a "Kelly" top hat and a beefsteak apron emblazoned with a picture of Harrigan's favorite character, Dan Mulligan. They roared through the Harrigan-Braham songs with the help of a German band, pausing only for short toasts to their hero. Victor Moore raised a glass to his old dad, who had dismissed every new

comedian with the same line: "He ain't as funny as Harrigan was."
Just before midnight, President Humphreys concluded the festivities with "the grandest announcement of his clarion-voiced career: 'His memory shan't die! Shall it?' He got his answer in quick order. The green-hatted house rose at him with a gladdening roar: 'Not on your life! No! No!' "

For the next ten years the club honored Harrigan's memory at least once a year at the Teutonia, at the Amsterdam Opera House on Ninth Avenue, or at Eagleton's Cafe in Greenwich Village, and with an occasional clambake on the beach. The celebrations were never solemn; they were raucous songfests, the kind of spirited evenings Harrigan would have enjoyed. Volume was accepted as a tolerable substitute for vocal skill as long as one knew the words —and everyone did. One reporter noted that the "chromos on Eagleton's walls quaked as three hundred voices whooped up 'Get Up, Jack, John, Sit Down.' " There was little speech making. The serious tributes were reserved for the souvenir program: "What more natural than that the old-time friends of that departed genius should wish to perpetuate in their own hearts the memory of this 'man among men.' " "Good nature wrapped him around like a garment of light. Sympathy shone from his eyes with gentle purity."[4]

There were others, not members of the club, who helped keep the Harrigan name alive: John J. Nolan's Double Concert Band regularly featured "Harrigan Nights" at the Bayside Casino at Sheepshead Bay. For the St. Patrick's Day celebrations at the Hippodrome, John Philip Sousa invariably drew on the Harrigan-Braham songbook. In July 1927, William Harrigan (his son) headlined the vaudeville bill at the Palace in a twenty-minute sketch "Memories of Harrigan and Hart" and according to *Variety* "scored with a zoop."[5]

And, of course, anyone who has sung with a barbershop quartette or a college glee club, or just kept his ears open, knows George M. Cohan's—

> H A double R I
> G A N spells Harrigan,
> Proud of all the Irish blood that's in me;
> Divil a man can say a word agin me.

> H A double R I,
> G A N you see,
> It's a name that a shame never has been connected with
> Har-ri-gan, that's me![6]

First sung in Cohan's *Fifty Miles from Boston* at the Garrick Theatre (formerly Harrigan's Theatre) in 1908, repeated in the Warners' motion picture *Yankee Doodle Dandy,* in the Broadway musical *George M.,* the song has never been forgotten.[7]

In the early forties, when Dorothy Parker and Nedda Harrigan (Harrigan's daughter) visited their husbands, Alan Campbell and Joshua Logan, on duty with the Air Force in Miami, they were greeted by a marching chorus charging toward them across the parade ground, singing "Harrigan." The cue was not lost on Dorothy Parker. She turned to Nedda and asked, "How did they know you were coming?"[8]

Harrigan's own songs have probably been sung as frequently as Cohan's "Harrigan"—two dozen were carried in the Victor record catalog until the mid-thirties[9]—though the quartettes, glee clubs, street singers, organ grinders, and parlor vocalists who rendered "The Babies on Our Block," "I Never Drink behind the Bar," or "My Dad's Dinner Pail" could not have named composer and lyricist. And one song, "The Mulligan Guard," outdistanced all the others in popularity. It was heard around the world, rendered by parading military bands on the Champs Elysées, in front of Buckingham Palace, and even on the plains of India. In Kipling's *Kim* (1901), Little Kim and the Old Lama hide behind a tree to listen to the regimental band and the marching soldiers singing "From Phoenix Park, We Marched to Dublin Bay." The original, "From Baxter (or Jackson) Street, We Marched to Avenue A" was easily altered.

In New York and across the land, and for some unknown reason particularly in the South, marching, even if a cappella, demanded "The Mulligan Guard."[10] It became the favorite of circus bands for their morning parades; of newsboys; of street merchants hawking peanuts, oysters, or ice cream; of children who learned the juvenile version from "The Ten Little Mulligan Guards"; for anyone called on "to oblige" at an impromptu entertainment and who was afraid to go it alone. Harrigan often said that if Braham's tune had been put to appropriate words it would have become one of our national airs, and a year before his death he estimated that it had been sung, hummed, or whistled by ten million people.[11] More millions have now been added.

In his own time, the last quarter of the nineteenth century, most everyone could render his latest hit songs, as most everyone knew that Harrigan and Hart was the funniest team on Broadway, that for an uproarious evening in the theatre nothing could match Harrigan's catastrophic "melees" and "general melees."

In *The Major,* for example, when Major Gilfeather tossed his cigar into Percival Pop's Fireworks Factory, the explosion sent the characters through the roof, and when they returned "you couldn't tell if you were burying a relative or a friend." And in *The Mulligan Guard Ball,* the Negro Skidmore Guard and its high-stepping partners crashed through the second floor of the Harp and Shamrock ballroom, "dropping in chunks" and smothering the Mulligans and their ladies who were dancing in the room below.[12]

Harrigan's plays were not, however, all horseplay, "knockdown and slambang," as his serious critics noted. In July 1886, William Dean Howells writing in *Harper's* alerted the literary world to Edward Harrigan, comparing him with Goldoni, Molière, and Shakespeare. Here was "the spring of a true American comedy, the joyous art of the true dramatist who loves the life he observes."[13] No playwright had ever explored New York's low life so lovingly, with such striking portraits of the Germans, the Italians, the Negroes, and particularly the Irish who inhabited Gotham's Lower East Side. Howells was not the only critic to class Harrigan with the notables. Others discovered resemblances to Zola, to Balzac; one declared that Harrigan's authentic views of the back alleys around Five Points were the work of an American Hogarth; and the *New York Herald* proclaimed his Mulligan plays "the Pickwick Papers of a Bowery Dickens."[14]

2

Running with "Old Tiger" on Corlear's Hook

So much of the "ould dart" clung to Harrigan's stage portraits that his followers were convinced that Harrigan had caught the first light of day in the land of St. Patrick, that New York's Little Ireland was his adopted home. Even later when the facts were known, when Harrigan's private life became public property, many Irishmen stuck to the myth.

Edward Harrigan saw Ireland only once, late in life. He was born in New York on October 26, 1844, at 34 Scammel Street, a byway that ran north and south between the waterfront and the intersection of Grand and East Broadway. The street no longer exists. Its roadway has been usurped by the playground of the Henrietta Szold School, P. S. Number 34.

From the windows of her East Side apartment, Nedda Harrigan Logan can look down the river to the spot where her father lived his early years, where the East River tugs, busy with their endless errands, swing around the easternmost border of Manhattan, where Corlear's Hook juts out into the river and the Williamsburg Bridge stretches to Brooklyn. From that high vantage point it is even possible to trace Harrigan's short journey inland to his first theatrical home on Lower Broadway. He never moved far from his birthplace.

His father William was equally ignorant of Ireland at first hand. He was born at Carbonear, Newfoundland, in 1799. The Harrigans' direct link with the homeland went back to William's father, who worked as a fisherman out of Cork until late in the eighteenth century, when he answered the call to Canada. That link, distant as it was, held Edward and his father bound to Ireland. Irish blood never loses its potency; sometimes it seems to run thicker on foreign soil. The tie to Newfoundland was never maintained, though when Edward had a home and family of his own he employed two shaggy Labrador retrievers to protect the children.[1]

Edward's father did not abandon the sea even when he rejected fishing as his way of life. He shipped out of Carbonear as a cabin boy on a Yankee clipper under the command of a New England Protestant who released him from his family bonds as well as from the church. He never returned to either and later fortified his break with Catholicism by joining and then becoming master of the Henry Clay Masonic Lodge. His son followed his religious lead, though with less vigor. Edward accepted the church as proper for weddings, christenings, and burials, and convent schools as suitable for the education of his daughters. His daughter Adelaide once raised the eyebrows of her nuns and brought tears to one when she presented an essay on the infidel Robert Ingersoll, one of her father's friends and heroes. She did not improve her standing when she tried to explain her father's skepticism of formal religions. He could not settle on one God when so many people of the world—Chinese, Hindus, American Indians, and Africans— worshiped different gods. Offering casual spiritual guidance was as close as Harrigan came to religion. He wrote to his son Ned in 1882, "Every night before you go to bed say 'God Bless Papa and Mama,' and when *The Blackbird* is played on the stage you can come and see the soldiers."[2]

William remained at sea during his early years, working up the nautical ladder until he became first mate on a square-rigger on the New York-to-Liverpool run. His vessel occasionally put in at Norfolk, and here, sometime in the early thirties, he met Ellen Ann Rogers, the young girl who was to become his wife.

Ellen was born in Charlestown, Massachusetts, in 1814, the daughter of Matthias Rogers. Rogers had died before she was born, of injuries received as a gunner on the *Chesapeake* when his commanding officer, James Lawrence, shouted, "Don't give up the ship" and the vessel was captured by the *Shannon,* which took it to Halifax. Shortly after his death and Ellen's birth, Mrs. Rogers moved to Norfolk, investing the federal pension she received as the widow of a navy man in a boardinghouse, where she specialized in Boston baked beans, clam chowder, and boiled dinners. William Harrigan may have first been attracted by the food in Mrs. Rogers's haven for New England sailors. He was soon more attracted by her pretty and gay seventeen-year-old daughter. And in the mid-thirties when Mrs. Rogers died, William persuaded Ellen to give up the boardinghouse, come to New York, and marry him, promising to give up the sea and find work on the waterfront.

William became a caulker, and they lived first at 8 Gouverneur Street where William, Jr., their eldest surviving child, was born in 1841. Two years later they moved a block east to 34 Scammel, and in 1845, a year after Edward's arrival, William withdrew his nest egg from the Little Bowery Savings Bank and invested in a home of their own, a two-story red-brick house across the street at 31 Scammel. (In many accounts of Harrigan's early days this address was mistakenly given as Edward's birthplace.) Although William was no more than a common caulker, he was a thrifty caulker who prided himself on his house. It was on the same row with those of captains and shipbuilders. His pride may have been damaged when he discovered his name was less respected than his neighbors'. In the early city directories he was invariably called "Harigan," and the 1850 census listed him as "Harrington." That he loved his wife and his home is clear from the record of progeny, thirteen children, only four of whom survived infancy. One of Edward's earliest memories was of the crepe that regularly decorated their front door.

William gave his children a strong start. He named his eldest son after himself, his second Edward Green in honor of the best sea captain he had served, Mary for her Biblical namesake, and Martha for Martha Washington. For the progeny of a naturalized citizen, an eager patriot, and a resident of Corlear's Hook, the names were singularly appropriate.

George Washington had been inaugurated as the first president just a few blocks inland at the residence of Walter Franklin, 1 Cherry Street, and the house had become known as America's first

White House. The Hook boasted of other notables. Col. Henry Rutgers, the founder of Rutgers College, had entertained Washington in his mansion there. Henry S. Brooks, one of the Brooks brothers who founded the clothing emporium, lived there in the early nineteenth century, and Robert Fulton built his first steamboat at the foot of Pike Street.

The name Corlear's Hook dates from 1638, when the Dutch West India Company granted Jacobus van Curler, councillor of New Netherlands, seventy-six acres bordering the river for a tobacco plantation. By the end of the eighteenth century, the area had shifted from farming to shipbuilding,[3] and on Sundays the waterfront was reserved for the Baptists' "practice of their rite of immersion."[4] A few blocks back from the river, remnants of rural life still existed. In 1824 the inhabitants of the Seventh Ward petitioned the Common Council "that the law regarding swine be so amended that they may run at large. The bell carts do not often come into that section, which makes it necessary that the swine should eat the garbage thrown into the streets."[5] The petition was granted.

When Edward Harrigan was discovering his boyhood world around Corlear's Hook, then more familiarly known as Cork Row, he was surrounded by a forest of masts. In the drydocks he could see the old broad-beamed monsters, whose rotting planks were gaping for oakum to give them a few more years, resting alongside the fresh keels of the new speed demons that would cut the trip to San Francisco to seventy-six days. Nestling against the wharfs, their bowsprits reaching for the dormer windows of the old sheds, were the packets from Liverpool and Hamburg and the tea ships from China and California. In the public slips he could observe the ferries preparing for their missions down the bay or over to Brooklyn. And across the river he could spy the warships waiting their turn at the Brooklyn Navy Yard.

In the fifties and sixties it was an exciting place for a youngster. By the end of the seventies, when Harrigan brought out *The Mulligan Guard Ball,* most of the shipyards had closed down and Corlear's Hook had become one of the most lawless sections of the city, its tenements crowded with gangs of thieves.

Law and some order prevailed in Edward's early years, though even then Cork Row was known as the toughest portion of the toughest ward in the city. The residents prided themselves on their reputation, and Edward and his young friends fearlessly roamed the streets and docks in search of adventure. He later recalled that he knew every pier and bulkhead around the Hook, every spot where it was safe to swim. Like all able-bodied men and boys he discovered the excitement of fire fighting. He even asserted his independence by carrying water buckets for Engine Number 6 instead of for Number 19, the Lafayette, where his father was foreman. Edward's Americus, or "Old Tiger," operated out of its house on Henry near Gouverneur and was commanded by William Marcy Tweed. Few youngsters were unaffiliated with some company, and when a boy ventured out of his home territory, a stranger did not inquire where he lived, he asked what hose he ran with.[6]

Edward did not spend all his time covering the waterfront and racing with the engines. Until he was fourteen his days were occupied by P.S. Number 31 on Monroe Street and after-school hours with miscellaneous errand-boy duties. When he abandoned formal education, he worked briefly as a printer's devil until his father got him on as an apprentice caulker. His father made stern demands on his time, never subscribing to the nonsensical notion that all work might make a dull boy. Fortunately his mother held different views.

Ellen Harrigan loved to dance and sing and had the talent to support her inclination. Even if she'd been no deeper South than Norfolk, her head was filled with Southern songs. In the evenings she would assemble the children at the square Sohmer piano in the parlor, and when the tune was fixed led them in a minstrel walk-around. "It was from her," Harrigan said later, "that I learned most of my Negro business and old songs. She had a capital dialect and could dance and sing 'Jim Crow' as well as I ever saw it done."[7] When he recalled her rich voice, her gay smile, and her easy natural swing as she danced, he often told his children that her talent should have been seen on the stage. And when his daughter Adelaide begged him to describe how his mother looked, he told her to part her hair in the middle, pull it back softly over her ears, tuck the curls up in back, brighten her smile, and look in the mirror: "You'll see your grandmother."[8]

Adelaide treasured other memory pieces from her father's child-hood. In the attic she had found old Kemmeier's Fine Shoes boxes filled with souvenirs of her grandfather's Masonic celebrations, of his outings at Fire Island, a tintype of her father in knee-length bathing trunks topped with a modest Sing Sing-like shirt and his mother in ankle-length flannel pants. On the piano, beside Edwin Booth as Cardinal Richelieu, there was a picture of grandfather William. The snowy halo of hair framed a strongly modeled head, a rigid chin, and a stern, firm face; the bare touch of a smile showed none of the easy warmth she knew in her father. Someone once said, add whiskers and Grandfather Harrigan could pass for Dr. Greeley. It was not a face to look kindly on singing, dancing, and strumming the banjo.

Edward's father advocated the hard-work ethic; he saw too many of his fellow Irishmen submit to their good natures and slide from frivolity to dissipation and to ultimate ruin. Even a youngster should not risk a step on the wrong path. Years later, as if following his father's example, Edward became possessed with a compulsion to work. He was always at his desk while his fellow actors were at play, though hard work never erased his inviting smile. He never duplicated his father's sternness and rigidity. "Lovable" and "genial" became the favored adjectives to describe Ned Harrigan.

In his early teens his nature found its comfort and support in his mother. He was delighted when she ignored her husband's grumbling, insisting that, if William commanded the day, she would preside in the evenings. She taught him to play the banjo and was always eager to listen and rehearse whenever he, or one of the other children, worked up a new routine. She was delighted when Ned and Mary invented a brother-and-sister act—*Little Church in the Greenwood* and *Belle of the Mohawk*—for the school Christmas program and when Ned produced a one-man show in the Harrigan cellar. She praised his first feeble compositions; only one trifle, a prophetic forecast, has survived:

> Win I am a man
> I don't give a damn
> But I will be an actor.[9]

She covered for him when he sneaked over to lower Broadway, just a few blocks from home, to Bryant's or Christy and Wood's Minstrels, to the Ravels' acrobatics or John Brougham in his burlesque *Po-ca-hon-tas* at Niblo's Garden, to the Bowery Theatre for Sam Ryan's Irish farces and S. W. Glenn's Dutch sketches or F. S. Chanfrau's revivals of *A Glance at New York* and *Mose in California.* Chanfrau's volunteer fireman Mose, dressed in a flaming red shirt and plug hat, always itching to fight a "b'hoy" or a fire, could have served as a model for Dan Mulligan, and the "Mose" series—*Mose in a Muss, Mose in China,* and *Mose's Visit to Philadelphia*—a forerunner of Harrigan's Mulligan plays.

Only once did he invade the other side of the footlights. Sometime around 1860 he savored one night of theatrical glory, when the amateurs were invited to Hitchcock's Old Concert Hall at 172 Canal Street, a stone's throw from where he would make his professional debut a dozen years later. Ned's stump speech in Negro dialect, "Newtown Creek," buried in the four hours of minstrel entertainment that Hitchcock offered for a dime, has not survived and apparently was not used again.[10]

Except for one brief interlude, Ned's boyhood was confined to the Seventh Ward waterfront. One day in the late fifties, his father was struck with an urge to change his way of life, to escape the water that always surrounded him. Or perhaps it was something in the Harrigan blood that challenged him to find a piece of land to call his own. That compulsion to own land was to run strong in Ned in later years. Whatever the reason, one day his father scouted New Jersey and announced that he had bought nine acres at Mead's Basin, between Newark and Paterson.

Ned often recited the adventure. He was put in charge of his grandmother and a wagonload of household goods, his father and mother having gone ahead. His grandmother was from County Cork, "as simple and severe as anybody that ever came over from the 'Ould Dart,' God rest her soul. She would sit straight up in her chair, with her prim white cap on, for hours at a time knitting and many is the time when she would forget her strength and welt me with her open hand in a way that would make me see stars. I suppose I deserved it all."[11]

As they were bouncing across the Jersey flats and easing out of the Newark marshes, his grandmother, who was nestled on a pile of bedding in the rear of the wagon, suddenly exclaimed, "Shtop the hourse!" Then, fumbling at her blouse, she pulled out a small bag. "Do yez see this, Ned Harrigan? Well, I have fifty dollars here, and I'll niver ask yure father to bury me. Drive an!" "There was a queer mixture of pathos and humor about this little affair that I have never forgotten," said Harrigan later.[12]

After a day or two on foreign soil—too much soil—William's rural fever subsided. Three weeks later they loaded up for the return trip to Corlear's Hook and the simpler life of caulking.

If any single event impelled Ned to desert the Seventh Ward, the only piece of the world he knew, it is now too deeply buried to be retrieved. In all likelihood a mixture of circumstances drove him away. If he needed reasons, he had plenty. His happiness at home had been centered on his mother. He rebelled at his father's steely commands. Now, in the early sixties, his parents were divorced—the official record of grounds for the dissolution have not been preserved—and his father hastily substituted a stepmother, a zealous Methodist, who pulled the reins even tighter.[13] The new Mrs. Harrigan, a widow in her middle years with two grown sons who had already broken away, reorganized the household, conceived a new Harrigan brood, two daughters and one son, and persuaded her husband to fix his attention on them and forget the others. Edward must have been thinking of her in one of his earliest songs, "A Good Fellow," when he wrote:

> Mother's sick; oh, that's tough
> And you are her only kid
> Don't use the old woman rough
> Might get a stepmother instead.[14]

His brother William might have made the domestic scene tolerable. He was three years older, an easygoing adventurer who was said to possess a roving eye that always discovered a pretty girl if one was nearby. Unfortunately, on March 3, 1863, William's name appeared on the "U. S. Provost Marshall's List of Persons Enrolled in the 7th Ward in accord with the act enrolling and calling out the national forces."[15] He joined Maj. Gen. Abram

Duryee's Zouaves (the Fifth New York Volunteers, an outfit that derived its name from its balloon breeches and short jackets, copied from the Algerian infantry in the French Army). Early in the war, William was captured and held at Andersonville, contracted malaria, and came home a walking shadow of the handsome young man who had marched down Broadway.[16]

Through some fortunate oversight Edward was not asked to join his brother—an oversight he accepted without protest. Fighting for fun he enjoyed; fighting in earnest offered dubious rewards. Still, he felt the urge to break with Cork Row. Every day as he plastered oakum into rotting planks, driven to speed up by captains who wanted their vessels in the water yesterday, he pictured the worlds beyond Corlear's Hook, where the ships were bound. Some vague yearning for distant ports may have circled in his blood, implanted by his father and grandfather.

One day a novice assigned to work with him became so energetic that the plank broke, and they were pitched into the East River. By the time they scrambled to shore and got back to work, they had lost a half day's pay. When Ned returned home, his father did not rejoice at his safety; he chastised him for cheating himself out of a full day's work.[17] Ned ran away that night, took a room in a sailor's boardinghouse on South Street, the next day bought himself a suit of clothes, exchanged his banjo for a newer one, and signed as a deckhand on a banana boat bound for New Orleans and points south. In New Orleans he fell in with an itinerant lot of "boiler makers" and traveled with them to Pensacola, to Mobile, and back to New Orleans, absorbing everything that he saw and heard, enjoying the new dialects and snatches of local humor and storing them in his memory. Harrigan always kept a sharp eye on the life around him.

Along the way he must have acquired considerable skill with boilers, a skill in great demand in the port cities, for he had stashed away $200 when he decided to return to New York. Money, of course, was not to be wasted on such frivolities as transportation. He registered as a steward aboard the clipper *Fearnaught* and apparently became so proud of his new occupation that he listed himself as "steward" in the New York city directory.

Back on the Lower East Side he did not rejoin his family; he took a room in a maritime boardinghouse at 36 Oak Street, just south of Chatham Square. He was shocked at the changes in the Seventh Ward. (Youthful eyes invariably detect radical changes in their native scenes, even after short absences.) Before his departure, he and two dozen of his cronies, "Gentlemen's Sons of Cork Row" as they called themselves, had sent out elaborately decorated Happy New Year cards on January 1, 1864.[18] Now these comrades had disappeared, were married and settled down, or "were rusticating at the expense of the State at Auburn."[19] His old world seemed impossible to retrieve, and his first taste of adventure had whetted his appetite for more.

He loafed around the ward for a few months, depleting his fortune, and then, sometime in early 1867, "cut sticks for the other side of the continent, landing in San Francisco friendless and without a cent." He never regretted his restlessness: "I look back upon those early rough and tumble adversities with a great deal of pleasure. They were the making of me."[20] He was not then, or was he ever, dependent on others. He drove ahead on his own, trusting his own talents and industry. When he made his mark, he wanted no creditors buzzing around to claim a share of his success.

3

San Francisco: Bella Union and Portsmouth Plaza

After a brief sojourn in New Orleans and a battle with malaria in Central America, Harrigan crossed Panama and boarded a freighter for San Francisco.[1] It edged up the coast and finally cut between the rugged rocky sentries that still guard the Golden Gate, where his eyes followed the long shoreline of the bay. The dreamy talk he had heard from the sailors at Corlear's Hook faded into shadow as he struggled to absorb the reality. Even now the sense-shattering seascape and landscape remain much as he saw them.

On shore Harrigan discovered a city permeated with an adolescent fervor that matched his own. (They were practically the same age.) He found a boardinghouse near the water below Mission Street in the area then known as the "Valley," and later as "Tar Flats,"[2] and just as quickly discovered that there was plenty of work for a caulker. He rammed oakum into the seams of decaying ferryboats and potato scows all along the waterfront up to Rincon Point and beyond, and sometimes took the Napa boat up to San Pablo Bay, to Mare Island and Vallejo.[3]

Serious thoughts of trying the theatrical line did not cross his mind, even when he kept his banjo busy in off hours. He recalled that some fellows formed a sort of club and hired a room in which to pass the evenings and "I began to string verses together and sing them to popular airs of the day." When he occasionally remained overnight in Vallejo, he tested his songs at the Cave of Harmony

17

saloon, and the spirited response, even if not all stimulated by him, encouraged him to seek a wider audience.[4]

Harrigan could not have missed the dozen or more entertainment halls clustered around Portsmouth Square; for its size and age San Francisco appeared to surpass New York in theatrical diversions. Not only were there high-class legitimate theatres—Maguire's Opera House, the Metropolitan, and the American featuring the latest Broadway stars and plays—the streets were dotted with melodeons.[5] These variety halls—Gilbert's, Butler's, What Cheer, New Mammouth, Bella Union, et al.—were attached to saloons and gambling parlors. The euphemism was well understood. Melodeon meant stag audiences. The females one encountered were employed by the establishment, and some of them were available for after-hours entertainment. A typical advertisement read: "Vocal and instrumental concerts, the latest songs, also choicest wines, liquors and cigars served by twelve beautiful young ladies. Go spend a few happy hours at Harmony Hall."[6] There were other diversions: Mrs. M. Field, the well-known orator, speaking on the Chinese question at Dashaway Hall; Bierstadt's painting, *Crossing the Plains,* in a viewing room on Montgomery Street; and also on Montgomery, near California, "Open daily, for gentlemen only, The Gallery of Natural History and Museum of Anatomy!"[7]

In 1867, with the melodeons competing for novelties and new talent, Harrigan was tempted to substitute burnt cork and grease paint for oakum. His caulking crew had urged him to take a stab at the stage, and one noon after his alfresco lunchtime turn, one of the boys shouted, "See here, Ned, you are a damned fool to work around here so hard, when you can get twenty dollars a week down in the minstrels." He took the advice in the fall, when the caulkers went on strike, and called on John Woodard, the stage manager of the Olympic.

Originally opened in 1859 as Gilbert's Melodeon on the northeast corner of Kearny and Clay, across from Portsmouth Plaza, the Olympic had become one of the most popular melodeons. (Now the Amparo Hotel and a porno book nook have taken over the location.) Harrigan had not expected good luck to strike so quickly. He was engaged, and in mid-October the ads in the *Daily*

Dramatic Chronicle carried a teasing announcement: "The indefatigable managers will shortly bring out two new performers."[8] And at the bottom of the Olympic program for Friday, October 18, 1867: "Monday—First Appearance of the Irish Comic Singer —Ed. Harrigan."[9] The astute managers did not reveal that they were testing a novice.

For an unknown, eight days shy of his twenty-third birthday, those bold letters must have seemed six feet high, more awe-inspiring than when "Harrigan and Hart" commanded the program at the Theatre Comique on Broadway six years later or when "HARRIGAN" was carved on the facade of his own New York theatre in 1890. Nor was his ego deflated when the *Daily Morning Call*'s Sunday announcement pushed him into second place: "Master O'Brien has arrived and tomorrow evening will appear in his great song and dance, 'Dancing Mad.' Also—Ned Harrigan, the Irish comic singer in a choice selection of the most popular of Erin's National Airs."[10]

Years later Harrigan recalled that opening night, October 21, 1867: "All the boys I knew came with their friends and handed me bouquets of oakum across the footlights. It was all done in a spirit of friendship and the hit that I made was so pronounced that I kept right on in the business."[11] Harrigan's memory is correct. Contrary to the often repeated reports that he was taken off after the first night, or after the third in another version, he remained on the Olympic bills nightly until the end of the year. After the first week, the *Dramatic Chronicle* reported that "the new clog dancer, Master O'Brien, and the Irish comic singer,[12] Ed. Harrigan, have proved themselves amply worthy of the public favor and the houses have been overflowing throughout the week."[13]

With the success of his comic songs he was soon given a second spot on the program, to sentimentalize over mothers and sweethearts in such teary numbers as "Mother Would Comfort Me," "Rock Me to Sleep Mother," and "Swing in the Lane." And as his place in the "Great Olympic Troupe" became secure, his duties expanded. He spoke a piece called "Bessie Bowman's Lecture," and he acted in the extravaganzas: *The Magic Shirt, Born to Luck,* and *Ireland and America,* a sketch that introduced him to what was to become his favored subject.

When the Olympic closed in January, Harrigan did not return to the waterfront. The theatrical bug had bitten too deep. He joined Master Alex O'Brien, John Woodard, and Otto Burbank, "the old war hoss," and answered the call of Piper's Opera House in Virginia City, Nevada. Piper's solicitations for talent appeared regularly in the San Francisco newspapers. Built by Tom Maguire in 1863, recently taken over by John Piper, a German saloon keeper, the Opera House—where "the trouble begins at eight o'clock precisely"[14]—provided the Virginia City miners a full range of theatricals: Lawrence Barrett and John McCullough in their famous roles, Ole Bull playing his fiddle, and Adelina Patti singing.[15] Harrigan and friends could manage only a few odd nights, when the stage was unoccupied by the stars.

As he later recalled the Nevada days, his memories did not focus on Piper's. He remembered the night he saw a miner lose his entire fortune at cards, including a diamond stickpin. The man went to the bar, tossed down two whiskeys, and marched out as proud as if he'd won a fortune. Harrigan said it was the grandest stage exit he had ever seen. Another night, when their luck ran out, he and O'Brien walked through a gambling house trying to sell his banjo. They were unable to penetrate the heavy concentration until one man dealing a hand of stud broke rhythm long enough to ask why the banjo was for sale. Ned told him they needed food. Without turning his head, and continuing with his deal, the man reached into his pile of twenty-dollar gold pieces, put two in Ned's hand, and told him to keep the banjo. Outside, they divided their winnings; O'Brien headed for a saloon and Harrigan for the hotel.[16] In future years Harrigan continued to sidestep the actor's beaten path from stage door to bar, not because he disapproved of liquor and friendly relaxation but most often because he had a song to finish or a sketch to work out. Unlike most of his fellow actors, Harrigan did have his eye on tomorrow.

Back in San Francisco late in the spring of 1868, he took a room on Washington Street where he could look down on the plaza and be near the theatres. Proximity was not enough. All he could manage were a few nights at Dashaway Hall. The Dashaways provided a showcase for up-and-coming talent, to draw an audience for their more serious mission. The Dashaway Society had been founded on January 1, 1859, by fourteen firemen from the Howard Engine Company who were determined to "dash away finally and forever the cup that poisons all who handle it." Their motto, "Death to King Alcohol," was emblazoned on a pennant above the building, and each evening's meeting opened with their theme song, to the tune of "America":

> Pure may our spirit be,
> As the wild currents, free,
> Happy and gay.
> With manly self-control
> We'll dash away the bowl,
> That would ensnare the soul
> To wine's dark sway.[17]

Even with no prospects for an engagement, Harrigan did not return to caulking; he was sure something would turn up. It did, with the help of Edward Buckley. Harrigan's daughter Adelaide got the story from Buckley in the 1950s when the old actor was in his nineties: "I first met your father outside a saloon on Kearny Street. Remember it well. It was raining cats and dogs and there was your Dad in a linen duster and with a straw hat, oblivious to the rain. I had seen him at the Olympic; I liked him and I knew he had talent." Ned Buckley was one of the minstrel endmen at the Bella Union, and he knew a replacement was needed for the other end. He arranged an audition with Sam and Madame Tetlow, the proprietors, pointing out that a "Ned" at each end would be a catchy novelty. They agreed to listen.

The first round of songs went badly. "Dutchy," the orchestra leader, swung around to the Tetlows, waving his violin and shouting, "Mein Gott in Himmel, the man can't sing; his voice is not in the violin." Harrigan refused to trust a foreign violin. He gave them some samples with his native banjo, adding a soft-shoe turn for extra persuasion. In spite of Dutchy's reservations, they hired him at twenty dollars per week, though Madame Tetlow, the treasurer, would have preferred eighteen dollars. When detachments from the waterfront began to appear at the box office and when they practically took over the Bella Union for Harrigan's first night, July 6, 1868, she felt more comfortable with her investment, and was sufficiently rewarded to raise his salary to fifty dollars by the time he departed two years later.

The Bella Union,[18] just a block from the Olympic and a half block from City Hall, had been a fixture on the north side of Portsmouth Plaza since 1849, first as a gambling palace and then in 1855 as a melodeon, a "little temple of merriment."[19] Madame Tetlow guarded the entrance—it could be reached only through the saloon or along a long, narrow hallway from the street—and Sam presided at the bar, "his genial countenance always visible behind the 'mahogany.' "[20] Easy access to stimulants often improved the performances, if sometimes adding an amusing unsteadiness to the performers.

Harrigan's repertoire was toned up and expanded. He sang "Irish Gems" and "Character Songs"—the characters were ininvariably Irish: O'Flanigans, Finegans, et al. He recited "San Francisco Sights," "Irish Comicalities," and "Jessie at the Bar," appeared in the finale sketches, *Fast Life in San Francisco, Ku Kux Klan* [sic], and at least once as an Irishwoman in *Bal Masque*. He helped make the Bella Union "the People's Resort—Something to Suit Everybody—Music, Mirth, and Wit, Combined."

If there was any question of his professional commitment, he settled it in the fall of 1868 by listing himself in *Polk's City Directory* as "Ned Harrigan, actor, Bella Union."[21]

Business was booming at the "Bellow Union," as it was known to the sailors who regarded a shore leave incomplete without at least one night at the hall, and the Tetlows responded to its popularity by constructing more sumptuous quarters around the corner.[22] And on Saturday, December 12, 1868, with Harrigan on the program, their new "Temple of Pleasure" was opened with a noisy complement of Harrigan's caulkers on hand. The site at 805 Kearny has been occupied by a theatre since that day, though the present far-from-new Bella Union, a decaying movie house featuring Chinese films, cannot match the original.

Harrigan was never a featured performer. Top billing was reserved for such forgotten ladies as May Carlton, "the celebrated and fascinating danseuse Cherry Belle (formerly Oceana)," and for the young California wonder Lotta Crabtree, whose name did make a mark. Everyone knew Lotta. With her career managed by an enterprising mother, her jigs, flings, and wild polkas made her a darling of the miners when she was barely in her teens. Now at the Bella Union, where she was billed as "a sunbeam," "a cataract," "a golden ingot," her father apparently got into the act and raided the family bank account. On June 21, 1868, the *Golden City* announced that there was "grief in the family of the Crabtrees." Lotta's father had decamped with his daughter's fortune, some $35,000. The newspaper writer speculated that the poor child must be revamping Lear's speech: "How sharper than a serpent's tooth it is to have a thankless father." Her California friends —at the Bella Union and elsewhere—quickly refilled her purse, and to express her gratitude Lotta gave the city a public drinking fountain. Erected in 1875, repainted and moved a few feet in the summer of 1974, the twelve-foot obelisk still stands at the intersection of Kearny, Market, and Geary, its spigots splashing fresh water into the basins. Now only the most curious passersby ever look up at her sweet face carved on the side and ask, "Who's Lotta?" Harrigan never forgot her. She taught him many tricks of the trade: a quick snap of the head, a gaze of wide-eyed wonder, an inviting lilt at the end of a line, guaranteed to bring a laugh, at least a smile.

During his two years at the Bella he added his own touch to Lotta's tricks, tested new songs and comicalities, mastered the Negro minstrel Tambo and Bones patter with Ned Buckley, perfected the fancy strut for the walkaround, and created a gallery of eccentrics in the latest farcical extravaganzas: *Higglety Pigglety; or, the Vatican in an Uproar; Don Juan; or, the Wild Boy of Bohemia; The Mermaids of the Cliff.* And such timely and local specials as *Santa Claus, The Demon of Saucelito* (that was the spelling then), and *Red Hot, Hottest.*

The acts were raucous and bawdy, geared to the miners and sailors seeking rest and rejuvenation. Some skeptics might not have been uplifted, as Bret Harte suggests in his poem "The Plaza":

> When the scrolls that show the playhouse nigh,
> In monstrous letters do feign and lie,
> Of "Fun divest of Vulgarity";
> When Bella Union is heard to rave
> O'er the last conundrum the minstrel gave;
> At home returning, do not snear
> If thou hast seen some things more fair.[23]

Among the more than a dozen newspapers then reporting the life of the city, only the *Police Gazette* and the *Dramatic Chronicle* (forerunner of the *Chronicle*) took account of the melodeons. And even they carried few lines on beginners like Ned Harrigan. They did note his "rollicking gaiety," declaring him "a comical favorite," and on January 30, 1869, the *Gazette* printed the most substantial notice of his San Francisco career: "What a delight to see the eccentric and versatile Harrigan on the end. He possesses a vein of humor so natural, and at the same time, so positive, that we believe he will soon work himself into prominence in the profession." After he had achieved that prominence a few years later, San Francisco hastily claimed him as a native son.

If the New Bella Union steered clear of vulgarity in its first year, it apparently rivaled its competitors in 1870.[24] Its pretty dancing girls were "just knocking spots out of things generally"; the Bella's cancan was the bounciest in town. The Tetlows paid for their folly, at least in some quarters; one unidentified reporter applauded "the many respectable persons who shunned the establishment."

If Harrigan was offended by the Bella's turn to bouncing flesh and shady stimulation, he never said so, though later his own shows were declared models of purity, one hundred percent safe for sisters and mothers. However, he did desert the Bella in the spring to team up with Sam Rickey in a duo act, *The Mulcahey Twins,* at the Pacific Melodeon, two blocks up Kearny at Pacific. Years later Harrigan said that Rickey was "the funniest man I ever saw," and after the partnership was dissolved, old Rickey admirers maintained that they saw the shadow of Rickey in Harrigan's sudden throwing back of his head, in the quick jerking double step he used for all his Irish characters, the walk that was later to become known as the Irish walk.

At the end of the season, with no strong prospects for fall on the horizon, Harrigan persuaded Otto Burbank to join him and Rickey in seeking the brighter lights in the East. Billing themselves as the California Comedians, they should stir wonder in Chicago and New York.[25]

The big dream of Broadway, of returning to familiar territory, salved most of Harrigan's regrets at leaving his first theatrical home, though he would miss his friends on the waterfront and

around Portsmouth Plaza, one of whom at a farewell gathering—
he overheard the remark—had called him the "incarnation of
geniality." He would also miss, for the time being, the chance to
advance acquaintances to friendships. He had met Mark Twain
and Bret Harte and the circle of nabobs, James Flood, James G.
Fair, and John Mackay, who had taken fortunes out of the Com-
stock Lode and were now investing their wealth in fancy homes on
Nob Hill.[26] Harrigan had good reason to look on the Bay Area as
his second home and to give San Francisco long engagements when
he later took to the road as a Broadway star.

4

Harrigan and Hart

From Portsmouth Plaza to Sacramento, Virginia City, Salt Lake City, and points east, the "Noted California Comedians" plodded slowly across the country, sharing quarters on a cattle train and making little impression on the theatrical landscape. Burbank battled for bookings to keep them moving, and Rickey's unquenchable thirst required more than his share of the profits. In Chicago they encountered an unsettling combination of competition and opportunity. The town was alive with Negro minstrels: Emerson's at McVicker's Theatre, Manning's at the Dearborn, and Bryant's at the Crosby Opera House.[1] The "Californians" found a spot on the Manning program for a few weeks until Rickey appropriated a pair of unattended trousers backstage, and it seemed wise to resume their journey. A few days earlier Rickey had pawned his own pants for the price of a drink, and the trio had survived on two pairs of trousers. The scheduling of who wore the pants when had become so burdensome that, when Sam spied the unguarded pants, the temptation overwhelmed his conscience.

When they reached New York in late October 1870, Otto Burbank persuaded the Spencer brothers to squeeze them in at the Globe,[2] an old theatre at 728 Broadway that Mark Twain called "a sort of half-frog, half-tadpole affair; it used to be a church and hasn't got entirely over looking like a church."[3] In the nineteenth century, as in recent years, churches were transformed to theatres and theatres to churches with astonishing rapidity. Some ten years later the Globe was to become Harrigan and Hart's Theatre Comique, and after concluding its theatrical life it relinquished the site to the men's clothing section of Wanamaker's department store. (In 1870 an H. Wannemacher was already on the premises, in the pit as musical director!)

Harrigan and Rickey opened on Broadway on November 21, 1870, and had two weeks in their own sketches followed by two in G. L. Stout's *A Morning with Judge Dowling.* The Globe patrons took little account of their presence, reserving their applause for old favorites: Professor Nelson and Sons "beautiful acts of posturing," El Nino Eddie "The greatest tight-rope walker in the world," and Mlle. De Vere's "Nymphs of the Carribbean Sea."⁴ The Broadway debut made a mark on Harrigan, if not on the public. Stout's play alerted him to the dramatic riches of the New York scene, to a gallery of characters drawn directly from life; in his own role, Frederick Vonhiskesier, he amply demonstrated the funny side of a thick-skulled German immigrant.

In January, with no new engagement in sight, with Rickey deep in his role as a "lushington," Harrigan returned to Chicago and Manning's Minstrels. Rickey stayed in New York, appeared occasionally in the "screaming Irish farce" *Bad Whiskey,* and finally lost his battle with the bottle in 1885. Harrigan recalled attending his funeral in the back parlor of a Spring Street undertaker's shop, where an old actor standing by the coffin turned to him and said, "Ned, that poor fellow lying there don't owe the world a cent!"⁵ Harrigan never missed a friend's funeral if he was in the neighborhood, and in later years he paid the undertaker's bill for many impoverished actors.

Before leaving New York he must have canvassed the Broadway theatres. They were crowded with diverse attractions, though none was clamoring for his talents. Edwin Booth, who was to become one of his stage heroes, was performing *Richelieu* in his new theatre at Sixth Avenue and Twenty-third. Dan Bryant's Minstrels were thriving just west of Booth's. Lotta Crabtree was in something called *Heart's Ease,* and the *Wee Willie Winkle* burlesque featured Annie Yeamans, Harrigan's future leading lady. And he couldn't have missed the town's sensation. No one missed *The Black Crook.*

This "delectable showy nonsense" was back at Niblo's where it had begun three years earlier when a ballet troupe from London was burned out of the Academy of Music and incorporated into Charles Barras's melodrama. Mark Twain described the outlandish hodgepodge in his *Travels with Mr. Brown*:

> The scenery and the legs are everything. Beautiful bare-legged girls hanging in flower baskets; others stretched in groups on great sea shells; others clustered around fluted columns; girls— nothing but a wilderness of girls—stacked up, pile on pile, away aloft to the dome of the theatre, diminishing in size and clothing, . . . girls dressed with a meagreness that would make a parasol blush. They change their clothes every fifteen minutes for four hours, and their dresses become more beautiful and more rascally all the time.[6]

Twain was sure that even Booth would have "to make a litttle change by-and-by and peel some women. Nothing else can chain the popular taste, the way things are going."

Less fancy girlie shows inhabited the concert saloons, New York's version of the San Francisco melodeons. One police investigator reported that some seventy-five of these "sinks of iniquity" were scattered throughout the city; twenty in the Broadway blocks between Spring and Fourth, with such inviting names as Kit Burns's Sportsman's Hall, Sultan's Divan, and the Black and Tan Concert Hall, also affectionately known as "Chemise and Drawers."[7]

Only one theatre other than the Globe offered an evening's entertainment that fit Harrigan's taste. Tony Pastor's had something for everyone: M. Dubosc, "The man who flies"; Mlle. de Granville, "The female Samson"; local sketches, *The Mysteries of Gotham, Escaped from Sing-Sing, The Bowery by Day and Night*; and always a song or two booming from Pastor's crescent-shaped chest. That season he was featuring *The Little Church around the Corner*, the true story of the old actor George Holland. When Holland had died his son could not find a church willing to risk a funeral service for an actor until he finally discovered a sympathetic clergyman at the Church of the Transfiguration on Twenty-Ninth Street, just off Fifth Avenue. It's still called "the little church around the corner."[8]

If Harrigan's theatrical ambition vaulted into the future, here was his model. Pastor had a fifteen-year edge on him, had been a child prodigy at Barnum's Museum, a circus ringmaster when he was sixteen, and in 1861 had become famous when he grabbed a flag and jumped to the stage at a Union rally at the Academy of Music and electrified the crowd with "The Star Spangled Banner."[9] Four years later he had his own theatre on the Bowery, where he inaugurated "legitimate variety." Legitimate meant wholesome.

If Harrigan later copied Pastor's theatre program, he never imitated his ostentatious attire. Pastor's bulky frame was invariably encased in full-dress clothes, and offstage he wore silk hats and mammoth fur-collared overcoats. Harrigan confined his "getups" to the stage; offstage he preferred to pass as one of New York's common citizens. If friends recognized him, it was because they knew his face, not his clothes.

Harrigan's five weeks on Broadway convinced him that he would return when the time was ripe, when his talents had ripened. Like any wanderer, searching his place in the world, he never guessed that chance and fate were plotting his future. When Harrigan left for Chicago, his partner-to-be had departed from Providence, Rhode Island, headed in the same direction.[10]

Before he embarked on his collision course with Harrigan, Anthony J. Cannon, not yet sixteen, had not set foot outside New England, though he had already earned his way as an entertainer for five years. He had abandoned home at an earlier age than Harrigan and under more compelling circumstances. When he was eleven his parents placed him in a reform school. Ten years younger than Harrigan, he was born in Worcester, Massachusetts, on July 25, 1855, in a small frame house on Hill Street, just back of St. Anne's Church. His ties to Ireland were stronger than Harrigan's. Both his parents, Anthony Cannon and Mary Sweeney, were born on Clare Island in County Mayo.

Before he started school, his parents detected a rebellious streak in his nature. Once their wishes were known, he struck out in the opposite direction. When teachers took over for part of the day, they soon learned that his soft, cherubic smile could not be accepted at face value. Notes from school deploring his disruptions or announcing his absences flowed steadily to the Cannon household. And though Tony did not possess the muscular prowess to support his inclinations, he terrorized the neighborhood. His sub-

dued moments at home were equally upsetting; he regularly proclaimed that he was going to quit school, quit Worcester, and
become a singer on the stage.

Like Harrigan he experimented with amateur shows. One of his
productions—young ladies admitted to the basement with a half
dozen pins, gentlemen one cent—ended in near disaster for a
supporting actor and did have disastrous consequences for him.
Anthony had cast himself as the sheriff, and when he strung up his
victim, he added an extra flourish, kicking out the box from under
the captive's feet. Fortunately the dangling villain's screams
aroused the sheriff's father, and the boy survived. The sheriff was
less lucky. The Cannons decided to invest their domestic tran-
quility in their other four children. Anthony was assigned to the
Lyman School, a state reformatory in nearby Westboro.

The rigors of his new life did not appeal to Anthony. If any
rehabilitation was to be accomplished, he knew it would not come
from the hard hands of his masters. He would have to heal himself. After carefully studying the security system for a couple of
weeks, he took French leave.

He headed first for Boston—how he got there he never revealed
—where he persuaded a saloon keeper to take him on as a cleanup
boy and part-time singer. Dissatisfied with too much glass polishing and too little singing, he moved to Providence where another
publican with a livelier ear for music christened him "Master
Antonio," a name designed to attract the Italian population. In a
few weeks he shifted to the old American Hotel on North Main,
where Billy Arlington heard him and gave him a spot with his
minstrels. Later Arlington said, "That voice once heard can never
be forgotten."[11] In a few years an army of admirers could never
forget that voice.

Somewhere on the New England circuit, M. B. Leavitt caught
Anthony's sweet soprano singing "Put Me in My Little Bed,"
watched strong men brush away tears, and persuaded him to
desert Arlington and join Madame Rentz's Female Minstrels.
Master Antonio stuck with Leavitt and his "females" (there was no
"Madame Rentz"), leaving a tear-filled path across the country,
until they reached Galesburg, Illinois. Here, according to the
manager, his boy soprano disappeared. Tony's roommate had
soiled their community towel. Tony tore off a piece of the counter-

pane from the bed as a substitute. The hotel keeper added five dollars to the bill, Leavitt withheld five dollars from Tony's salary, and Tony departed for Chicago.[12] Tony could never tolerate such high-handed interference.

A breakdown in any one of the turns of chance that brought Anthony Cannon from Worcester to a shoe-shine stand in Chicago, or in Harrigan's journey to the same spot at the same time, could have deprived an American generation of its favorite theatrical team.[13] For the next fourteen years their names were to be so inseparable that many of their noisy fans believed they were named Harriganandhart.

As their shoes were polished, the actors exchanged notes on their current misfortunes. Harrigan was eager to quit the Mannings. *A Trip around the World,* the present offering at the Dearborn, gave him little opportunity, though one scene, "Castle Garden and the Landing of Emigrants," had been tucked in his memory for future use. He had turned his talents in a new direction, had taken a cue from Frank Kent, the Mannings' popular female impersonator, had written a singing act, and was now searching for a partner who could look and sound like a girl. If he could work up the act, he'd quit the Mannings.

When Cannon admitted he was at liberty and eager to try anything, they adjourned to Harrigan's room. Ned pulled out his banjo, and, when the baby-faced Tony flavored the female lyrics of *The Little Fraud* with his sweet falsetto, they quickly agreed to join forces. During the next few days, as they rehearsed the act, they searched for a catchy billing. Harrigan and Cannon in either order didn't sound right, didn't look right. According to the apocryphal story circulated by later publicists, Hart's christening occurred on a Chicago street when they were stopped by a panhandler and Tony, whose generosity was easily touched, handed the man a dollar. A passerby, viewing this rash encouragement of indolence, turned to the pair and remarked, "Boy, you've got some heart."[14] The incident may have settled them on the euphonious combination Harrigan and Hart, but they also knew the theatrical ubiquity of the name: Josh and John Hart at the Globe in New York; B. C. Hart, the Pittsburgh manager; and Bob Hart, the famous stump speaker who was then appearing at the Dearborn in his *Senator Hart on the Darwin Theory*. Hart had always been a good stage name, and audiences liked easy, familiar names. (The name has continued in favor, most conspicuously with William S., Lorenz, and Moss Hart.)

For their debut the partners set their sights low enough to assure success, selecting the Winter Garden at Clark and Monroe, a creaky bandbox of a room on the third floor of a dilapidated office building. Struggling to pass as a theatre, the place had little support from the queer triumvirate who posed as managers: an ex-woodsman out of the Northwest, an ex-auctioneer, and a little hunchback of unknown occupation. This trio carried on a running battle with other tenants of the building, particularly with a quack doctor on the floor below. One cold night the doctor became so incensed that he hosed the stairs until the icy treads became too slippery for the Winter Garden patrons, and the performance was canceled.[15]

Harrigan and Hart ignored the hazards and for three weeks concentrated on *The Little Fraud*. Harrigan had borrowed his tune from J. P. Webster's "Little Maud," making the song his own by substituting the comic patter of a pair of lovesick young Germans for Thomas Bailey Aldrich's sentimental yearning for his "dainty, darling Maud." Hart appeared in a long seersucker skirt, an overlaid blouse of matching stripes, white cotton stockings drooping over his oxfords, and a tight bonnet crowned with a fancy bow; Hart's own curly ringlets decorated his forehead. Harrigan wore prison-striped pants and a vest under a frock coat, a winged collar, and a black skullcap. Their ridiculous costumes set the tone for their comic antics, for Hart's coy transvestism—only the program revealed his sex—and for their strenuous jigs that punctuated the verses. A small sample gives proof that the act depended more on Harrigan and Hart's stage business than on the text:

> HE: Oh, vere is dot leetle deicher darling
> Der pootiest leetle vaiter gal of all:
> Oh, vere is der pickles by der garten,
> Der mock organges hanging by her wall.
> How sweet she used to vait on der table
> Mit sarsparilla vater by her tray;
> Und sometimes put bottles by her tables,
> Ven efer de boss he vas avay.

> *Chorus.*
>   BOTH: Little Fraud
>   SHE: Chews terbaccer
> Little Fraud!
>   SHE: Dunner vater
> Vas der pootiest little deicher gal of all.
> *Dance.*

Harrigan had uncovered a gold mine in his new partner. According to one reporter, Hart found wonder and fun in anything Harrigan wrote. His sweet voice and infectious smile warmed the coolest house on the coldest night. His female impersonation seemed to come naturally, without any swishy, sissy swing. He walked and danced like a girl, his pudgy dimples made him look like a girl, and his sweet soprano sounded like the voice of a girl. Yet no one questioned his virility, and a good many ladies found him less safe than they had imagined. Years later—any fan could recite the story—a Pinkerton detective was fooled and refused to admit his mistake until Hart took him to his dressing room, peeled his blouse, and dropped his skirt.[16]

More telling for their future success was Hart's natural stage magnetism. He could capture an audience as soon as he came on. Mrs. Edward Harrigan once said, "Tony lit up the stage like an electric light in an era of gas lighting."[17] And the actor Nat Goodwin, one of Hart's closest friends, wrote in his memoirs: "Hart sang like a nightingale, danced like a fairy, and acted like a master comedian. His magnetism was compelling, his personality charming. He had the face of an Irish Apollo; his eyes were liquid blue, almost feminine in their dove-like expression. His head was large and round and covered with a luxurious growth of brown curly hair which clustered in tight curls over a strong brow; his smile was almost pathetic. I loved three men in my life; he was two of them."[18] Another friend said he looked like an angel on a valentine.

With a strong new partner, with *Little Fraud* bringing more laughs at every performance, and with test trials of three other routines to be perfected later—*The Big and Little of It, The Day We Went* West, and *You 'Spute Me*—Harrigan was ready to move back East, if not to New York, at least to the fringe of Broadway. They decided to attack Boston.

5

Love, Music, and the Brahams

In mid-April 1871, Harrigan and Hart auditioned for John Stetson at the Howard Athenaeum—that cherished landmark of many later Harvard generations who journeyed to Scollay Square to feast on female flesh. Stetson thought them worth a trial, and on Monday, May 1, the Howard program announced: "First appearance in this city of the California Artists, Harrigan and Hart, who will appear in their character songs and their original act 'The Little Fraud.' "[1] No one need know that Hart had never been farther west than Galesburg. Although they shared the evening with seventeen acts, Stetson gave them the third spot and bolder billing than their reputation warranted. The following week they had become the "Great versatile artists, received nightly with screams of laughter." The third week they added another duo act, *The German Emigrants,* and on May 22, they became full-fledged members of the company with roles in the finale extravaganza, *High Jack the Heeler.* On June 19, during the last week of the season, Stetson scheduled a benefit, billing them as the "Non Pareils in their original artistic Terpsichorean Masterpieces." Apparently more comic dancing had been added. In two months they had become Boston's favorite triple-threat artists. No one could match their walkarounds, their jigs and clogs, Harrigan's trembling tenor and Hart's tender falsetto, and above all, their joyous and extravagant clowning. They always seemed so happy with each other. When the season closed, the partnership was firmly fixed; their theatrical future seemed secure.

Unfortunately security was soon threatened. Tony Pastor, who had played the Athenaeum the week before their debut, caught their act, and decided to bring them to New York the next season. Stetson got wind of the scheme and, having discovered that Hart was still AWOL from the reformatory, filed a complaint. Tony was haled into juvenile court—he was not yet sixteen.[2] Harrigan went along to the hearing—it was not the last time he would protect Tony from himself—pleaded with the court to give the boy a chance, and showed the judge how much they depended on each other by performing *The Little Fraud* routine. If Tony were left in his charge, he would look after him, make a man of him. The judge was persuaded. The partnership was preserved.

Stetson apologized for his prying by boosting their salary from $75 for the act to $100 for each—later advanced to $150; and when the Athenaeum reopened in August, Harrigan and Hart took over a larger share of the program. In addition to their duos, they appeared as "character artists" in the extravaganzas: Harrigan as the Irishman McSwegan in *Boston by Daylight and Gaslight,* as Folshe, a Congo dancer, and Hart as Sun-de-See in *Kim-Ka.* And once Harrigan usurped Tony's transvestism, playing Hannah Lightfoot in *Life on the Plantation.*

Boston provided more than a rich theatrical training ground. They met Johnny Wild, later to become a stalwart in the Harrigan and Hart company, and Harrigan made his first acquaintance with the Braham family. John Braham led the Athenaeum's "superb orchestra, twelve first-class musicians," and when they left Boston, John gave Harrigan a letter to his uncle, David Braham, leader of the orchestra at Broadway's Theatre Comique; David would be a good man to know. He was right.

When they said farewell to the Athenaeum and headed for New York in mid-November, they did not fully appreciate the devotion of their fellow actors. After their exodus, Jennie Worrell and Adah Richmond kept their names alive in Boston by appropriating their *Little Fraud* act, a gesture that alerted Harrigan to a hazard he had not anticipated.[3] Thereafter he discouraged such friendly flattery by keeping a tight hold on his scripts. Generous as he was with his purse, he drew the line at sharing his stage material. When he wrote a sketch, song, or play, he wrote it for Harrigan and Hart and no one else.

Although the fill-in week at New York's Union Square Theatre added little to their professional standing, the visits with David Braham shaped more of Harrigan's future than he could then have realized. Not only did he receive a warm welcome from David, he caught sight of the Brahams' daughter, a pretty black-haired lass who was busily tending the stove in the kitchen. Later Ned told his children that this "little gypsy" had enslaved him immediately: "I fell in love with your mother's ankle when I first saw her swinging a poker at 86 Carmine Street; it was a moment that could never be forgotten."[4]

With the prospect of another glimpse at Annie, he found an excuse for returning most every day to talk with David about music. He wanted to know how he wrote his songs. Did the words come first or the tune? Would Braham be willing to fit a tune to some of Harrigan's words? As the week rapidly slipped away, Harrigan noticed, or thought he noticed, that Annie deserted her duties in the kitchen more often each time he appeared. She seemed to be fascinated by the conversation in the parlor. He even fancied that her dark eyes met his more often as the days went by. She might be a twelve-year-old child to the Brahams. To him she was a young beauty who had turned his head to thoughts of love and marriage. Once the week was ended, he knew that her smile would stick in his memory and haunt his dreams until he saw her again.

Lady Luck was riding with Harrigan in these years. Pure chance had crossed his path with Tony Hart's in Chicago. A simple letter of introduction had brought him to his future wife, to the composer who would write the music for all his songs and preside in the pit when he opened his own theatre.

The Brahams were a musical family. David and his brother Joseph had come from London in 1856, had begun as fiddlers in various New York minstrel halls, and when Harrigan appeared, David was the orchestra leader at the Comique and Joseph at Tony Pastor's. For the rest of the century, the ubiquitous Brahams almost cornered the market.[5]

Three of Joseph's boys made their careers in Boston: John at the Athenaeum, then as musical director for the first American production of *Pinafore*; Albert and William with the Boston Symphony. Harry stayed in New York, conducted at the Madison Square Theatre, at Wallack's, and finally at the Brooklyn Park, though he achieved greater prominence as the first of Lillian Russell's four husbands.

David's two sons (he also had five daughters) stuck with the New York theatre. David, Jr., began as a musician and then turned actor. George managed the pit for David Belasco and, after his father died, replaced him as musical director and composer for Harrigan. There were also two Braham nephews in pit orchestras. No other single family matched the Brahams' record.

Harrigan's collaboration with David Braham developed quickly and easily, and though Braham was ten years his senior and even after Braham became his father-in-law, Harrigan could never address him as "Mr. Braham." From the beginning they were like brothers, always David and Ned to each other, and they soon discovered that professional habits as well as natural affection bound them together. When they were not in the theatre, they were working at home. Braham had adopted a rigorous routine of work even before he met Harrigan. At night he crawled into the pit; during the day he searched for the tunes to match the lyrics of G. L. Stout, Jennie Kemble, and now, Edward Harrigan.[6]

After the week with the Brahams, Harrigan was happier than he had ever been as he and Hart barnstormed through New England and upstate New York, brightening the theatres in New Haven, New London, Providence, Springfield, Albany, Rochester, Syracuse, and the villages in between. The provincial managers, duly impressed with their six months at the Athenaeum, billed them as "the celebrated Harrigan and Hart," and the newspapers came on stronger than the managers. In Syracuse, where they played the month of February, 1872, at Wild's Opera House, the *Daily Standard* wrote: "Harrigan and Hart are certainly artists of unparalleled fame, in their splendid performance. They were called out no less than six times, and favored each time with an entire change of dress and songs. The female personations of Hart are almost perfect and defy the closest scrutiny to detect by voice or action the real man."[7] As they walked the streets in towns neither had ever seen, they began to hear their own names on the lips of strangers.

Pleased as he was at the new attention, Harrigan was not fired by dreams of fame and fortune. His own inner fire, ignited on Corlear's Hook, refueled at the Olympic, Bella Union, Globe, and Athenaeum, and most recently at the Brahams', supplied all the drive he needed. Whatever the rewards, he simply had to unlock all the talents within him. He worked constantly as they moved from town to town, fixing the pattern that was to stick with him throughout his life. When he wasn't onstage or rehearsing some new business, he was writing. When he wasn't writing, he was roaming the streets collecting scenes and characters that might later find a place onstage.

In January he sent Braham the words for his famous song "The Mulligan Guard" and in February wrote his first serious play. Although the play never reached the stage, Harrigan cherished the manuscript and ordered a printed title page to paste on the notebook, the title in fancy gothic and each line in a different type face: "*Shamus O'Brien* / at Home / An Irish Sketch by Ned Harrigan / In one act and one scene / Syracuse, February 8, 1872."

The simple melodramatic story duplicated many Irish family histories. Nora Brady's Shamus O'Brien "was drove from Ireland because he was willing to stand up and die for his country." When he returns to save her from the lecherous landlord, he is filled with the wonders of America: "a home for all downtrodden people on the face of the earth, where charity and friendship flows as steady as the River Shannon."

Primitive as it was, the play forecast Harrigan's fascination with the Irishman's patriotic and comic view of America and with Irish melodrama—though he quickly discovered that his melodramas never gained favor until he subdued the weepy heroines and black-hearted landlords and gave the stage to the comics.

Twice during the season they returned to Chicago. In March and April they created an "unparalleled and unprecedented furor" at the West Side Opera House, a theatre that had been quickly erected at Randolph and Jefferson after the devastating October fire. In July they had four weeks with Tony Pastor's company at

Nixon's Amphitheatre, a gigantic circuslike building on Clinton Street near Randolph.

During that Chicago summer Harrigan filled his notebooks with gags, sketches, and songs.[8] Hardly a day passed without a new entry. New songs for the lovesick Germans. Irish songs—one about two immigrants who were misled by Horace Greeley. Songs about an Italian fruit seller, a colored senator, a Jewish clothing dealer, and even a hymn for the feminists, "Women Have Rights":

> We won't make any speeches
> We have thim all alone
> For we women are the creatures
> Have rights we call our own.

He wrote pages of comic patter for the Negro minstrels Tambo (Harrigan invariably called him Sam) and Bones, recitations for the stump speakers. *What I Know about Farming* could have served W. C. Fields or Robert Benchley:

> A farm my friends is composed of mud or dirt and is called by some eminent philosophers, Land. . . . In the balmy Indian summer, you can set by your Wigwam like Minnehaha and get drunk on pressed cider, only 5 cents a pail.

Not and Shot resembled the *Who's on Second; What's on First* routine that can still be heard from time to time on TV:

> One Mr. Not and one Mr. Shot into a quarrel got. . . .Mr. Shot, their tried revolvers got. . . . Not was shot and Shot was not, and Shot the glory got.

Some sketches evolved slowly. One day he wrote under "Gag items": "A widow visits a spiritual meeting, calls for the spirit of her departed husband—asks him if he wouldn't like to come back to his lovely widow—he answer—No it's hot enough where he was." A few pages later the idea is fleshed out:

> BONES: . . . She buried him in a lovely grave with no one to keep him company but the soup dish from which he had souped and the last ham bone he chawed on. . . . She brought in a medium to take in de spirits.
> SAM: You had a spiritual meeting at your house?
> BONES: Yes she cleared off de supper table wid a fly duster, and de medium went into a slumber, and pooty soon

all de tables commenced to bounce. . . . She spoke right out, am dare any spirits here and a voice replied dare am, de spirit of your departed husband. Den Miss Clawson took a pull at de gin bottle and asked: My dear long lost darling, won't you come back and live wid your dead wife? . . . He said no. It was hot enough where he was.

When Harrigan and Hart decamped from Chicago, bound for Broadway, Harrigan's notebooks were crammed with new material, and his head was filled with new ideas waiting to be recorded. As long as he had a fresh supply of notebooks and pencils and his two favorite actors on hand to play whatever he wrote, his imagination continued to run at full steam.

New York gave them a rousing welcome, first at Pastor's in the 1872–1873 season, then at Josh Hart's Theatre Comique, and for the next nine years—except for 1875–1876 on the road, occasional nights in Brooklyn, and summers in the provinces—the Comique became their home. In a brief year and a half, Harrigan and Hart had climbed to the top, and audiences soon discovered that they offered a new kind of program. Most variety houses rejuvenated their weekly bills by a complete change of performers. Harrigan and Hart relied on fresh turns from their in-house writer. Now more than ever, Harrigan had to keep up his feverish activity, onstage every night except Sunday and every day at his writing table. And stimulated by his return to his home town, he abandoned minstrel gags and shifted to New York scenes and characters, laying the ground for his later plays, and turning out over forty sketches in their first three seasons at the Comique.

6

"Welcome Mulligan Guard"

Harrigan and Hart hit Broadway at a good time. Tony Pastor and Josh Hart were riding high, edging out the concert saloons with wholesome entertainment guaranteed not to offend. "Hart's stage," according to one reporter, "is never desecrated with a can-can dance; never seeks to undermine the morals of the youth of this city by presenting a crowd of half-stripped women in lascivious poses."[1] And regularly the ads proclaimed: "Pure Fun Only. The Favorite Resort of Families. Ladies and children always welcome."[2]

Off-color diversions were, of course, still available. An enterprising voyeur could feast on the *Lady Godiva Can-Can* at the Arion Cafe,[3] or on *The Female Bather, or, Fun at Long Branch* at Robinson Hall: ". . . a dozen women come down to bathe, stripping to the buff—or pink, for such is the color of their tights—and then are chased around the stage. When the pursuers have each clasped in his arms one of these brazen females, the size of whose limbs and the liberality with which they expose such other charms as nature has bestowed upon them constitute their claim to popular favor."[4]

Ladies and gentlemen at Hart's Comique (514 Broadway, just below Spring) were never threatened by lusty Amazons. His actors made them shake with laughter, gape in wonder, but never blush, and in the early seventies Harrigan and Hart's "inimitable personations" provided a big share of the laughter at the Comique. Wonder was supplied by: Harry Sefton, "The Dancing Spider";

Neil Warner's comic lecture, "In Africa; or, How I Found Livingstone" (Sir Henry Stanley was then lecturing in New York); and the astonishing Professor Gilbert and his birds, "the best performing birds ever seen," each a master in his line: Chere told the day of the week, the month, and the year, with the aid of a calendar. Phenix brought flowers to the professor and distinguished the flags of all nations. Charles, the ladies' favorite, selected from a deck whatever card was called for by the audience. The Boy of Paris ran up a post three feet high and took down the flags, while Jaques fired a cannon.[5]

With such remarkable spectacles plus Harrigan and Hart, the Comique was outdistancing Tony Pastor's. Even during the panic year of 1873, the place was crowded nightly with a thousand happy customers, while Pastor could not half fill his house, even with door prizes: hams, barrels of flour, and "on Saturday, ten tons of coal."[6] The Comique's success was no accident. Hart had outbid Pastor for talent, offering $150 per week each to Harrigan and Hart and his other top artists, and the gamble had paid off.

New Yorkers who wanted more variety than Hart and Pastor offered, more theatrical thrills, more culture, had plenty to choose from. Bryant's Minstrels and Madame Rentz's Minstrels. "Brilliant pageants, splendor and magnificence augmented beyond recognition" at Barnum's Hippodrome. Barnum had remodeled the Harlem Railway buildings on Madison Avenue at Twenty-Sixth Street after the terminal was moved to the new Grand Central Station on Forty-Second Street. For western adventure there was Oliver Doud Byron in *Across the Continent,* Frank Mayo in *Davy Crockett,* or Buffalo Bill in Ned Buntline's *Scouts of the Prairie.* For tears and melodramatic chills: *East Lynne, Bertha the Sewing Machine Girl, Under the Gaslight,* and *The Two Orphans.* And, as always, Shakespeare: Edwin Forrest, in his final public appearances, reading from the podium at Steinway Hall; Edwin Booth as Hamlet, Richard III, or Macbeth, his final season in his own theatre; and the fiery Italian Tommaso Salvini in *Othello.* And for those who shied away from the theatre, lectures by such notables as Bret Harte and Mark Twain.

None of these competed with Harrigan and Hart. They operated in another league.

Recognizing that his prosperity rested on the partners he had captured from Pastor, Josh Hart gave Harrigan a free hand to rehearse and readjust the program as he wished, test new acts, and send Braham into the pit with fresh tunes as fast as they came along. Harrigan had renewed his visits to the Brahams, spending more time there than in his rooms in Brooklyn, working with David, mooning over Annie, and discovering that his life in the theatre and out entwined more and more with the Brahams.

The collaboration with David seemed permanently fixed almost immediately with the sensational success of *The Mulligan Guard*. The act became a fixture in the Harrigan and Hart repertoire, led Harrigan to his famous *Mulligan Guard* plays, and made the Mulligan name synonymous with Harriganandhart.

Harrigan got the "guard idea" in Boston in the winter of 1872, wrote the sketch and lyrics, and when Braham sent him a tune shaped to his lyrics, he tried to persuade William A. Pond to publish the sheet music, hoping to get the song in circulation before the act got on stage.[7] It was a promotional stunt he was to use successfully in later years. Pond declined, then changed his mind after he heard Harrigan and Hart perform the number. He offered fifty dollars for the rights, and Harrigan accepted. For the rest of his life, Harrigan bemoaned his youthful indiscretion: "I let him have it! I let him have it!"[8] Why couldn't he have learned his lesson just as well on a less popular song?

The Mulligan act featured a marching troop of two, one modeled on a tailor in the Seventh Ward named Dan Mulligan and the other on Capt. Jack Hussey, a baggage master at Castle Garden who was said to have the "awfulest gnarled, dead-looking face that Darwin ever saw,"[9] but whose chest was decorated shoulder to shoulder with medals awarded for the rescues from drowning he had performed along the East River. (Hussey's wife Cordelia would later serve as the model for Dan's wife Cordelia in the Mulligan plays.) Harrigan had already begun to draw his characters from life.

He also drew the military routine from life, and though Harrigan insisted that his burlesque of a target company excursion was intended to help eradicate a "New York nuisance,"[10] the antics bore little resemblance to a social crusade. However much he ridiculed this "jolliest lot of local trash that ever held the boards,"[11] as one reporter described them, Harrigan loved his two guards and their Negro target bearer and sympathized with their frustrating attempts to master the maneuvers prescribed by the manual.

Enough of this early ten-minute sketch has been preserved to know how primitive it was, how much it depended on "gags and business." It was first tried out when the Comique company played Chicago in May and June 1873, and much of the staging was probably derived from "Charles and Carrie Austin in their terrific Zouave Drill and Bayonet Combat," on the program with them at the Chicago Academy of Music, and also from W. C. Burton and Minnie Rainforth's *Lightning Zouave Drill* which had shared the stage in Boston the previous season.

The setting was simple: a backdrop with two windows; one marked "Midnight Club" and the other "Mulligan's Saloon," with a banner stretched between them reading "Welcome Mulligan Guard."[12] The miniature army marched in from the wings: Hart as Captain Hussey, Harrigan his platoon of one, and Morgan, the little Negro, dragging the target and rarely managing to raise it above his head. Hart, in a tight army jacket, a bib encircled with brass buttons, and a generous expanse of white shirt bulging above his shaggy pants, balanced a gigantic, moth-eaten bearskin shako on his head. Harrigan wore a pair of massive epaulets three sizes larger than his shoulders, a gold-braided fez, and a wide belt tucked up under his armpits to accommodate the huge sword that touched the ground and continually got caught between his legs. They were guaranteed a howl of laughter as soon as they entered, even before they began their grotesque drills, Tony Hart with his giant rifle and Harrigan with his recalcitrant sword. Here's a sample of the buffoonery:

> TONY: *(Taking sword.)* Aisy sir, aisy.
> NED: I'm as aisy as you are.
> TONY: Salute me when you spake to me.
> NED: It breaks my heart to call ye captain.
> TONY: I'll break your head if you don't.
> . . . .
> NED: You never would have been captain but you kept the company drunk for a week to get their votes.
> TONY: I couldn't get you drunk, a river of gin wouldn't fill you.

. . . .

TONY: Attention, by the left, no, no, I mane by the right. *(Pulls
out book.)* What the divil does the manual say about it. Shoulder
arms. (NED *drills awkward.)* You haven't it. You haven't it.
Put it down, put it down. No put it up to your shoulder.
NED: It's not the way we drilled last year.
TONY: It's the new style.[13]

The incredible popularity of *The Mulligan Guard* cannot be
attributed to the dialogue. It derived from the swing of the tune,
the lyrics, and Harrigan and Hart's ridiculous stage business.
Throughout the seventies, the partners stumbled through the
manual of arms, discovering new misadventures for sword and
rifle. And when Harrigan advanced from sketches to plays, he
could not abandon the proved box-office magic of *The Mulligan
Guard.* He incorporated "Mulligan Guard" into the titles of his
full-length plays.

When the act reached New York, word spread like wildfire
around the city: no theatrical team had ever created such an uproar; nothing as funny as Harrigan and Hart's drill had ever hit
Broadway. The routine struck a familiar chord for most of the
Comique audience. *The Mulligan Guard* celebrated and satirized
the ridiculous pseudomilitary target companies that were manned
by the immigrants who were excluded from the regular militia.
With more than a hundred groups in the city, every loyal, patriotic, able-bodied man who loved to march, shoot, and carouse
could join the Cleveland Light Guards, Lafayette Battery, Oregon
Blues, First Ward Magnetizers, Mustache Fusileers, or Washington
Market Chowder Guard. And a volunteer fireman automatically
affiliated with the auxiliary attached to his engine: the Gulick,
Atlantic, or Columbia Guards.[14] (The craze has not completely
disappeared. Most Republican congressmen boast of membership
in Washington's Chowder and Marching Society.)

Most of these guard companies marched on Sundays, though
one New York visitor in the late sixties said he watched them from
his hotel room almost daily as they paraded on Broadway.[15] Usually they assembled at the neighborhood engine house, squirmed
into formation, marched to the home of the leading politician for
his blessing, and then headed uptown to Jones's Woods or to
Harlem, or down to the Battery for a boat to Staten Island or

Hoboken Heights. A drum and fife corps, hired or improvised from their ranks, kept them in step. A target decorated with flowers and carried on "the stalwart shoulders of a herculean specimen of the African race" displayed the proud name of the organization.[16] (Harrigan's Negro was far from "stalwart.") Their homemade uniforms rarely matched. Wives and sweethearts striped their trousers with whatever ribbon was at hand and manufactured chevrons or shoulder straps to fit their imaginations. Ingenuity, pawnbrokers, and secondhand shops supplied medals, boots, bearskin shakos, leather aprons, and leggins. Military hardware was usually borrowed for the occasion. The companies' morning manuvers, even before the disrupting influence of beer, were as individualized as their costumes, though one reporter found some units so well drilled that they "would put to blush the best militia companies."[17]

The few military historians who have footnoted these companies have assumed that they evolved to accommodate the boys in blue when they returned from the war. The record reads otherwise. In 1860 the *Herald* reported that on many days ten to fifteen companies passed the newspaper's office, and on Thanksgiving and Christmas, as many as a hundred.[18] On March 16, 1861, Charles Dickens noted that "These incessant street processions allow no omnibus, van, or barouche to break their ranks, leaving Broadway traffic benumbed. . . . They wear a rude sort of shako covered with oil skin, red flannel shirts, with black silk handkerchiefs blowing gaily (as to the ends), tied around their throats in jaunty sailor's knots. They affect a certain recklessness, so as not to appear to be drilled or drummed about to the detriment of their brave democratic freedom uniform. . . . They have been over on a 'target excursion' to Brooklyn. Tomorrow, there will be a paragraph about their excellent shooting, the number of bull's eyes they made, the 'clam chowder' they partook of afterwards, and the 'good time' they had generally."[19] In 1849, Giuseppe Garibaldi watched the red-shirted parades on Staten Island, and later, when he adopted the uniform for his Italian troops, the red shirt became known as the "Garibaldi."[20]

The climactic event in the guards' history apparently occurred on April 23, 1857.[21] All business was suspended, stands were erected along the line of march, and everyone turned out to cheer the massed assembly of 127 companies, some twelve thousand men, as they paraded up Broadway. It was the grandest and longest parade ever witnessed in the city prior to the war.

Harrigan probably saw the big parade. Certainly he had watched the marching of the Americus Guard (the auxiliary of Americus 6, his engine company), knew at first hand the typical day's routine of a target outing, and compressed the happy journey into the lyrics of his famous "Mulligan Guard":

> We crave your condescension,
> We'll tell you what we know
> Of marching in the Mulligan Guard from Sligo ward below
> Our Captain's name was Hussey, a Tipperary man,
> He carried his sword like a Russian duke,
> whenever he took command.
> *Chorus*
> We shoulder'd guns, and march'd, and march'd a-way,
> From Baxter Street, we march'd to Avenue A,
> With drums and fife, how sweetly they did play,
> As we march'd, march'd, march'd in the Mulligan Guard
>
> When the band play'd Garry Owen,
> Or the Connamara Pet;
> With a rub a dub, dub, we'd march
> In the mud, to the military step.
> With green above the red, boys,
> To show where we come from,
> Our guns we'd lift with the right shoulder shift,
> As we'd march to the bate of the drum.—*Chorus.*
>
> When we got home at night, boys,
> The divil a bite we'd ate,
> We'd all set up and drink a sup
> Of whiskey strong and nate.
> Thin we'd all march home together,
> As slippery as lard,
> The solid min would all fall in,
> And march with the Mulligan Guard.—*Chorus.*[22]

Harrigan and Hart did not retain a monopoly on the Mulligan Guard. Others demanded a share of their spectacular success. In 1874 Collin and Small published *The Illustrated History of the*

Mulligan Guard, "a full authentic record, thirty-one pages for fifteen cents."[23] According to this anonymous historian, the guard was organized by Michael Hussey to honor "Terrence Mulligan, the Assistant Alderman of the red-hot Seventh and the best Irishman in Ameriky." (If Harrigan did not lend a hand with the story, it was certainly concocted by someone who had seen his act.)

Hussey, armed with a jagged saber said to have been worn by the Duke of Wellington, and Paddy McGloin, his one recruit, with a musket retrieved at Waterloo, held their first drill at Widow Mahoney's grocery and liquor emporium. It ended in a shambles. As Hussey tried to manipulate his saber and read from *Hardee's Tactics* simultaneously, Paddy, "nussed too much from the Widow's bottle," stuck his bayonet in the ceiling and the widow, "showing the effects of the milk," stumbled and brought Paddy down over a tub of pickles and a box of smoked herrings, "banging his nut up and down in the briny confusion." (A Harrigan melee!)

On their first target excursion to Jones's Wood, on the East River at Sixty-sixth (the first proposed site for Central Park), no one could hit the target. Hussey remedied the misfortune with a small auger and each man—the company had grown—inscribed his name opposite a hole. They celebrated their success with "a regular Seventh Ward lay-out: a pound of crackers, a pound of cheese, and a square gallon of whiskey," and as they began their homeward march Captain Hussey and his troops "gloried in the inspiration of success and whiskey, two of the greatest incentives of our natures. . . . There are great and momentous occasions when the spirit of a people will culminate in a song or hymn that will decide their destinies and create character for the future historian. 'God Save the King,' 'Yankee Doodle,' 'Shoo Fly,' 'Tramp, Tramp, Tramp,' and other immortal hymns, are evidences of this spasmodic inspiration. So also in this instance. The words of the 'Mulligan Guard' were not written; they sprang into wild and burning existence on this occasion."

The Seventh Ward rang with huzzas when they returned, and had it not been for some of her female friends Widdy Mahoney "would have stood on her head; in fact, she attempted it several times, and was exceedingly indignant that she was not allowed to have her own way in expressing her excessive delight." Drinking and dancing continued until "the dust had been rattled out of the cracks in the floor and everybody voted it the happiest occasion that ever was, and a fit finale to the first day's triumph of the Guard."

A companion volume, published the same year, was aimed at the small fry. With words, music, and pictures, *Ten Little Mulligan Guards* supplied complete instructions for playing the Mulligan game: "Let ten little boys (if there are not boys enough in the party, the little girls can play instead) get such household articles as brooms, dusters, etc., using them for guns. Form in single file, singing the song, at the same time keeping step, and march around the room. At the end of each verse one falls out, to make one less, until none are left. By following these directions a highly interesting and amusing game can be played."[24] The verses offered opportunity for spontaneous juvenile violence, not indicated in the directions:

> The boiler burst, and up we went
> Like bees out of a hive,
> And of the Little Mulligans
> It left us only five.
>
> When Pat Malone was shooting,
> We heard a dreadful roar;
> He'd shot a Little Mulligan,
> And then we had but four.

No Harrigan and Hart routine caught fire like "The Mulligan Guard" or stimulated so many imitators, and none of the Harrigan-Braham songs ever traveled so widely. The partners could probably have made a life work of their outlandish drill, but Harrigan, already wise to the dangers of overexposure, refused to take the chance.

He conceived alternative misadventures for himself and Tony. Sketches were intertwined, characters reincarnated to face new troubles, and many characters and incidents that reached maturity in the long plays appeared first in the early twenty-minute sketches. He took his first whirl at Irish-German slambang. In *Who Stole the Monkey?* Harrigan as Peter Pimblelock collided with Hart's Hercules O'Flanigan. *The Mixed Couple* featured domestic explosions between Hans (Harrigan) and Bridget (Hart) Roebecker. This German couple would reappear as Gustav and Bridget Lochmuller in the *Mulligan* plays.

Some sketches were loaded with the nonsense and horseplay that would become Harrigan trademarks. *Muldoon, the Solid Man* foreshadowed his fascination with lunatics and undertakers. An old actor has gone mad on Shakespeare, a common affliction according to Harrigan. Another lunatic imagines himself a kite and shouts, "Fly me! Fly me!"[25] The undertaker is overjoyed at the prospect of the final wholesale slaughter: "A whole world dead! Lord, what a fat job that would be!"

There was more marching. In *The Day We Celebrate* (later called *St. Patrick's Day Parade*), Conroy and Johanna weave around Union Square (four chairs), along Second Avenue (a bench), and past City Hall (a washtub). Hart was always at his best swishing a skirt around his ankles. *Regular Army, O!* introduced the high-stepping Skidmores, the blackfaced guard that was to march and sing through the *Mulligan* series. *Down Broadway* featured the "Gallant 69th Boys" and Harrigan as a country bumpkin. He's overwhelmed by Washington's statue in Union Square: "That's the man—when he was a boy said to his father, 'Take back the meat ax I can't tell a lie. I broke the window with a brick.' "

The Irishman's fascination with liquor propelled many sketches. *The Terrible Example* documented a Temperance Society meeting. Harrigan and Hart (president and secretary) valiantly deny their own parched throats while lubricating Jimmy Lush, their "terrible example." When Harrigan reads from the bylaws, "Any member of this society dying within its confines will receive $50 after his death," the members drop dead. When he announces, "in case of sudden recovery ye can come forward and take a drink," they storm the podium.

Harrigan celebrated the Hawaiian King Kalakaua's visit with *Fee Gee,* a hodgepodge of observations on missionaries, cannibals, and contemporary events. The cannibal king from County Sligo (Harrigan) advises his daughter Mutton Chops (Hart) that

Heathentamer has been sent by "the Young Men's Christian Association the cannibals to convert/And give 'em all a clean white shirt." If the cannibals weary of hearing him screech, they can "Go to Brooklyn / Hear Talmadge preach."[26]

Apparently Harrigan cherished the manuscripts of these sketches; on the flyleaf of *Innocence at Home,* a short sketch about a husband's torments in keeping the pledge while still accommodating his thirst for medicinal comfort, he wrote:

> Should this book from me
> E'er stray away
> Be kind enough my friend to think
> That from this work
> Comes food and drink
> For one poor actor
> Return it, do be so kind
> The owner you can easily find
> That's your most obedient Harrigan
> Twill ease your conscience
> When tis done
> Send it to Lorimer St. 301
> Brooklyn, E. D. [Eastern District][27]

The partners did not restrict themselves to Harrigan inventions in these early years. Harrigan played Uncle Tom and Hart played Topsy in an abbreviated *Uncle Tom's Cabin.* Both appeared in *The Italian Padrone* and in G. L. Stout's controversial *The Skibbeah.* When Dion Boucicault claimed *Skibbeah* was stolen from his *The Shaughraun,* and the *Spirit of the Times* alternated its columns between the Stout-Boucicault and the earlier Shakespeare-Bacon controversy,[28] Harrigan took account of both in a song, "The Scandal Club":

> We'll find out who wrote Shakespeare
> If we don't it isn't our fault
> Twas wrote by Poole and Buffalo Bill
> And claimed by Boucicault.

He experimented with one full-length play, *Eureka,* in collaboration with John Woodard, the stage manager who had given him his start in San Francisco, mixing melodrama with Harrigan and Hart shenanigans. Although it was never produced, two routines were set aside for future use. In one, a deranged actor has become an accomplished "Sundayambulist"; he can read the newspaper and eat his midnight snack while continuing to snore. The other bit was borrowed from Molière's *Doctor in Spite of Himself*: "When you ax him if he's a doctor, ten to one he'll say no and refuse to go with you. Then just give him a whelt or two across the back and he'll folly you as gently as a sucking pig."

When the Comique closed in May 1875, the partners moved to Wallack's for three weeks in an anonymous farcical melodrama, appearing as Michael and Nora Donovan in *The Donovans*.[29] Here, after rescuing the heroine from a blazing tenement and her child from the railroad tracks, Harrigan and Hart quick-changed to their uniforms and marched *The Mulligan Guard*.[30] They loved the evenings when they could change costumes, shift dialects, and play more than one part. In one early sketch, Harrigan changed a half-dozen times from a German to an Irishman and back and at one point argued with himself offstage, alternating between German and Irish dialects.

Josh Hart gave up the Comique at the end of the season. His successor, T. Allston Brown (better known now as a historian of the New York stage), appeared vague about their future, and so Harrigan and Hart decided to try the road and capture some of the cash that was flowing into the opera houses and town halls across the country.

Neither thought of striking out on his own. In three years of experimenting with new twists and turns, exploring an album of stage portraits (more than many actors tried in a lifetime), and perpetually being astonished by the steady demand for *The Mulligan Guard,* Ned and Tony had become partners for life, or so they believed. And in his writing Harrigan had discovered most of the characters, scenes, and mad adventures that would serve him for the next thirty years.

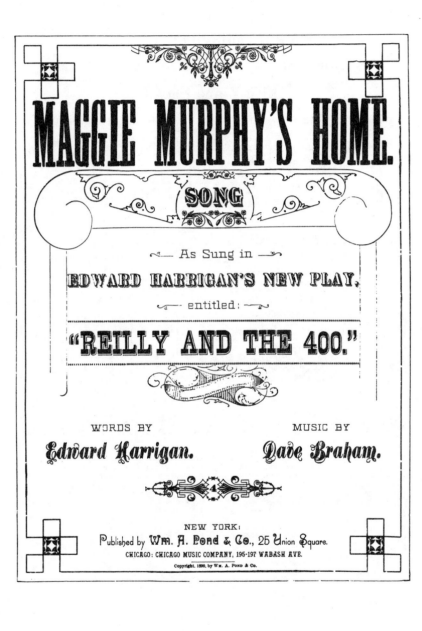

MAGGIE MURPHY'S HOME.

SONG

— As Sung in —

EDWARD HARRIGAN'S NEW PLAY,

— entitled: —

"REILLY AND THE 400."

WORDS BY
Edward Harrigan.

MUSIC BY
Dave Braham.

NEW YORK:
Published by WM. A. Pond & Co., 25 Union Square.
CHICAGO: CHICAGO MUSIC COMPANY, 195-197 WABASH AVE.

MAGGIE MURPHY'S HOME.

As Sung in Edward Harrigan's New Play, Entitled:

"REILLY and the 400."

Words by EDWARD HARRIGAN. Music by DAVE BRAHAM.

1. Be - hind a gram - mar school - house In a dou - ble ten - e - ment, ...
2. Such danc ing in the par - lor, There's a waltz for you and I, ...
3. It's from the o - pen win - dow At the noon - time of the day, ...
4. I walk through Ho - gan's Al - ley, At the clos - ing of the day, ...

.... I live with my old moth - er .... And al - ways pay the rent ....
.... Such mash - ing in the cor - ner .... And kiss - es on the sly ....
.... You'll see the neigh - bors' chil - dren ...... So hap - py at their play, ...
.... To greet my dear old moth - er .... You'll hear the neigh - bors say, ...

12496—3.

A bed - room and a par - lor............ Is all we call our own,
O bless the leis - ure hours............... That work - ing peo - ple know,
There's Jim - my with his Nel - ly............ To - geth - er romp and roam,
Oh there goes lit - tle Mag - gie,............ I wish she were my own.

And your wel - come ev - 'ry eve - ning At Mag - gie Mur - phy's home........
And they're wel - come ev - 'ry eve - ning At Mag - gie Mur - phy's home........
And they gath - er in the school - yard Near Mag - gie Mur - phy's home........
Oh, may bless - ings ev - er lin - ger O'er Mag - gie Mur - phy's home........

Chorus.

On Sun - day night, 'tis my de - light And pleas - ure, don't you

Maggie Murphy's Home.   Wm. A. P. & Co.   12435—3.

see,.............. Meet - ing all the girls and all the boys, That work down

town with me,.................. There's an or - gan in the par - -

lor to give the house a tone, And your wel - come

ev - 'ry eve - - ning, At Mag - gie Mur - phy's home..................

Maggie Murphy's Home WM. A. P. & Co. 12.425—3. WM. B. Everns & Co. 973 Arch Street, Phila., Pa

5

PADDY DUFFY'S CART.

As sung in Edward Harrigan's Comic Play "SQUATTER SOVEREIGNTY."

Words by Ed. Harrigan.

Music by Dave Braham.

1 The ma - ny hap - py eve - nings I spent when but a
2 We'd gath - er in the eve - ning, all hon - est work - ing
3 Oh, a mer - ry lit - tle maid - en, so nob - by, neat and

lad On Pad - dy Duf - fy's lum - ber cart, quite safe a - way from
boys, And get on Pad - dy Duf - fy's cart for no one marr'd our
coy, A - smil - ing up at Duf - fy's cart up - on her sweet - heart

dad; It stood down on the cor - ner, near the old lamp-
joys; All seat - ed in the moon - light, laugh - ing 'mid its
boy; It made a jeal - ous feel - ing, a qui - et piece of

rit.

light. You should see the con - gre - ga - tion there on ev' - ry sum - mer night.
rays. Oh, I love to talk of old New York, and of my boy - ish days.
chaff; But all in play it died a - way and end - ed with a laugh.

rit.

CHORUS.

Oh, there was Tom - my Dob - son, now a sen - a - tor;
Oh, there was Hen - ry Glea - son, now a mil - lion - are;
Oh, there was Lar - ry Thom - son was a chum of mine;

a tempo.

W. A. P. & CO. 10551.

Bil - ly Flyn and John - ny Glyn, oh, they were kill'd in war: All
Cur - ly Rob and Whit - ey Bob, they're liv - ing on the air: All
Lem - my Freer and Sand - y Greer, they died in for - ty - nine: All

mer - ry boy - ish com - rades, re - col - lec - tions bring All

seat - ed there in Duf - fy's cart on sum - mer nights to sing.

*CHORUS after Verses 1 and 3.

Twink - ling stars are laugh-ing, love, laugh-ing on you and me;

While your bright eyes look in mine, Peep-ing stars they seem to be.

*CHORUS after Verse 2. what's the mat - ter, she chews to -

Lit - tle Fraud, Lit - tle Fraud,

W. A. P. & CO. №551.   * By permission of Messrs. O. Ditson & Co.

PHILIP P. ARMSTRONG & CO., MUSIC TYPOGRAPHERS, Philadelphia.

I NEVER DRINK BEHIND THE BAR

AS SUNG IN

ED. HARRIGAN'S

NEW PLAY,

"THE McSORLEYS,"

EMBRACING	
I never drink behind the bar.	McNally's Row of Flats.
The Old Feather Bed.	The Charleston Blues. *March and Chorus.*
The Market on Saturday Night.	Salvation Army, oh !

WORDS BY

ED. HARRIGAN,

MUSIC BY

DAVE BRAHAM.

NEW YORK:
Published by WM. A. POND & CO., 25 Union Square,
Broadway, bet. 15th & 16th Sts.
Chicago: CHICAGO MUSIC CO., 152 State St.

I never Drink behind the Bar.

SONG.

Words by EDWARD HARRIGAN.

Music by DAVE BRAHAM.

Piano.

1. I used to own a
2. Oh, like a pink I
3. Oh, I could mix a
4. I'd stand a lot of

fine sa - loon with mir - rors on the wall, The
mix a drink and toss the glass in style; This
lem - on - ade, a cock - tail, or gin - fiz, 'Twas
coax - ing, and take taf - fy, too, you bet, But

M764—3

fin - est class would nev - er pass but just drop in and call;
round on you a dol - lar due, I whis - per with a smile;
giv - en out that none a - bout could beat me at my biz;
if they'd try to hang me up, the house was not to let;

Good morn - ing, Pete, they'd say to me, your look-ing slick ta - ta, Oh,
Oh, don't go home, I'm quite a - lone, you've time to catch a car,— Try
Oh, your a lal - ly cool - er, Pete, a reg' - lar la - di - da,— They'd
You know me, Pete, they'd say to me, you al - so know my pa,— I'm

will you jine? I must de - cline while I'm be - hind the bar.
one with me, oh, don't you see that I'm be - hind the bar.
wink at me, and bet a "V" I'd drink be - hind the bar.
good for all, come, take a ball! 'Twas cash be - hind the bar.

never drink behind the bar.

W. A. P. & CO. 10764—3

My Dad's Dinner Pail.

As sung in Edward Harrigan's New Comic Play entitled:

"CORDELIA'S ASPIRATIONS"

Words by
ED. HARRIGAN.

Music by
DAVE BRAHAM.

1. Pre -
2. When the
3. If the
4. There's a

-serve that old ket - tle, so black - en'd and worn, It be -
bell rang for meal - time, my fa - ther'd come down, He'd
day should be rain - y, my fa - ther'd stop home, And he'd
place for the cof - fee, and al - so the bread, The

14072 - 3

long'd to my fa - ther be - fore I was born, It
ate wid the work - man a - bout on the ground, He'd
pol ish his ket - tle as clane as a stone; He'd
corn beef and pra - ties, and oft it was said: "Go,

hung in a cor - ner, be - yant on a nail, 'Twas an
share wid a la - b'rer, and say he'd go bail, You would
joke wid me moth - er, and me he would wale If I
fill it wid por - ter, wid beer, or wid ale". The

em - blem of la - bor was Dad's din - ner pail.
ne'er reach the bot - tom of Dad's din - ner pail.
just put a fin - ger on Dad's din - ner pail.
drink would taste sweet - er from Dad's din - ner pail.

REFRAIN.

It glis - ten'd like sil - ver, so spark - ling and bright, I am
fond of the tri - fle that held his wee bite; In
sum - mer or win - ter, in rain, snow or hail, I've
car - ried that ket - tle, my Dad's din - ner pail.

Respectfully dedicated to
COL. CAVANAH, AND THE OFFICERS
AND MEMBERS OF THE 69TH REGT N.G.S.N.Y.

HARRIGAN & HART'S

NEW SONG AND CHORUS

THE GALLANT SIXTY-NINTH.

SUNG BY

TONY HART

AND

CADET CORPS.

Words by **ED. HARRIGAN**   Music by **DAVE BRAHAM.**

NEW YORK.

Published by **Wm. A. Pond & Co.** 25 Union Square.

MILWAUKEE,   SAN FRANCISCO,   BOSTON.   CINCINNATI O,   NEW ORLEANS.
H. N. HEMPSTED.   M. GRAY.   CARL PRUFER.   C. Y. FONDA.   L. GRUNEWALD.
Entd according to Act of Congress in the year 1875 by Wm A. Pond & Co. in the office of the Librarian of Congress at Washington
By the same authors, "Mulligan Guards", "Patricks Day Parade", &c. &c.

THE GALLANT

"69th."

SONG AND CHORUS.

Words by ED. HARRIGAN.

Music by DAVE BRAHAM.

Allo Marciale.

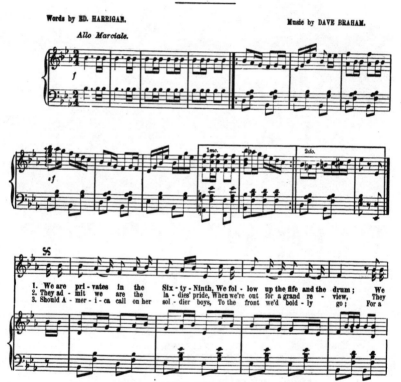

1. We are pri - vates in the Six - ty - Ninth, We fol - low up the fife and the drum; We
2. They ad - mit we are the la - dies' pride, When we're out for a grand re - view, They
3. Should A - mer - i - ca call on her sol - dier boys, To the front we'd bold - ly go; For a

4

can't for-get our old com-rades, And their glo - ry at Bull Run. It was
shout huz - za from near and far, At our I - rish boys so true; With
right - eous cause, our Na - tion's laws, Give bat - tle to the foe. We'll

there with bay - o - nets brist-ling, In the thick - est of the fray, Where the
col - umns so - lid as a wall, Bright uni - forms neat and clean, We are
ne'er for - get old Ire - land, But keep our pow - der dry, "Faugh a

shot and shell were whist-ling, Our boys help'd gain the day.
one and all sons of E - rin, From the land of the Sham-rock green.
bal - lagh" our cry, clear the way, To con - quer or to die.

CHORUS.

We march be - hind the band, True sons of Pad - dy's land, The

5

I - rish boys for style are ex - cel - lent; The green a - bove the

red, With mar - tial step we tread, In the gal - lant Six - ty -

Ninth Reg - i - ment, We ment.

1mo.

2do.

D. C. al Fine.

THE MULLIGAN GUARD.

Composed and arranged by DAVID BRAHAM.

Captain's name was Hussey, a Tipper - ra - ry man, He carried his sword like a Russian duke, when-

-ever he took com - mand. We shoulder'd guns, and march'd,and march'd a - way, From

FORWARD MARCH. f

Bax - ter street, we march'd to Avenue A. With drums and fife, how sweet - ly they did

play, As we march'd,march'd, march'd in the Mulligan Guard. We Guard........

1st. 2d.

Dal Segno

After the Second Verse.

f

The Mulligan Guard. 8504,-3.

When the band play'd Garry Owen,
Or the Connamara Pet;
With a rub a dub, dub, we'd march
In the mud, to the military step.
With the green above the red, boys,
To show where we come from,
Our guns we'd lift with the right shoulder shift,
As we'd march to the bate of the drum.—CHORUS.

2

Whin we got home at night, boys,
The divil a bite we'd ate,
We'd all set up and drink a sup
Of whiskey strong and nate.
Thin we'd all march home together,
As slippery as lard,
The solid min would all fall in,
And march with the Mulligan Guard.—CHORUS.

3

The Mulligan Guard.   8504,-3.

Harrigan

Schloss —

Harrigan

Harrigan

Hart

Ned Harrigan Club

SOUVENIR PROGRAMME
BEEFSTEAK DINNER
NED HARRIGAN CLUB

"The Mulligan Guards"

TEUTONIA ASSEMBLY ROOMS
158 THIRD AVENUE, NEW YORK

THURSDAY, MARCH TWENTY-SIXTH
NINETEEN FOURTEEN

COMPLIMENTS
JOE HUMPHREYS, PRES

Credit: Museum of the City of New York

H&H as Mulligan Guards

Harrigan's Guard Costume   Hart's Guard Costume

The Ten Little Mulligan Guards

Ten Little Mulligans

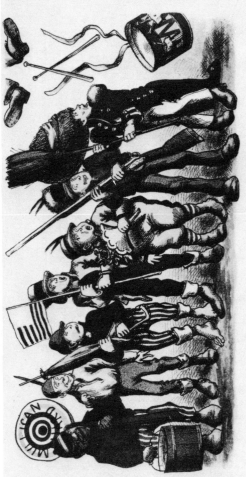

'Twas gaily then we marched along
  Until we reached Broadway,
And there we all presented arms
  To get a sweet bouquet.

Then Tommy Snapps he burst his straps,
  And flew straight up to Heaven,
And of the Little Mulligans then
  We only had but seven.

Ten Little Mulligans

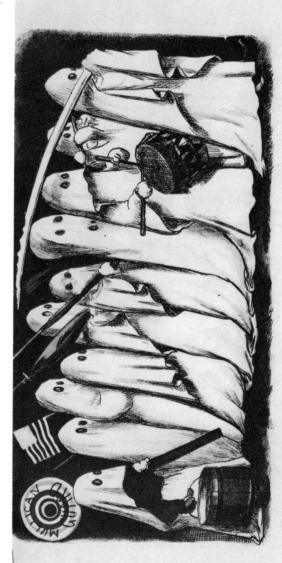

'Tis sad to read this story,
  But yet, one Summer's night,
I saw these Little Mulligans
  All dressed in spotless white.

Their band was playing gaily,
  His sword the Captain swung,
And to the stirring music
  This chorus then they sung.

Chorus.—Swords and guns and flags a-flying free, &c., &c.

Ten Little Mulligans

NEW
BELLA UNION

Kearny St., One Door North of Washington St.

PROPRIETOR .... SAMUEL TETLOW
STAGE MANAGER .... JAMES DOWLING | ACTING MANAGER ....HARRY CORBYN
MUSICAL DIRECTOR .... E. ZIMMER | BALLET MASTER .... M. AUGUST LEHMAN

Re-appearance of
GRACE DARLEY

KATHLEEN O'NEIL
MINNIE CORBYN
ADA HARCOURT

Ida May, Minnie Fillmore,
May Carlton, Mattie Thorne,
Nellie Brooks, Sallie Thayer,
Ned Buckley, Ned Harrigan,
Fred Howson, Will Bark,
Mat Kelly,
Aug. Lehman & Young America,

THE STAR ACROBATS.

THURSDAY EVENING, APRIL 22

Bella Union Program

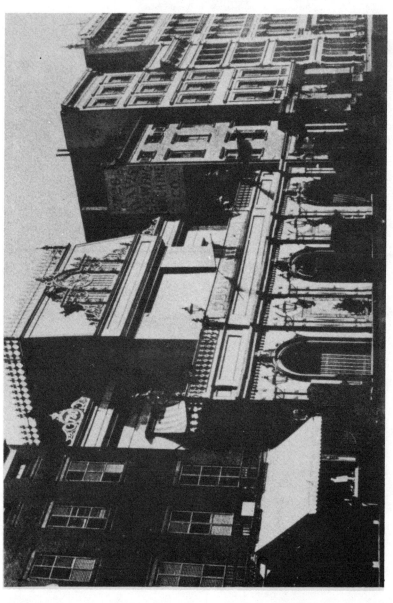

Globe Theatre

Little Fraud

Credit: Nedda Harrigan Logan

You 'Spute Me

1874 Comique Company

St. Patrick's Day Parade

Comique Army

Martin Hanley

Dave Braham

Harrigan and Hart in *Doyle Bros.*

The original Harrigan and Hart

H&H Combination Composite

Hart and Harrigan in *Old Lavender*

Dan Mulligan

Harrigan in *The Major*

H&H New York Boys

7

Letters to Annie

Harrigan and Hart had come up in the theatrical world. Three years earlier the Nonpareils, alias California Comedians, had tracked the circuit with *Little Fraud* and little more than their Boston record to attract the managers. Now they claimed the endorsement of Broadway, and they carried a full evening's entertainment with their Harrigan and Hart Combination, a company of thirty-seven actors, musicians, and marching boys, the "Gallant 69th."

The Brahams lent strong support to the enterprise. Harrigan spent most of his off-duty hours in New York with them, working up new songs with David and edging ahead with Annie, and he met more Brahams. Joseph and Harry now joined him as musicians, and Martin W. Hanley, Mrs. Braham's brother, became business manager. "Genial Mart" Hanley, a charming, picturesque man with a mass of black hair and perpetually rosy cheeks, was endowed with a natural magnetism, suavity, and unfailing good humor that invited friendship.[1] He seemed to know everyone, and everyone liked him. Certainly much of the success of the tour and of Harrigan's later career resulted from his industry and tact.

Two years older than Harrigan, Hanley was born in Tipperary, began in the theatre as a super at the Bowery, joined the famous French pantomimists, the Ravels, first as Harlequin, then as manager. Two years before meeting Harrigan, he had deserted the Ravels, married their vivacious niece Marietta, a tightrope dancer, and managed her career until she retired into domesticity. When he signed on with the new combination, he cast his lot with Harrigan permanently. From then until his death in 1905, except for one brief interlude, Harrigan's friends counted on a pastoral welcome in the lobby from "Father" Hanley, a sobriquet he acquired by reversing his collar. (He discovered the trick before David Belasco.)

Mutual respect and affection bound them together. Hanley once told a *Dramatic Mirror* reporter that no angry word had ever passed between them; "Ned is the soul of honor, a gentleman in every sense of the word. I don't think you'll find his match in the history of the American theatre."[2] And in a letter to Annie, Ned wrote: "What a good faithful man. He is all business and it is to his intelligence and business qualifications that we owe our success. You know I am Mart's confidante. He tells me everything, certain I won't tell anybody. And so faithful to his family. He sends all his money home, except for buying what he actually needs. God bless him." Harrigan prized the Hanley virtues and tried to cultivate them in himself.

The traveling troupe for the new Harrigan play had meshed so easily and casually that no one realized what a winning combination they had with Hanley out front, music by Braham, sketches by Harrigan, stage madness by Harrigan and Hart, tricky marching by the boys, and all woven into *The Doyle Brothers,* a detective thriller of murder, fearless pursuit, salvation, and final justice. An ideal program for the provincials who doted on *Uncle Tom's Cabin* and *East Lynne,* who filled their halls for Tony Pastor's Combination or Haverly's Minstrels. Here was a full bundle of terror, tears, and uproarious laughter, all for one price and in one evening.

The Doyle Brothers[3] came from the same mold as *Eureka* and *The Donovans.* Woodard may have sketched the story—Hanley once hinted as much—but clearly most of the final version belonged to Harrigan. The action moved easily from a melodramatic chase to miscellaneous variety turns, some lifted from earlier sketches, with Harrigan and Hart as Darby and Lanty, a theatrical team turned detectives. And as if that transformation would not keep the partners occupied, each had four other roles: Harrigan as an Irish Gentleman, Wabert from London, Old Uncle Pete, and Italian Joe; Hart as Johanna McCann, Hedwin of the Alhambra, Mrs. McGillicuddy, and Luce, a Colored Cherub. More than half the parts were played by Harrigan and Hart. It was the kind of energetic evening they loved.

Comic routines alternated with chills and thrills, a rescue from the train tracks in a "rocky pass out west." Darby climbing from the window of a flaming building with a lady draped over his shoulder. And the finale in the courtroom with Darby, as prosecutor and witness, confounding the judge, exposing the villain, and inspiring the hero's "colleen, a female girl of the feminine gender," to pronounce the final tribute: "Of all earthly treasures there are none we hold so dear as the loyal friendship of the Doyle Brothers." Loud cheers for Harrigan and Hart!

The cheers began in Boston on August 16, 1875, and followed them as they zigzagged across the country to a final two weeks at Mrs. John Drew's Arch Street Theatre in Philadelphia the following June. Harrigan and Hart were never away from New York that long again.

Newspaper reports, programs, and most of all the steady stream of letters from Ned to Annie Braham recount their daily triumphs, the rigors of jumping from city to city, his frank revelations about himself, his homesickness for the Brahams, and in every letter dreamy thoughts of Annie.

After a week in Boston they began the westward trek, stopping at Albany, Troy, Cohoes, then into Pennsylvania, Danville and Scranton. This was followed by a week at the Holliday Street Theatre in Baltimore, "the most successful week since the theatre opened," and a week at Ford's Theatre in Washington. Then after engagements in Wilmington, Paterson, and Newark, they returned to New York for a day's rest. A strenuous five weeks.

Annie's letters cheered Harrigan and kept him at top form. His first from Troy on September 4, 1875, was typical of the many to follow.[1] He reports that he's in excellent health, has gained 4 pounds, now weighs 138. "Hearty eating and plenty of fresh air works wonders." She should follow his example, get out and walk around more. He could indulge himself and write a lot of "soft nonsense," but that would take up lots of room and he knows she's a good sensible girl. Still he hopes she'll not be offended if "once in a while I tell you how much I think of you."

Four days later from Danville, Pennsylvania, he wonders if she misses him in the evening, as much as he misses her. If only he had a gigantic cane to reach her window, to tap when she's lonely. Her Uncle Martin is getting stout, "looking fresh and happy as an English squire and pulling his moustache as often as ever." The 69th boys are in splendid condition, working handsomely, and wearing out their uniforms as fast as regular New York soldiers. Luckily Hanley had scheduled only a single night in Danville; the workshops are closed, over five hundred houses unoccupied. They'll be fortunate if they get out with expenses.

What a contrast in Baltimore, where they "made an immense hit," in spite of competition from the circus and two variety theatres. In mid-September all he can think of is being home in two weeks for Sunday dinner with the Brahams. Hope she doesn't mind that he invites himself, a reward he deserves for being a good boy: "I am behaving like a saint, no beer, or any running around and I feel all the better for it."

Most of his letters were written on small sheets of lined paper, though in Baltimore he snitched an official letterhead: "The Original / Harrigan and Hart / M. W. Hanley, Business manager." Before he came for dinner he wanted Annie to be impressed by their eminence. Two months later, when Hanley ordered new stationery in Cleveland, he discovered that the partners' names were not as well known as he had thought. Harrigan was relieved of one *r,* and on the programs, as if the same printer were trying to correct his error, the *r* was restored but into "Harrison." The same spelling problem that had confounded Harrigan's father.[5]

Harrigan savored the Sunday in New York, every moment of his reunion with Annie, knowing that when he departed on Monday they would not see each other again until the following April. The pain of breaking away had become almost unbearable.

The second leg of the tour took them to New Haven, to Providence, across Massachusetts and New York to Buffalo, through the corner of Pennsylvania, Erie and Meadville, to Cleveland and Dayton, where the manager billed them as Harrigan and Hart's Minstels. Then, after backtracking to Pittsburgh and Wheeling, they headed west again into Ohio and Indiana, had Christmas week in Detroit, and hit Fort Wayne and Logansport before beginning a week in Chicago on January 3, 1876. Everywhere they were announced with Hanley's fanfare:

> UNPRECEDENTED ATTRACTION / THE ORIGINAL / HARRIGAN AND HART / WITH THEIR GRAND COMBINATION / AND / THE GALLANT 69TH OF NEW YORK. Having concluded their highly successful engagement on Broadway, where their wonderful versatility and artistic performances were received with acclamation and delight by the elite of the metropolis, they will appear, supplied by a COMPANY OF DRAMATIC ARTISTS and splendid orchestra, in their new and beautiful drama, THE DOYLE BROTHERS, unequivocally transcendant in mirth, provoking dialogue, and laughable situations. HARRIGAN AND HART will introduce their world-renowned Musical Sketches, of which they are the originals.[6]

Few could resist Hanley's invitation. All along the way the houses were jammed, and when they crossed paths with Frank Mayo in *Davy Crockett,* Haverly's Minstrels, John T. Raymond as Colonel Sellers, Buffalo Bill's show, or Tony Pastor's Combination, they held their own or outdrew the competition. And the local reporters were as extravagant as Hanley: "Every creation of these versatile artists a gem." "Nothing ever so funny as the court scene."[7] "The 69th a great hit—audience demanded three repeats." "They deserve great credit and full patronage for introducing such a moral entertainment."[8]

Harrigan's letters glowed with their success. "You wouldn't believe the reputation we are making throughout the country, besides making money." All signs pointed to easier years ahead and more money, yet he kept his fingers crossed. "Fortune has been kind to us; yet I know she may turn fickle at any moment." Annie must not believe the malicious lies in the *Dramatic News.* Those reports of financial disaster were composed by Josh Hart and T. Allston Brown. Let theatrical jealousy turn old friends to enemies; he would not join the battle. When he heard that Josh Hart had appropriated *Down Broadway* and featured a miniature Seventh Regiment of one hundred boys, he asked Annie to say nothing: "I wouldn't have anybody think I would notice." Harrigan was always charitable toward his competitors.

Prosperity had not gone to his head. He was being a good boy, sticking to work—"you know I aint lazy am I?"—and guarding his money. Regularly he reported on his good health—by the time they reached Dayton he had gained thirteen pounds and continued to thrive in spite of miserable rations. In Detroit "we sat down to the leg of an old veteran turkey who must have died from starvation." How he longed to sit down for dinner with the Brahams. He could picture Annie in the kitchen, "getting the greens out of the oven or sticking the fork in the beef." From Cleveland he begged her to send him the wishbone from their Thanksgiving turkey.

In spite of the rugged routine—never to bed until after midnight and most of the time up at five or six for the trip to the next town —he never missed a performance and only once complained of any affliction. In Cohoes he suffered from a boil on his neck which he was sure came from the constant blacking up and washing for the "Old Pete" number.

His good-conduct reports, personal and financial, were part of his courtship. Only once, on a Sunday morning in New Orleans, he confessed to a headache from three or four glasses of wine "with the solid men of the city." It was the first time he'd failed to give Tony and the others the slip after the show. "They won't catch up with me again."

He always inquired about her parents and sent his greetings. She must excuse him "for calling your father Dave. It comes to me so natural I cannot help it." If her father was upset at misreading their telegram from Pittsburgh, he needn't be. When Uncle Joe arrived to play second violin instead of Harry, it didn't really matter. Might even be better. Harry is sometimes too "nice to the ladies, too willing to let them under his umbrella."[9]

Money was rolling in and not much rolling out. He repaid a debt to her brother and was now clear with the world. Harrigan had a passion for staying out of debt. Although his sisters never wrote, he mailed them money every week. "I won't write unless they do but will continue the allowance. I suppose that's better than letters to them." Harrigan always shared his prosperity with his family. Apparently he had found some kind of job in the company for his father, though his duties were never detailed and only one letter alludes to his presence. From Meadville he wrote that his father had caught cold and would probably have to go home.

She should know that that spendthrift Tony has bought some splendid diamonds, a ring and pin for $300, and "what fun he is having over those diamonds." Let him have his fun, "I shall buy mine in dirt, a good house, beds, carpets, etc." As naturally as their inclinations meshed onstage, offstage Tony and Ned did not see eye to eye. Tony lived for the moment, confident that the next hour, the next day would take care of itself. Ned was always looking ahead, preparing for tomorrow, conscious of his Horatio Alger obligations. Like Annie, "sensible little woman that you are," he stuck to his motto, "Face the music. Go in and win." He managed to stay happy no matter what came his way, confident that "Ned will really be an actor by and by."

He was always working up new material, a new Irish act to replace the "Parade," and in Fort Wayne they introduced *Broadway Statuettes*. "I have my hair parted in the middle and wear an elegant new suit, red necktie, and piccadilly collar. For a homely fellow they say I am a darling. As for Tony he looks like one of those painted angels you see in valentines." In Pittsburgh he devised a new drill for the 69th, "forming some of the prettiest pictures you ever saw." It was no accident they were called the 69th. The gallantry of the real "fighting 69th" at Gettysburg, at the Second Battle of Bull Run, at Antietam, Fredericksburg, and Chancellorsville was well known.

The 69th kept things lively on stage and off. In Pittston, Pennsylvania, the "little fellows slushed through the snow in the St. Patrick's Day parade." From Providence, Harrigan reported, "Martin has just gone to church with the boys. How is that for an advertisement? The Gallant 69th singing hymns, imagine that. Ain't it splendid?" Landlords regularly complained about their ravenous appetites, grabbing two dumplings when the quota was one, and in Elmira when two of the boys got "too fresh," they were sent home and replaced by two eager country lads.

Much as Harrigan revealed about himself and day-to-day affairs, he revealed more of his growing love for Annie, now that his "little girl was sweet sixteen at last." He went to sleep thinking about her letter and wondering what made her think he was cross. "I never get mad, with anyone I like." Doesn't she know he keeps her picture on his trunk, to look at every morning. And at night, "I can't see you to kiss you so I kiss your picture. Ain't I silly—

well we can't all be wise." If she only knew how much he cherished her letters and how long he lingered over his reply. "The longer we tarry at the gate the better. You know how long I used to stay over to your house at nights. Well if I did not admire someone I would have retired earlier."

When the company left Chicago for St. Louis and points south, Memphis, New Orleans, Mobile, Montgomery, Atlanta, Chattanooga, and Nashville, and then headed back toward New York, the letters were warming to a proposal. She knows how fond he is of her parents, how familiar he's become in their house, as if he belonged to the family. He's making hay while the sun shines because he has something to live for, and he might want a nice home of his own by and by. Her parents probably won't ever move from Carmine Street, but "you will some day, won't you?" Why does she say she's bashful? She must get over that. Haven't they been acquainted more than three years? And why does she apologize for the picture she sent? She might be getting stout, but he likes a good strong constitution; it keeps people alive. And after he's slept through a fire in Scranton, he speculates on marriage and fire bells: "I know if I was a married man there would be an awful kick, but I hardly think I would run to fires then. Oh dear, what am I saying?"

As melancholy as he often seemed in wanting "to set down by her and look in her dear black eyes," his letters were never gloomy. He found plenty of sunshine in the theatre. In New Orleans, "the rebel country where everybody looks down-hearted and sad—on bad terms with themselves," they were given a glorious reception. One night he and Tony were presented with gold medals from a man in a private box who "talked for an awful while and we had to stand like two gawks and listen." When he finished, "I bowed and spoke a polite thank you, but Tony killed the act, muttering, 'I don't know what to say,' and stuck." With all the medals we've accumulated—enough to dress like Christmas trees, Tony should have done better.

New Orleans taught him he could win an audience against its will. When he appeared in *The Blue and the Grey,* a new hands-across-the-border sketch, dressed in the uniform of a 69th New York Volunteer, singing of his loneliness on the Potomac, the audience greeted him with a hateful stare. Harrigan stared back, marched to the footlights, broke out his warmest Irish smile, and pleaded, "For the love of God, won't you give the Yankee a hand?" Much as every loyal Southern son despised his blue coat, they could not resist Ned Harrigan.[10]

Before leaving New Orleans, Harrigan had his picture taken for Annie, "trying not to look so much like a minister or the fellow who has lost his sweetheart . . . a bit of a low comedy smile, yet serious enough to look like a manager." When he put the photograph in the mail, he begged her to remember "it isn't always the best lookers that can do the best act, is it dear?" Harrigan never encouraged comparison with the matinee idols. He was not a clotheshorse actor.

After covering the South, they slowly retraced their path through Indiana, Ohio, and Pennsylvania, then circled back to New York State with return engagements in Elmira, Ithaca, Auburn, Utica, Troy, and Albany. Everywhere the theatres were crowded with repeaters, and everywhere the reporters welcomed them back: "Their bill is simply immense and the drill of the young lads in the 69th and the Mulligan Guards reflects great credit upon this superb combination."[11] Practically every town from the Atlantic to the Mississippi now knew Harrigan and Hart.

As they neared New York at the end of March, Harrigan thought mostly of the Brahams and his future. He would spend the precious hours with Annie and on his own work, not "running around the city talking to one guy and another, those guys who grab your coat and tell you what you ought to do and if you take their advice you will be president." Harrigan always avoided the theatrical blowhards. From Auburn he wrote on March 27, 1876, that he would leave right after the Saturday night show, get in early in the morning before she's up, "but I shall call first at your house and then go over home in Brooklyn and stay until ten or eleven—then to your house—all afternoon and night to talk and tell you lots of things. On second thought I think it is best I eat breakfast at your house. What a cheek I've got ain't I? Don't want to lose sight of you all day. Ain't I hoggish?"

With a week together they must have shared serious thoughts about the future. Perhaps a solemn man-to-man talk with David, a down-on-the-knees proposal? No solid evidence supports this speculation, only what can be read into such subsequent lines as those from Lowell on May 6: "Oh, if I only had my Annie with me which I shall if I don't die. Well bless me, I am talking like an undertaker"; and from Lawrence, "Home in eleven days after Danbury—Home Sweet Home!"

The final months of the year on the road were more hectic and less rewarding. They began in Albany, backtracked to Newburgh, Trenton, Newark, then to Bridgeport, where Hanley lost his temper for the first time: "Oh, he was mad." The property boy had left the 69th's uniforms and belts in a trunk in Newark, and the Gallants had to march in mufti. Fortunately their gear caught up with them in New Haven. They had another mishap in Newburyport when the scenery missed the schedule. After Providence, Hartford, Worcester, and Springfield, they struggled through one-nighters in Portland, Manchester, Concord, Nashua, Fitchburg, and Leominster. "What a long time these five weeks among the bean eaters." The mill towns appear devoid of men, only an army of girls who work ten hours a day. "There must be a million old maids in New England" who seem to have neither the means nor the inclination to finish their day in the theatre. Harrigan found only one consolation: Tony Pastor and the other troupes fared no better.

The bleak New England memories quickly evaporated when he returned to "home sweet home," and the Combination "fresh from their unprecedentedly successful tour of the States" took over Brooklyn's Park Theatre for a week. Every night, hundreds were turned away. Their long absence plus the intelligence that had filtered back from around the country had aroused the public to a climactic welcome. Remembrances were exchanged among the company, and the marching boys, now stretching the last inch out of their uniforms, pooled their savings and presented Hanley with a "gold watch and chain worth at least $500."[12]

Following the Brooklyn triumph, they had a week in Jersey City and two final glorious weeks in Philadelphia. While they were still playing at the Arch Street Theatre there, Hanley rushed back to New York to negotiate for 514 Broadway, and, on July 15, the Spirit of the Times announced that Harrigan and Hart, with M. W.

Hanley as manager, had taken over the Theatre Comique. "Their success is assured; they will raise the tone of the house; the Comique will again become a favorite resort. These gentlemen by their industry and talent have, in a short time, made themselves very popular, and they certainly deserve their extraordinary success."[13]

8

Wedding in Greenwich Village

When the Comique opened on August 7, 1876, with *The Blue and the Grey* and the gallant boys, now in blackface, singing "Ginger Blues," Harrigan and Hart took their trunks to the attic. New York was now to be their permanent home. The Comique was scrubbed clean and freshened with paint, the lobby window to Sandy Spencer's bar opened for business, David Braham was ready in the pit—to accompany the aerialists, gymnasts, banjoists, dancers, and diverse eccentrics (Stewart Dare, the one-legged gymnast; Harry Parker's dogs). "The three H's"—Harrigan, Hart, and Hanley—promised to eradicate whatever unsavory odors clung to the Comique from its previous season of Matt Morgan's Living Statues.[1] They would supplant the statues with high-class specialities plus extracts from *The Doyle Brothers* and, for most every Monday night's opening, fresh sketches from the Harrigan notebooks.

Old friends rushed to the box office. New recruits joined the stampede. Every night the house was jammed to capacity, a thousand strong roaring their welcome. Go early, one reporter advised, or "you won't find a seat for love or money. Harrigan and Hart have done miracles at the Comique. For unbounded hilarity they can't be beat. You will laugh till you cry over the mightiest and merriest of entertainments."[2] Nor did the enthusiasm fade after the initial excitement. Throughout the year, Hanley's beaming welcome in the lobby told the story: the ticket racks were bare; the cash drawer was filled.

Harrigan had uncovered a new talent: serving as general manager. Today he would be called an artistic director. He arranged and rehearsed the entire bill. Every week he assembled a fresh mixture, old acts and new, with always enough of the new to delight his steady customers. No one could boast of seeing the Harrigan and Hart show until he had seen the current week's offering. How Harrigan squeezed his heavy load of writing, rehearsing, and performing into each day without collapsing, without giving himself a breather, remains a mystery to contemplate with envy and empathic exhaustion. He was blessed with incredible energy and a knack for never wasting a moment.

How else could he have progressed with Annie? Their courtship had reached its climactic moments. Before Thanksgiving they would be married. If his timetable had allowed for contemplation, he might have questioned his temerity in acquiring a theatre and a wife all in the same season. The thought never crossed his mind.

Sketches moved constantly from his desk to the stage. He was never trapped on dead center. His imagination never ran dry. It helped that he revisited scenes and characters he'd already tested, in *S.O.T.* (Sons of Temperance), *Bold Hibernian Boys,* and *Walkin' for Dat Cake,* an authentic copy of a Negro cakewalk he'd seen in the South. But he also wandered into new territory with *Bar Ber Ous,* a madcap backstage burlesque of an amateur troupe getting up a show. And in *Malone's Night Off, or, the German Turnverein* he advanced another step toward the *Mulligan* plays with recognizable locales on the Lower East Side, Irish-German skirmishes, and a grand turnverein finale: Awfulback Gilmore (Harrigan) pursuing the band through the "William Reilly Overture," baton in one hand, a flag in the other.

Through the fall months, Harrigan was also at work on a long play, convinced that if he were to advance as a writer he must subdue the temptation to turn everything to fun. The result was *Iascaire* (the Gaelic word for "fisherman"), "a new and original Irish romantic drama in one act and nine tableaux," a tale of villainy and dispossession—a familiar, true-to-life story for many Irishmen[3]—with Harrigan playing the villain's deformed son and

Hart a loquacious fisherman who saves the family. New roles for both of them, demonstrating their versatility and showing that they could handle pathos and heroics as well as hilarity.

The O'Sullivans are about to be dispossessed. Their son Jerold is a fugitive for having joined the "uprising agin the sogers." Cornelius Lynch, the villainous lawyer—"when St. Patrick carried the snakes out of Ireland in a basket that one must have dropped out" —will stay the eviction and call off the pursuit of Jerold if the O'Sullivans' daughter will marry him. She refuses, and Lynch announces, "I'll tache you Oona O'Sullivan my proud beauty." Lynch is a relentless demon. His leather whip repeatedly lashes the back of his deformed and illegitimate son Michael (Harrigan).

Shaun O'Kelly (Hart), a sweet-talking fisherman, is in love with Oona, protects the family, and engineers Jerold's escape. All hands assemble at a ruined chapel on the coast where a boat is to take Jerold to France and then to America. Signal lights flash in the darkness, Jerold descends from his cell on a rope, Shaun appears in the boat. Lynch gags Oona, tangles with Jerold and then with Michael. Finally, Michael stabs his father: "You brought me into the world to send you out of it." Harrigan knew how to capture tears and cheers.

A christening party at Squire Brady's provides the Harrigan hilarity. The squire performs his game-leg gig on the table top, and Shaun lubricates the festivities with a hamper of liquor disguised as fish: "cognac flounder, Marseilles wake fish, and Holland gin herring."

With the demands of his new role, with the careful rehearsals required for a full-length serious play, Harrigan compressed his honeymoon into a weekend. *Iascaire* opened on Monday, November 20, 1876. He was married on Saturday, November 18.

Annie and Ned spoke their vows before Father Fritz Harris and a small gathering, family and a few friends from the theatre, in St. Joseph's Church on Sixth Avenue at Washington Place.[4] The ceremony matched the simplicity of the church, a neat Greek-revival structure built in 1833 and now the oldest Roman Catholic church in New York. Neither of the Brahams was Catholic, though Mrs. Braham turned to the church for ceremonials and when she sought spiritual guidance. David knew only the ecclesiastical vestiges that survived in some of the Broadway theatres. His father, of Orthodox Jewish heritage, had deserted the family home in Frankfurt-am-Main in the eighteenth century and married a gentile in London.[5]

After the ceremony, the seventeen-year-old bride and the busy bridegroom, fifteen years her senior, stepped into a hired carriage (Tony Hart might well have supplied this accommodation: he loved private transportation) for the three-block ride to the Brahams at 22 Varick, where food, drink, and best wishes celebrated the union.[6] The Braham home became the Harrigan home for the next five years: the following year at 26 King Street, then at 30 King. Even when the families separated in 1881, both remained in Greenwich Village, the Brahams at 175 West Tenth, the Harrigans in a three-story red brick at 14 Perry, where they lived for the next ten years.

The Harrigans began early to follow the Brahams' example in begetting children, and the resulting scramble for beds, rather than any domestic turmoil, eventually forced them to adopt separate establishments. Seven Braham children and three Harrigans were too many for a single dwelling. One Harrigan baby had already died in infancy, and two more were to follow that sad example after the move to Perry Street. Finally the Harrigan brood would equal the Brahams, as if Annie were competing with her mother. Unlike the Brahams, most of whom stuck with music, only three of the Harrigans who reached maturity stayed in the theatre: Edward, the firstborn, whose death at seventeen cut a sadness into his father's heart from which he never fully recovered. William, who became a distinguished actor, appearing in such productions as *The Great God Brown* and *Mister Roberts.* Nedda, who had a successful career in the theatre while married to the actor Walter Connolly; after his death she appeared in Joshua Logan's revival of *Charley's Aunt* and retired from the stage when she became Mrs. Logan. Adelaide, who married a wealthy Philadelphian. And three other sons, who added distinction to the name outside the theatre: Anthony, a doctor; Philip, a coal merchant; and Nolan, a banker.

The Harrigan family circle bore other similarities to the Brahams. Love and loyalty subdued domestic tensions before they ever caught fire. Outsiders who crossed the threshold invariably remarked on the family pride shared by all Harrigans, on the affection that passed so easily between them. Children climbed over their father at will, and he always found snuggling room for the last arrival. Only when Annie announced that time was up did he release them. Annie managed the household firmly but never harshly. And almost immediately after their marriage, her voice carried into the theatre.

She always maintained a happy home and a ready welcome for him and his friends. While Harrigan was at the theatre in the evening, she laid a fire in their second-floor sitting room, laid out an after-the-show supper, repaired what damage the day had inflicted on her gypsy vivacity, and slipped into her cashmere Mother Hubbard to greet her husband. Her father and Ned rarely came alone and often brought a carton of fried oysters to add to the table. The food was supplemented with beer, a small glass of Zinfandel diluted with water and a teaspoon of sugar for her, and ale for David. David's ale was never poured until his pewter mug had been heated on the coals.[7]

Harrigan never built a wall between home and theatre. He wrote at home, tried out songs and speeches on whoever was handy to listen—he once said he adopted the habit from Molière—and shared the daily events with the family. Whenever big decisions had to be made, they waited until Annie spoke her mind. As his career advanced, as prosperity brought new problems at the Comique, he depended more and more on her. Writing and rehearsals he could handle alone. She had a better head for business.

Annie's stamina and efficiency were as astounding as his: waiting out ten pregnancies, mothering seven youngsters through childhood afflictions, and, just as she faced the arduous task of guiding their school days, "the Duchess," as she became known in the theatre world, took an even more active role, if behind the scenes, in Ned's theatrical affairs. It was a remarkable union of two remarkable people.

When Harrigan returned to the theatre from his brief honeymoon, he hoped his successful engagement at the church would be duplicated with *Iascaire,* his bid for attention as a serious dramatist. The press was kind, compared him favorably with Dion

Boucicault, the recognized master of Irish melodrama, but the public did not respond. Harrigan accepted this judgment, abandoned the play after two weeks, and settled the Comique and himself into the old routine.

Before the end of the season, more than a dozen Harrigan sketches reached the stage, ranging over the New York landscape and challenging the partners to fresh lunacies. Hart became a sleuth and Harrigan a Jewish clothing dealer in *Callahan, the Detective. My Son Dan* featured a mad burlesque of the *Romeo and Juliet* balcony scene—it would be used again. And *Matrimonial Ads* explored the risk of bigamy or sudden divorce when roving husbands and restless wives are tempted by the "personals" in the newspapers.

On March 19, 1877, Harrigan's *The Telephone* got a month's jump on the "eminent artists" who were scheduled to sing "Home Sweet Home" and the "Last Rose of Summer" in Philadelphia and have their voices carried by wire to New York's Steinway Hall. The telephone was still an astounding curiosity. Alexander Graham Bell had transmitted the first telephonic communication —"Mr. Watson, come here, I want you"—on March 10, 1876. And just before Harrigan brought Bell's invention to the stage, Judge Henry Hilton, owner of the A. T. Stewart department store, had agreed to test an instrument in his establishment, providing it was installed without charge and did not disrupt business.

Harrigan's telephone, a gigantic funnel-shaped instrument, is installed in the outer office of a divorce lawyer. He specializes in divorce cases because they are "thicker than strawberries." Assorted husbands and wives feed their questions into the funnel, and the lawyer transmits his replies from his inner sanctum.

A month earlier Harrigan had taken account of another local phenomenon. In November 1871, the Russian Grand Duke Alexis had paraded up Broadway with a National Guard regiment, attended a ball at the Brooklyn Navy Yard, had his picture taken at Brady's Gallery, and, on a slumming excursion to the Five Points, had been taken to a cellar theatre in a tenement on Baxter Street that was operated by ten newspaper boys. When the duke and his entourage gave the boys a standing ovation, they echoed his extravagance by naming their theatre "The Grand Duke Opera House," although the place could hardly be called grand.[8]

A slippery wooden staircase led to the catacomb tunnel where the cashier collected three cents admission. Snaking into the rugged benches, one scraped one's head on the ceiling. The stage, sunk a foot below the benches, was illuminated by three kerosene lamps that doubled as houselights. The *Spirit of the Times* reported that the drop scene of a Greek temple did not conform to the pervading atmosphere, suggestive of drains and Italian cooking, nor to the stage spectacle: an Irish biddy addicted to the bottle and a heavy brogue gets pitched out the window by a German bully. A Negro is demolished by the umbrellas of two Hibernians. Siamese twins are sold to Mr. Barnum for ten dollars and then dissipate their value by separating.

Horatio Alger's Julius, the street boy, reported that when he visited the opera house he saw a "laughing gas" sketch and a marching chorus singing that "celebrated local song, The Mulligan Guards," and that Dave, the stage manager, told him that all the acts were copied from Harrigan's Comique.[9]

Harrigan returned the compliment, saluting the juvenile thespians with *The Grand Duke Opera House*, a sketch about a quartette of Blackwell's Island lunatics: Geleary, a champion walker; Skyhigh, the kite man; Bucphalus, who fancies himself a horse; Macready Booth, a decayed actor; and The Quite Man, a paragon of good sense who loves everyone except his mother-in-law.

Even with the surefire success of the minifarces, Harrigan was again working on a full-length play, and on January 1, 1877, a week later than intended, *Christmas Joys and Sorrows* opened. Farce sprinkled with melodrama was the new game. Death, near death, abduction, and unjust incarceration alternated with the farcical misadventures of Berrian Suil, "Berrian by name and Berrian by nature"; Jeremiah McCarthy (Harrigan), the happy undertaker; and the blackfaced Caroline Long (in later plays called Rebecca Allup), Tony Hart's most famous creation.

Jeremiah appears in most every scene flashing his advertising card: "Jeremiah McCarthy, Undertaker, funerals promptly attended to. Country orders filled." He eyes everyone as a prospect, and whenever he and Berrian meet in the cemetery to share a bottle—"nothing like having spirits all around you"—they exchange notes on their latest professional adventures. Jeremiah boxes and refrigerates their clients, and Berrian escorts them on the final journey and sometimes even resurrects them late at night "to introduce them to a doctor for a five or ten."[10]

Certainly Master Antonio in his Providence days would never have guessed that burnt cork and a skirt would bring him fame and fortune. Hart struck gold with his Negro transvestite Caroline Long. Audiences marveled at Caroline's rhetorical dexterity and her speedy recovery from widowhood. Her late husband "was eating clams in de fore part of the evening, den he took a lunch about nine of some raw lobster and green watermelon, wid a bowl of goat's condensed milk and de supposition is dat he died from a weak stomach." When a greedy mourner inquires if the deceased left any old clothes, she reports that he had only two changes, "Off and on!"

Other Harrigan trademarks were foreshadowed. Meticulously detailed scene descriptions were to become standard, and when words failed him, he wrote, "See Model."[11] McCarthy's dogged attempts to persuade his mother-in-law to respect his calling gave Harrigan and Annie Yeamans the first of the snappy verbal battles that would delight audiences for the next twenty-five years. Margaret O'Dooley (Yeamans) taunts Jeremiah about his competitor who beat him out of "two odd fellows, a free mason and a son of temperance." When he tells her that his latest client opened one eye when he started to screw down the lid, then both eyes, she deflates him as a mother-in-law should: "Tell that to the marines."

Imitations of McCarthy and Berrian's tombstone chatter would enliven many later plays. As they celebrate the triumph of virtue with beer in the belfry, they toast the season and bring down the curtain with the "Undertaker's Song":

> McCARTHY: Christmas comes but once a year. Here's to the undertaker that likes his bier.
> BERRIAN: Here's a Merry Christmas to those living wherever found. Here's a Merry Christmas to those lying under ground.
>
> . . . .
> You should see the big funeral of Casey depart,
> It rivaled in glory the great Bonyparte.
> I had out my white hearse on top I did ride,

While Patsy he lay like a fairy inside.
With plume on the hearse, a German brass band,
The multitude shouted, by Heavens! It's grand!
Saying, there's no undertaker so artistic as ye,
From the city of Limerick to Pennsylvany.

A taste of tearful torment and a heap of hilarity spelled success. The play ran for a month, returned again in May, and was revived regularly during the next two years.

Harrigan and Hart could not have asked for a better first season on their own. Business held strong from beginning to end, and with *Christmas Joys* they turned the Comique into a new kind of Broadway house—a house where a full-length play and variety turns occupied the same stage at the same time and all for one price. Prospects for fall looked bright!

For the summer they headed into New England with an assortment of sketches, but when Harrigan discovered in Boston that the market for variety had collapsed (probably because "the people in New England are awful poor—awful") he considered dismissing the troupe and organizing another *Doyle Brothers* combination.[12] "Our names and reputation must be kept before the people," he wrote to Annie, and "I won't work for nothing." When the company got wind of his plans, they volunteered to cut their salaries. Harrigan accepted their gesture and set out across Massachusetts and New York. In Syracuse he again thought of quitting but knew it would injure the troupe professionally if it came off the road in the middle of the tour. Harrigan and Hart were now valuable theatrical properties, to be handled with care.

There was one cheerful note to Annie from Boston. *Old Lavender,* an expansion of *Old Lavender Water,* or, *Around the Docks* would be ready for fall, and Harrigan wrote, "I think it will be an immense hit." He was right.

His personal messages to Annie, often written with David on the other side of the table, were filled with solicitude for her condition—she was pregnant. She "must have nourishment so she can bear up against her suffering." She mustn't go around the garden in slippers and get her feet wet. Another bottle of brandy might help her sleep later. And regularly, the dutiful husband—did she need money?

In late July from Chicago he reported that the tour was ending in prosperity and happiness and with Ned Harrigan remarkably reformed: "Would you believe it, I actually hang my coat up on a hook when I take it off. I love you, you rascal."

After a week in St. Louis, they rushed home to begin the new season at the Comique on August 20, 1877, with a revival of *Christmas Joys and Sorrows*.

9

Old Lavender

The uncertainties that had hounded Harrigan in Boston evaporated when the company settled in at the Comique, and for the next four seasons he and Hart swung merrily from one success to another. Perseverance and talent had brought them to the top, but even there Harrigan knew the footing was slippery. They could not mark time, fattening on past triumphs. The nightly jury was eager to update its verdict.

Harrigan's pencil raced through his notebooks faster than ever, discovering fresh madness, and when his family of comedians fleshed out the text, the Comique was declared New York's favorite family funhouse. Everyone now knew Harrigan and Hart, the songs were heard everywhere, and a playback of Comique highlights was available on the neighborhood corner, or, with improvements, in the local saloon.

For the new season and for the next couple of years, Harrigan stuck to the tested routine: plays, sketches, and variety turns balanced out in fairly equal portions. Having been declared public property, he could not shift his ground too quickly. Old favorites —*The Blue and the Grey, S.O.T., Malone's Night Off,* even *The Doyle Brothers* and *St. Patrick's Day Parade,* were dusted off and alternated with the new: *The Rising Star, The Pillsbury Muddle,* and *The Coloured Baby Show.*

Specialty acts boasting astounding and ingenious dexterities filled out the programs. They came and went in rapid order: Miss

77

Alice Sommers, "artistic evolutions and musical emotions"; the gymnasts Levantine and Earl "in their pleasing illustrations of Grecian sport"; Harry Cerenie in his leaps over chairs; and Young Ajax, the boneless wonder.[1] Where they all came from and where they went is a theatrical mystery. The Comique's offerings became so abundant, often extending to three hours—all for fifteen to seventy-five cents—that performers were restricted to two recalls, and the audience was urged to restrain its enthusiasm.[2]

Gradually, and without disturbing Hanley's box office, Harrigan phased out the variety acts, scattered the sketches more sparingly, and turned to full-length plays. The change on the printed program was hardly noticed onstage. Songs, dances and acrobatics had not disappeared. They simply acquired a new setting, a panorama of the Lower East Side, as if the back wall of the theatre had been cut away, opening to a view of Corlear's Hook, Cherry Hill, Baxter Street, or Five Points. The shops, alleys, and tenements, the men and women who raced in and out, were strikingly familiar. And the harebrained schemes, the domestic battles, the loud and spicy joshing, which climaxed with a knockdown showdown among or between the Irish, Germans, Negroes, and Italians, though equally familiar, had never seemed so uproarious in life as on Harrigan's stage. Even when snatches of sadness broke the surface and bodies rolled across the floor and bounced through windows, endangering life and limb, the laughter did not subside. Grim, ugly reality never had a chance. Harrigan found fun in the shabbiest tenements, in the darkest alleys, among the sorriest specimens. And once he began roaming the streets he had known as a youngster, among the people who had shared his world, he found a remarkable gallery of places and faces, enough to supply more than thirty plays. Only rarely did he turn to other scenes; he held to the ground he knew, pledged to a life-long mission of showing New York, New York.

When *Old Lavender* failed to match his prediction, he returned it to his study for revision and expansion (in September it played less than an hour), and when he brought it back in April 1878, it caught on immediately, ran for the rest of the season, and became the first firm fixture in the Harrigan repertoire, "the gem among the plays," according to Hanley.

The seedy and lovable reprobate, Old Lavender, copied after

an eccentric who had achieved celebrity on Corlear's Hook, was one of Harrigan's finest portraits. His counterpart might be found among the soggy inhabitants of any waterfront saloon, but few devout drunks could match Lavender's astonishing resistance to inebriation and to the deprivations of poverty. His elegant circumlocutions emerged in greater profusion with each dash of lubrication, and his natural dignity was unimpaired by his damaged top hat, his ragged frock coat, and his fingerless gloves. Harrigan had spotted the costume on an old man on Lower Broadway.

Beloved rogues, surefire stage favorites for centuries, have been discovered in unlikely places. Harrigan was the first to find one among the East River docks, "a rogue as sweet as the fragrant herb from which he takes his name," according to one friend.

Old Lavender's lowlife companions, though not so fully sketched, are equally at home in his Dickensian world: Pop Jones, proprietor of the waterfront coffee and cake saloon, the downtown branch of Delmonico's where Old Lavender pauses "to refresh the inner man with the nutriment which is dispensed by the connoisseur who presides over this cafe." (W. C. Fields would have savored the line. In fact, much of Fields's loquacious arrogance seems derived from Old Lavender and from Harrigan's later creation, Major Gilfeather.) Dick the Rat, bootblack and Old Lavender's Sancho Panza, the only character who dares to puncture Old Lavender's ballooning soliloquies, insisting that he sounds "de way dem actors talk when I go to de theatre and set in de gallery." Hart as the Rat could be sure of strong support out front. Mark Twain observed a few years earlier that the city was crowded with shoeshiners, as if every little ragamuffin in New York had bought a brush and a foot box and gone into the bootblacking business, and when not polishing boots commanded the galleries of every theatre in town.[3]

Old Lavender's retinue also included Smoke, a Negro who scavanges the docks for dogs and cigars—he rejoices when it rains, "den de cigars group in de gutter," and Mrs. Crawford, proprietress of a boardinghouse called the Stranger's Rest. Her "aural appendages are entirely useless."

The other characters required to propel the story appear shadowy compared with Old Lavender and his crowd: theatrical creations who have never been exposed to the true light of day.

Philip Coggswell, banker and self-righteous teetotaler, slams the door on his brother George (Old Lavender) when he detects the evil odor of liquor. Laura, Philip's wife, overwhelmed by the gaudy blandishments of Paul Cassin, home breaker and forger, elopes with him, is abandoned, pursued, and finally tossed in the river, fortunately next to Old Lavender's shack, where Rat is ready to rescue her.

Old Lavender could have joined the pathetic army of waterfront bums, surviving on pity and handouts from the upper classes, when he's evicted by his straitlaced brother. Not Old Lavender. However severe the tortures, regardless of the load of juice he carries, he walks and talks like a king, endowing the simplest thoughts with a mighty ring: "I must hasten home 'ere the soda crackers which the daily tenant of our domicile kindly leaves in store for my supper are devoured by the lowest of the animal tribe the dock rodent —four squares more—then I am in the arms of morpheous." Rat and Lavender share their quarters with a retired seaman who transforms it to a galley in the daytime, dispensing a fluid advertised as clam soup.

Old Lavender's head and tongue thrive on sweet reason. He developed his aversion to water when he discovered a gold mine on one of his western adventures, and just as he had begun to dig out his treasure, nature fouled the cave, flooding it with water. While watching a Liverpool boat being loaded, he soliloquizes on American foreign policy: "The millions of souls in the old world turn with a longing eye to this great American nation and cry for bread. The mighty West with its prolific acres answers these calls. The republic may stagger financially, civilly, or morally, but the herculaneum energy of the American people will prop her up and there she'll stand firm as the Rock of Ages."

Occasionally Old Lavender reminds Rat that his rhetorical gifts are not exclusively natural endowments. In the song "College Days" he recalls that some of the culture and intelligence that has helped him "to rise through poverty's cold ways" was acquired at Harvard College, where he was "fitted for the bar or bench / a linguist too besides."[4]

Harrigan toyed with *Old Lavender* most of his life. In 1885 he added more songs: "Poverty's Tears Ebb and Flow"; "Please to

Put That Down"; a salute to liquor, "When sorrow sits down on your brow, / and sadness peeps out of your eye, / don't stop to think but take a drink"; and one of the swingingest Braham-Harrigan tunes, "Get Up, Jack, John, Sit Down." And in 1897, taking account of the proliferation of men's clubs around New York, Harrigan introduced an elaborate opening scene in the Owl Club where Mrs. Crawford works as an attendant. Dick the Rat, now her adopted son, peddles newspapers singing "Extra, Extra, read all about the Fenians in Canada, about Gladstone and his gout." And Old Lavender, the senior owl, raises his glass and invites his fellow owls to join him in soaring aloft. Owls need liquor. Water is meant for ducks.

Even with the added attractions, Old Lavender remained center stage. Harrigan loved his loquacious rebel, loved to slip into his ragged outfit. Like Joseph Jefferson's Rip—with whom he was often compared—Old Lavender kept the house brimming with laughter even as he tugged at the heartstrings. He was one of nature's noblemen. Harrigan often said that Old Lavender made him proud of the human race, proud that a man's true nature could not be clouded by a vapor of liquor or buried under shabby clothes. It was one of the wonders of the world that comforted him. "I think Old Lavender fits more of my own individuality in stage characterization than any other part I ever played. I never could see his rags. He was the sort of fellow who could be welcomed anywhere, and was man enough to set off a little from the rest of the crowd. With his conversational powers he could hold his audience. He drank not for drink's self, but for sociability—and I've seen many Lavenders."[5]

The two other plays that season—*Sullivan's Christmas* and *The Lorgaire*—did not remain in the repertoire, though the first, with its four snappy scenes of Irish and German domesticity, foreshadowed the *Mulligan* series.

Kate and John Sullivan and their son Dan are preparing a turkey dinner, their first in five years. Overcome with the spirit of the season, they invite Captain Krautsmeir to join them. The captain refuses. He prefers his hasenpfeffer, five plates of red cabbage, and two roasted pigs that his band is going to share with him. The band members lose their directions and appear in Sullivan's parlor, and John tosses them downstairs. Action more than words supplied the fun, though Kate did have one good line. When John is struck with an idea, she advises him to "hould on to it, if it gets away it will make an epidemic in the community." More of a sketch than a play, *Sullivan's Christmas* took less than an hour to perform.

The Lorgaire, brought out on February 18, 1878, was an extraordinarily long play, three acts and multiple scenes, laid in and around a fishing village in County Galway on the west coast of Ireland. In Gaelic a *lorgaire* is a searcher or pursuer. Harrigan's lorgaire was a detective from Scotland Yard.

Even though there was a generous assortment of exciting escapades—the detective trapped in an underground vault; the leap for life; the rescue of the heroine from the lake—Harrigan's audience was more fascinated by the new album of songs and by Harrigan's quick changes. Among the songs, introduced at a christening party: "Dolly, My Crumpled Horn Cow," extolling Dolly's milk-producing prowess. "List to the Anvil," a paean to hard work. And two hymns to Irish whiskey: "The Mountain Dew" and "The Irish Smuggler."

Harrigan's detective, Cornelius Dempsey, appears alternately as a peddler, a blind piper, and a schoolmaster. His disguises never fool the audience but utterly confound the other characters. Many friends slipped into the theatre regularly just to observe him thrashing about in the academic world: "I am Dyonesious Kavenagh, Professor of the Learned Languages, also a *Homo Factus Ad Ungeum,* and teacher of bookkeeping, geometry, trigonometry, stereometry, mensuration, navigation, galvanism, ventilation, explosion, and cholera morphus. *Quas Enumerare Longum Est.*"

Harrigan often remarked that *The Lorgaire* was one of the best plays he ever wrote, a claim that rested on his pride in having matched, some said beat, Boucicault at his own game.[6]

Three plays had filled the theatre night after night, often with standees four deep at the back, outdrawing the uptown legitimates two to one, according to one reporter, and mainly because Harrigan guaranteed three hours of wholesome fun for twenty-five cents to a dollar. "What a comforting testament to the advancing taste of the present generation," the *Dramatic News* noted, "to observe the crowds at Harrigan and Hart's Comique and to see the empty seats at *Romeo and Juliet,* that sickeningly obscene play, crammed so full of nastiness."[7]

Capacity houses plus Harrigan and Hanley's eagle eyes on the treasury gave them an enviable bill of health, $45,000 clear profit at the end of the season and that with a payroll of eighty to ninety. The next season would be even better: over a hundred employees and a $60,000 surplus. Unique solvency for a theatrical enterprise at any time.[8] In the 1870s and in every decade since, Broadway productions have invariably skirted the edge of disaster. One Wall Street genius of the time proposed a Managerial Insurance Company underwritten by the theatre managers to assure rents, royalties, and salaries for all plays that failed to make the grade with the public.[9]

Not all the crowd was out front at the Comique. Actors lined up at the stage door seeking a place in the company. The mysterious hookup that has always kept actors informed had carried the word that Harrigan offered good salaries, even paid for rehearsal time—an unheard-of bonus, guaranteed a full season, and provided a fifty-fifty chance of a summer tour.

Though Harrigan restricted his plays to the New York scene, as an actor he never confined himself to Broadway. If provincials could not make it to him, he went to them, alternating his summers between Boston and New England, Chicago and the Midwest, San Francisco and the Far West. Not until his move to the second Comique did summers become vacation time; in the early years he worked the year around.

In 1878 he struck out with the Gallant 69th Boys plus forty actors and musicians for Chicago, Council Bluffs, Omaha, Ogden, Salt Lake City, five weeks at the Bush Street Theatre in San Francisco, and the southern route back to Broadway, to begin the Comique season alternating the attractions he had had on the road, *The Doyle Brothers* and *Old Lavender.*[10] San Francisco convinced him that he was indeed a favored son, and Tony an honorary favored son. They outdrew Joe Jefferson's *Rip,* and when their weekly gross continued to surpass $30,000 in their fourth and final week, the manager held them over, forcing Tony Pastor to cool his heels in Nevada.[11]

The new year at the Comique would be the Mulligan year. It was a turning point for Harrigan and Hart, even though the Mulligans did not strike gold their first time out. In September Harrigan lifted the title from the old marching routine, and hitched it to a forty-minute sketch, *The Mulligan Guard Picnic.* The play "turned away hundreds nightly" and ran for a month, but Harrigan was not satisfied. He withdrew it, returned to short sketches, in January tried again with *The Mulligan Guard Ball,* and hit the winning bell. *The Ball* ran for the rest of the season.

Harrigan kept two notebooks on his writing table, one for the Mulligans, the other for fresh farcical fragments from the life of the city. In *My Wife's Mother,* a husky, strong-minded feminist pursues her eloping daughter to Coney Island. For good clean Harrigan fun, there was no place like Coney Island. *The Rising Star* explored behind the scenes at the theatre: an alligator tries to crash the stage door, says he's booked for next week's pantomime. On stage a Romeo forgets his lines and smashes a violin on the orchestra leader. Harrigan had used this turn before and would again. When baby shows invaded Gilmore's Garden, with prizes for the sweetest mother, the baby with the most teeth, Harrigan burlesqued the fad with a *Coloured Baby Show.* The craze for chicken fights propelled *The Pillsbury Muddle.* On the sleeper to Albany, passengers exchange berths with such bewildering speed that it's impossible to know who's a senator, an author, a critic, who on his way to the state assembly, who to the chicken fight. The conductor concludes that "half de Irish population's crazy"; and Harrigan reduced everyone to a common denominator with an explosion. He took his first look at the Italian immigrants, at lawyers and politics in *The Italian Junkman; O'Brien, Counselor at Law;* and *Our Law Makers.*[12]

Most all of these characters and scenes would be used again. Harrigan had been preparing for the Mulligans, testing his actors to see how they suited up in Harrigan portraits, sizing them up for Mulligan's Alley, and harnessing himself to his life's work: chronicler of the carnival revelry among the immigrants on the Lower East Side.

10

The Mulligan Guard Ball

Three months after *The Mulligan Guard Picnic* experiment, the Mulligans took over the Comique:

The Mulligan Guard Ball—January 13, 1879 (first
performance)
The Mulligan Guard Chowder—August 11, 1879
The Mulligan Guards' Christmas—November 17, 1879*
The Mulligan Guards' Surprise—February 16, 1880*
The Mulligan Guard Picnic—August 9, 1880
The Mulligan Guard Nominee—November 22, 1880
The Mulligans' Silver Wedding—February 21, 1881

Nor did the saga terminate with *Silver Wedding*; many of Harrigan's later plays, sans Mulligan in the title, included Mulligans and friends in the cast.

With these seven, crowded into little more than two years, Harrigan caught the eye of the serious critics. They discovered his plays were pervaded with "an atmosphere of friendliness and sweet temper," a "high quality of truth," "an authentic history of our life and times." He was compared with Balzac, Dickens, and Zola, and one enthusiast wrote: "America has produced nothing more national, more distinctly its own, than these plays of the Irish in New York."[1] Harrigan took theatrical eminence in his stride. Pleased as he was to be taken seriously, he knew better than to take himself

---

*"Guards' " here; in the other plays, "Guard."

seriously and let the praise go to his head. A swelled head would kill the fun, and fun was his business.

Luck had contributed its share to the Mulligans' success: the luck of being reared on the Lower East Side, of commanding the Comique. As he traveled the country, Harrigan had often observed that no city possessed such true local flavor as New York; and the New York elite, unlike the stern upper crust in Boston and Philadelphia, were fascinated by the life of their inferiors in the downtown wards, and no theatre could survive without the dressy crowd's buying out the boxes and dress circle.

That he began the *Mulligan* adventures with a picnic was not surprising. New Yorkers loved picnics; the Irish loved picnics. Two-thirds of the inhabitants—some said 99 percent of the Irish —left the city every Sunday for Hoboken, Fort Lee, Coney Island, or Fort Hamilton. And apparently the passion for outings persisted; Peter Dunne's Mr. Dooley once remarked, "Be hivins, if Ireland could be freed by a picnic, it'd not on'y be free today, but an impire, begorra."[2]

Neither the story nor the casting of the first *Picnic* resembled the later *Mulligan* plays. Dan Mulligan, reportedly drowned at Coney Island, has returned in whiskers to badger his widow, now enamored of the "terpsichorean voice" of her dancing master. Dan thwarts her advance to the altar by pitching the dancing master overboard. Hart played Dan Mulligan, Harrigan a minor character, and Annie Mack, Cordelia Mulligan. The later casting was invariably: Harrigan as Dan; Hart, Tommy Mulligan and/or Rebecca Allup; and Cordelia always Annie Yeamans. Only one episode documented a continuing phenomenon in the life of the city. When the Mulligan Guard is halted by a mud pile, the captain orders them to wait for the street commissioners to remove the obstruction. His lieutenant has other plans for his life: if they wait for the commissioners, they'll wait till Judgment Day.

When his trial balloon had floated along for a solid month, Harrigan decided that the Mulligans deserved more spectacular adventures, and by the end of the year the Comique company, now cast in their lifetime roles, were busily into rehearsals of *The Mulligan Guard Ball.*

When *The Ball* opened, a little more than ten years after Harrigan had made his professional debut, the hardiest optimist could not have predicted its sensational success. On April 9, the ladies in the audience received a satin program commemorating the 100th performance; on May 24 it closed the season with 153 performances. (All the Mulligan plays, except *Silver Wedding*, with 80, topped the 100-performance mark.) In recent years, when the Broadway theatre has been dominated by long runs and when a play can not claim success until after 100 performances, *The Ball*'s record appears less spectacular. In 1879, it was an astonishing feat. Theatres like the Comique and Tony Pastor's invariably introduced new programs each Monday night; legitimate theatres might sometimes run a play for six to eight weeks; only occasional oddities like *Uncle Tom's Cabin* and *The Black Crook* held the stage for long runs.

Even after *The Ball* closed, its songs were still in the air. A Judge W. E. Horton from Detroit recalled that, when he went to Manhattan Beach with Harrigan on a Sunday afternoon in July, the leader of Gilmore's Band spotted Harrigan and struck up "Babies on Our Block." A dozen bathers joined in immediately and, within fifteen minutes, as the band retraced the melody, "over one thousand were whisking around on the sand, singing the song."[3] And when the play was revived, as it was regularly until the end of the century, many declared it Harrigan's funniest play.

The Mulligan Guard Ball was loaded with Harrigan hilarity on every page, in every minute on the stage. He climaxed his previous exploits in slambang, melee, and general melee when the Negro Skidmore Guard plunged through the ceiling of De Harp and Shamrock and crashed on the Irish Mulligan Guard dancing in the ballroom below. The pileup of arms and legs, smothered in plaster and entwined with the chandelier, created an astonishing spectacle —and a dreaded nightmare for the stage mechanics. There were also milder melees: Dan Mulligan's exploding cigar, Lochmuller's butchers flailing the air with cleavers, a suckling pig jumping from the table to escape its fate, a stray rat tormenting the ladies, Bridget and Cordelia mopping the floor with their husbands before tackling each other. Harrigan actors had a bruising evening.

The divertissements were augmented by a simple *Romeo and Juliet, Abie's Irish Rose* story. The Mulligans' Tommy woos and marries the Lochmullers' Kitty, a calamitous, unnatural union. Bridget Lochmuller can't bear to see her daughter repeat her own mistake, "a dacent Irish girl from County Cork, that had her twelve dollars a week in a feather factory" being taken in by Gustav, "a bologna pudding merchant," and Dan Mulligan threatens to lick every German from Hamburg to Gowanus before "the Divil a Dutch drop of blood will enter this family."

The Mulligan-Lochmuller clash was not a stage figment; it came straight from life. Everyone on the Lower East Side knew the daily eruptions when the "impulsive Celt" met the "plodding Teuton," and according to Harrigan his Gustav Lochmuller was modeled on a "bologna butcher" on Pearl Street.[4] Dan Mulligan typified "the honesty, wit, humor, and bonhomie which underlie the great army of Irishmen who have crossed the ocean and prospered in the metropolis of the West. My friends often told me that they knew Dan in real life and have named the man he was copied from."[5] In Harrigan's time most everyone knew a Mulligan. The city directory listed two columns of them.

The Irish-German skirmishes were, however, only a warm-up for the main event, the showdown between Dan's Mulligan Guard and the blackfaced Skidmore Guard, commanded by the barber Simpson Primrose and by Brother Palestine Puter. Puter is chaplain of the Ancient Order of Full Moons, "de colored secret society pledged to prevent the Irish from riding on the horse cars."[6] The Skids tolerate the German and Irish foreigners as long as they keep their place, though Puter favors "stricter quarantine or stronger fumigation."

The collision course is set when Mr. Garlic rents his Harp and Shamrock ballroom in Bleecker Street to the Mulligans, and his assistant schedules the Skids in the same room, the same night. Only a stupid Italian could make such a mistake.

The Mulligans' ball proceeds peacefully through the intermission and Dan's "Babies on Our Block," a song Harrigan said had come to him when he threaded his way home through the mobs of Irish children—Phalens, Whalens, Clearys, Learys, Brannons, and Cannons:[7] "Come over with me socially / In the first ward, near the dock, / Where Ireland's represented / By the Babies on our Block." But just as the Mulligans swing into a fancy quadrille, the

Skids arrive. Captain Primrose orders his troops to plant their muskets in the hat rack but keep their razors at the ready: "Dar's no telling how many Irish will be in hambush dare."

With Mulligans and Skids jamming the dance floor, catastrophe is inescapable: "Grand rush to Center. Business of fight. Women scream. Negroes draw razors, general melee when Mr. Garlic enters." The free-swinging combat was not improvised on the spur of the moment nor was it as mild as the stage directions seem to suggest. Harrigan provided meticulous choreography at the rehearsals.

Garlic finally shouts the dancers into a truce and proposes a compromise. The Skids can use the Red Men's Lodge room upstairs with ten dollars knocked off the rent. Simpson accepts the "boisterous propersition." The two balls can proceed "widout interfering and as long as we're upstairs—we're above de Irish—and I know dat suits every Full Moon in de company." The Skids' departure is short-lived. They have just led their partners onto the floor when the boards begin to sag and they "come down in chunks" through the ceiling. It was Harrigan's grandest melee.

Even though the Irish-German-Negro confrontations held the center of attention—described in Bostonese by the *Traveller* as "demonstrating the animosity between the Celtic, Teutonic, and Ethiopian races"[8]—the evening was enriched with the customary Harrigan cornucopia of recognizable, well-detailed scenes (models provided): New York streets, Primrose's barbershop backed against Maggie Kierney's hairdresser's studio, each fully equipped, and the ballroom decorated by Dan and his lieutenant, Walsingham McSweeney: "A row of American flags on the right hand, with the Irish flags blending between them. Then a row of wax candles on the balcony with a sign, 'Look out for the drip,' and about thirty-three canaries and some blackbirds in cages, hung on the chandeliers." Primrose and Puter's specifications for the Skids were equally festive: a chromo of Abraham Lincoln surrounded by "gorgeous flural tribunes," and with Lieutenant Newlimber's sister Ruth posing on a pedestal as de Goddess of Liberty. Music was to be rendered by "De El Dorado Reed Striding Military Cotillion Brass Band." Delmonico's was proposed for refreshments, but since the intermission would not come till one "and de victuals is very bad den in restaurants," Puter settled for the corner grocery where they could "munch a few crackers."

There were other diversions. Dan and Cordelia introduce snatches of Gaelic for the benefit of the Irish fresh off the boat and also to confuse Lochmulller, who thinks they are talking Russian or Greek.[9] After tumbling through the ceiling, Primrose appears with a white eye. When a rat scoots back and forth across the room at the Mulligan supper, the ladies scream and the Guards pelt it with miscellaneous scraps of food. Dan thinks he recognizes the beast as a neighbor from Mulberry Street.

The Theatre Comique outclassed its Broadway rivals. It provided something for everybody. Harrigan had discovered that bits and pieces from his repertoire could be pulled together under one umbrella, if the umbrella was stamped "Mulligan Guard." And if a few stuffy souls resisted the horseplay, none could resist the songs: "Babies on Our Block," "The Hallway Door," "Skidmore's Fancy Ball," and "The Mulligan Guard."

Throughout the spring, until *The Ball* moved to Brooklyn and Boston, audiences jammed the Comique and reporters rhapsodized on the Mulligan fun. Some nights standees were stacked so tightly it became impossible to get in. Speculators cornered blocks of the best tickets, and one reporter who had fulminated against these leeches advised, "Pay them; it's worth it."[10] Another wrote, "Postpone everything else and see it. Harrigan and Hart are inimitable, and the whole performance is a credit to the American stage."[11]

Never had Harrigan been given so much space in the press, so much detailed and serious attention. One reporter wrote about the parade of the Skidmores: "A mere description cannot but do injustice to the antics of the ten or twelve artists, not supernumeraries, who represent that doughty and dusky corps."[12] Sweet words for Harrigan. He prided himself on his stage discipline, insisting that his supers be as qualified and as well trained as his principals. And he couldn't have missed the comparison with the competition: "The characters are as unique as Dundreary in *Our American Cousin,* funnier than Twain's Colonel Sellers [in *The Gilded Age*], and the play more distinctively American than Bronson Howard's *Saratoga.*"[13]

The Mulligan Guard Ball was not yet a full-length play (and did not become one until four years later); its six scenes took up only about two-thirds of the program. Miscellaneous acts filled out the evening: Fryer's Dogs; Fred A. Plaisted, "champion oarsman and club swinger"; Andrew Gaffney, "a towering form of symmetry and strength"; and a Harrigan sketch, *The Great In-Toe-Natural Walking Match*. All for fifteen cents in the gallery, thirty-five in the dress circle, fifty in the parquet, and seventy-five for an orchestra chair.

These low prices undoubtedly were a factor in Harrigan's decision to try longer plays. Hiring a company of actors came cheaper than hiring a dozen or more specialty artists, particularly when the same actors who appeared in the play could also perform in sketches like the *Walking Match*.

Harrigan kept an eye on events in the city that might be burlesqued on the stage. He didn't miss the International Pedestrian Contest at Gilmore's Garden.[14] Night and day over eighty thousand spectators, enticed by newspaper accounts of near calamities and predictions of dirty work at the track, watched the walkers cover the one-eighth-mile sawdust circuit. One night some opera boxes left over from the Arion Ball collapsed, and several spectators were rushed to the hospital. Fistfights erupted among the rowdies as they cheered their favorites and bathed the competition in tobacco juice. One reporter feared that, if this sporting insanity were not arrested, newspapers would be announcing: "All theatres will be closed this evening in consequence of the Astley belt walk. . . . Reserved seats with railroad coupons attached, for Henry Irving's performance of *Hamlet* at the Boston Theatre, for sale at all principal hotels. N.B. Mr. Irving will not visit New York this season in consequence of the great dog fights now in progress at Spuyten Duyvil Square."[15] In late March, one week after the agony was over and New Yorkers had "returned to their neglected homes and offices,"[16] Harrigan brought out *The Great In-Toe-Natural Walking Match*, with his Peg Bunion, sawed-off Charley Row-well, and Gallant Dan O'Lear-eye raising dust on the Comique track.[17] It proved a worthy companion for *The Ball*.

Considering the Mulligans' phenomenal popularity, it was clear that they must return in the fall. Suddenly everything had jelled for

Harrigan and Hart. They hit the top of their form just as Harrigan found the formula for filling most of the evening with frolicking adventure in familiar places, with Irish, Germans, Negroes, and Italians from the Lower East Side who bore a striking resemblance to the Comique actors. Like Molière, with whom he was often compared, Harrigan molded his characters to his actors until it became impossible to know where Harrigan left off and Hart, Yeamans, Wild, and the others began.

Dan Mulligan, the amiable, garrulous, fun-loving, high-spirited Irish adventurer, was shaped to fit Harrigan. Two parts were created for Tony Hart—sometimes he played both: Tommy, the Mulligans' son, tricky, pugnacious, ambitious, and sometimes boy-scout dutiful; and in later plays, Rebecca Allup, the boisterous Negro wench, who toyed with suitors and the English language with remarkable dexterity. Rebecca acquired her given name from a Negro washerwoman who appeared with her tin pail at the saloon at Prince and Crosby so frequently that the neighbors christened her "Rebecca at the Well." Her surname derived from her pathetic cry when she had journeyed to the well too often: "Well, it's all up."[18] Dan's faithful Cordelia, played by Annie Yeamans, obeyed her husband and extolled his virtues, particularly when his inclinations matched her own. When he was wrong, she helped him recover. If he was stubborn, she let him suffer alone. Gustavus Lochmuller, the bombastic, thickheaded German butcher and his loquacious wife Bridget were played by Harry A. Fisher and Annie Mack. Michael Bradley was Walsingham Mc-Sweeney, Dan's right-hand man; Johnny Wild and Billy Gray the burnt cork pair, Sam Primrose and Palestine Puter, fancy talkers, schemers, and majestic officers of the Skidmore Guard and the Full Moon Union. This was the first rank in the company and in the plays, and though each had wandered widely over the theatrical map, once settled in the Harrigan family they stuck with him throughout their careers.

Harrigan never hired actors with big names; they could make their names with him. As he once remarked, "I had such queer parts to fill, I had to look for people to fill them, not for actors who were set in some line of business."[19] Yet his performers had to know their trade, come equipped with a stock of tricks, be willing to add more, and above all be steady and untroubled by dreams of top billing. Incompetents, even in the minor roles, were quickly dismissed.

He chose a remarkable group. With Harrigan lines and Harrigan business, they turned the theatre into a madhouse. For rolling spectators in the aisles, splitting their sides, pushing laughter to tears—the common description of an evening at the Comique—they had no equal.

Mrs. Annie Yeamans led the ladies, and many thought she should have shared star billing with the partners. Yeamans never took up this cause; she was satisfied as Edward Harrigan's leading lady, friend, and ardent promoter. She was among the first to tell reporters that some day he would be accounted a man of genius. In the Harrigan household she was a member of the family, invariably on hand for all celebrations, and when the family joined her sixty-seventh-birthday party in 1902, Harrigan embraced her and said, "Annie, God bless you. I am going to kiss you. I don't care if my wife and daughter are looking on."[20] The kiss had not yet become the common salute in the profession. Apparently she shared Ned's social restraint. William Harrigan once recalled that when at age five he shared Yeamans's dressing room, she shielded her costume changes from his view; that when he came to her hotel when she was eighty, she was just as fastidious. When he called from the lobby, she said that she would ask him to come up but she was afraid she might be criticized.[21]

In the theatre her inhibitions evaporated. She bubbled with good feeling, her explosive, good-natured Irish smile triggering the audience to join the fun. Three smiles to one tear, according to a friend. She was just naturally funny, inside and out. She loved to make people laugh, as long as the jokes were wholesome, uplifting, and ennobling, and her open flexible face seemed always brimming with humor. She was not "cursed with the fatal gift of beauty," as one reporter put it, a deficiency that did not disturb her. She once told an interviewer that the rewards for a funny woman may not be as great "as those accruing to the dazzling Venuses with alabaster shoulder blades and colossal legs, but the rewards are more enduring and make the stage a great place for an old lady."[22]

For the women in the audience, she fulfilled their Mitty dreams of escape from domestic drudgery—children, pots, pans, and washing up—to the world of shouting, laughing, and playing the fool. They loved her. And the men did too. Husbands wondered why their wives couldn't let go now and then, like Cordelia, knowing full well they would have pinned their ears back if they tried.

Annie Yeamans had had an adventurous apprenticeship.[23] Born on the Isle of Man of a Manx mother and a Welsh father, she was taken to Australia as a child when her parents sought their theatrical fortunes down under. At fifteen she signed with a circus and learned to ride bareback—a deceptively profitable introduction to the theatre, as she often recalled. Circling the ring, she was pelted with gold nuggets from the bulging pockets of miners. Two years later, she married Harry Yeamans, an American clown, and for the next ten years traveled with him and the circus around Australia, to Java, China, Japan, the Philippines, and finally to San Francisco, where Yeamans died. She moved to New York in the late sixties with her children and appeared with George L. Fox's *Humpty Dumpty* at the Olympic, in various pantomimic spectacles, in Daly's *Under the Gaslight,* and as Aunt Ophelia in *Uncle Tom's Cabin.* Often her daughters, Jennie, Lydia, and Emily, joined her onstage, as they did after she became Harrigan's Cordelia Mulligan.

For over twenty years, Yeamans and Cordelia were inseparable, and the Harrigan-Yeamans duets, with their verbal thrusts seeming to glance off each other in midair, highlighted the evenings. Richard Harding Davis once wrote, "We could never replace her coquetry or her brogue or her red wig and her bashful wiggle and shiver of pleasure when she is told how beautiful she is. She makes such an excellent foil to Harrigan with her excited, bustling garrulousness, the opposite at every point to the star's calm, easy confidence."[24]

Annie Mack acquired her brogue for Bridget Lochmuller naturally.[25] She was born in Dublin, came to New York at fourteen, got her first job with John Brougham, married Edward Mack two years later, played Ophelia to Edwin Booth's Hamlet in Albany, and toured the country with Joseph Jefferson as Rip's wife Gretchen. In 1879 she and her husband enlisted with Harrigan, she for Bridget and he for an assortment of minor roles.

Harry A. Fisher made his New York debut in *The Irish Outlaw* in 1876. The next year he joined Harrigan, and for most of his life he devoted himself to the bullheaded butcher Gustav Lochmuller. As the last survivor of the original company, he was always on hand to render "Babies on Our Block" at the Harrigan Club meetings.

Michael Bradley started as a super at the Comique when he was fifteen and remained with Harrigan until his death in 1888, a member of the family at home and in the theatre. His funeral at the Harrigan home was "one of the saddest occasions in my life," Harrigan told a reporter, "particularly watching young Ned cry as though his heart would break." Bradley had been teaching Ned his trick of dancing up and down a flight of stairs. "What a sterling performer he was; his angularity, eccentricity, and peculiar mannerisms fitted him to the life of Walsingham McSweeney, one of the finest Irish stage creations I ever saw."[26] Harrigan buried McSweeney with Bradley, as he had Palestine Puter when Billy Gray died six years earlier.

Billy Gray began with Bryant's Minstrels, teamed with Wild in a duo at Josh Hart's Comique and, according to Harrigan, was one of the funniest men he ever met, his Reverend Palestine Puter "a genuine masterpiece in the black-face line."[27]

Generally audiences rated Johnny Wild as funnier than Gray, a close second to Tony Hart. Richard Harding Davis wrote, "There is no one else who combines his gallant susceptibility to women with a disregard for the ownership of overcoats and hats, who can show such shocked surprise when some other gentleman's boots are found upon his feet; and with what philosophic contentment he accepts and excuses the fact that 'a man's got to keep a-lying to live two lives.' "[28] Wild had also apprenticed with the minstrels and like Yeamans was endowed with a humorous temperament that couldn't be concealed. His inexpressibly sad eyes—pop eyes some called them—were just too sad to be taken seriously. And when he marched on as the Skids' Captain Primrose, buttons polished to mirrorlike brilliance and with creamy words floating from his tongue, the audience roared, as they did when he soaped his way into Rebecca Allup's affection or became the solemn high priest in the Mystic Order of Full Moons. None of the stage scalawag carried into his private life. When he died in 1898, Yeamans said that he was "not a man upon whom anecdotes hang. He was a most domestic fellow who went home right after the performance every night."[29] He spent his offstage hours reading literature, returning to his favorite, *Uncle Tom's Cabin,* every six months.

This small tribe of Harrigan and Hart clowns, as loaded with fun as any group ever assembled on Broadway, was ready for Mulligan's Alley as soon as Harrigan opened the territory. Characters and actors were made for each other and, as each new play unfolded, as their smiles expanded and their antics became more outlandish, they knew they had staked their claims on the future in the right place.

11

Slambang, Melee, and General Melee

The Mulligan Guard Ball had settled Harrigan's future, and it made the fall opening at the Comique a major Broadway event, an event to be exploited by the press. When the *Spirit of the Times* sent its man to the Comique, three days in advance of the opening, he found the place bright and neat as a new pin, the front and vestibule glowing with fresh paint, and Harrigan, "a slim, handsome, young gentleman of about thirty," pacing the company through final rehearsals and eager to talk about *The Mulligan Guard Chowder*.[1] No expense had been spared "to please the patrons who have done so nobly for us," and, though at first this third volume of the Mulligan Guard chronicles had seemed too crowded to handle, with four races—the Irish, Germans, Africans, and Celestials (Chinese)—it had come out all right. Harrigan knew the risk in "following successful fun with new fun; but I have just let the Mulligan family work out its own history naturally. Supposing the Mulligans to have existed—and Tony and I have several thousand very solid reasons for thinking so—all the story follows natural as life."

Dave Braham would be back in the pit with new music, the Skids with more fancy marching, and two new characters had joined the fun: John Chinaman and Tony Hart as an old Negro woman. And a new scenic artist, Charles W. Witham, had been lured to the Comique. Harrigan could have gone on about Tony. Rebecca Allup would become Hart's masterpiece. Even now in rehearsals the company broke up whenever Rebecca came on. And everyone who had seen the new backdrops and "practicals" knew they had acquired the best painter in the business.[2]

Witham had done the scenes for Edwin Booth's *Hamlet* and *Romeo and Juliet,* had been Augustin Daly's principal artist, and now he became a permanent addition to the Comique family with his authentic pictures—a chowder on the Jersey beach, Allup's dingy room, and Mulligan's Alley—capturing with paint and canvas what Harrigan had imagined. The Alley would be the most famous of the Harrigan-Witham creations. Like the town squares that have served so many dramatists, ancient and modern, Mulligan's Alley was a place where anything and everything could and did happen, in the pileup of tenement rooms, in the ground floor courtyard, in Lochmuller's Butcher Shop and Beer Saloon, in McSweeney's Rectifying Distillery.

Catastrophe struck early on opening night, August 11, 1879, marking *The Chowder* a worthy sequel. Captain Primrose ignores Lochmuller's warning about straw in the cellar—"the whole neighborhood is too damp to burn"—lights the initiation candle, and orders the novitiate to swallow the flame, swearing she'll "walk through fire to keep down the Irish." The victim rebels and knocks over the candle. The conflagration arouses the volunteers. Their hoses flood the courtyard, as does a cloudburst of mattresses, chairs, and crockery from the upper stories. When the smoke clears, Hog-Eye, perched in a window flirting with Rebecca Allup across the yard, excites such languishing sighs that Primrose fears Rebecca will enter "de connubial state wid a assisattic." Palestine Puter, now a fugitive for having "bezzled from the Baptists," is hidden in a converted-icebox coffin, left over when Rebecca sold her husband's corpse to a surgeon.

Beer, chowder, and songs—"The Skids Are Out Today," "Oh! Girly, Girly!"—pyramid the Mulligans, Skids, and Lochmuller's Fat Men's Club into an uproar on the Jersey Beach. During the final melee, a dozen cats jump out of the chowder pot, Puter's cortege arrives, and Puter pops out of his box, grabs the beer keg, and heads for the woods.

Harrigan struck another familiar chord with the new offering.

Chowders were popular events on New York's social calendar.[3] In the summer they were held on the shore, in the winter at the firehouses on Saturday nights. The Big Six on Henry Street declared it had the best in town: chicken and oysters, salmon and clams, fish and eel.

When "Volume the Third of the Mulligan Progression" closed on November 15, Volume the Fourth, *The Mulligan Guards' Christmas,* was waiting in the wings to take up the story the following Monday. Sticking with Mulligans, Lochmullers, Skids, and Mulligan's Alley did not dull Harrigan's fancy. Whenever he offered a fresh "what if," his actors sailed into the new escapades with irrepressible zeal, eager for fun and with careless disregard for comfort and safety. As each chapter unfolded, some acquaintance with past events was helpful, but Harrigan never held to a rigorous, soap opera continuity. Each story stood on its own, and though his people cherished and preserved their antipathies, they shifted occupations, changed life-styles, and acquired new enthusiasms. No playwright before or since ever captured such a rich gallery set against a true-to-life panorama of New York's Lower East Side, and all brought to the Comique stage in three seasons.

The Mulligan Guards' Christmas took the Skids and Mulligans (now called the Mulligan Braves, the Tammany influence) to Spuyten Duyvil for a holiday shoot, Cordelia on an excursion to Albany for her sister's wedding, and everyone to a disastrous Christmas dinner at the Mulligans.

At Spuyten Duyvil, Primrose misses the target but hits the engineer of a passing train, Dan confounds Cordelia with an Indian war dance, and Macauly Jangles, a living-statue specialist in Cordelia's entourage, poses as "Jonah escaping from the whale," "Daniel in the lion's den," "Joan of Arc behind the hay wagon," and at the Christmas dinner, "Pocahontas in the surf at Coney Island." When an officer arrives to return him to the insane asylum, Dan is astounded; he thought he was a college student.

At the holiday feast, Primrose and Puter steal the ducks as fast as Rebecca brings them in. An elephant sticks his trunk in the window and squirts the guests; a giraffe snags the turkey. (Circus animals are quartered next door!) And for the finale, Dan races to the roof to watch a fire, loses his footing, slides down the chimney, and returns to the Christmas dinner a shadow of his former self.

The Mulligan Guards' Surprise, February 16, 1880, struck more familiar notes: Most every Irish family knew, at least at secondhand, the joys and sorrows of social elevation, of abandoning shanty for lace curtains, and few had escaped a mass visitation from a wife's relatives—invariably the wife's, never the husband's.

Cordelia has deserted the Alley, moved uptown to "Lafertee Avenue" (Lafayette), forced Dan into high society, and crowded her "French flat" with relatives, fancy furniture, and, to protect the carpet, eight spittoons—"stevedores" to Dan. Rebecca, now a dusky parlor maid, can't understand why it's called a French flat, "when everybody's Irish in it 'cept me, and I'm a Puritan clear through." Rebecca hates to see a "shipboard of emigrants" sponging on Dan and does her best to help him. When he hangs his favorite picture of Saint Patrick and Cordelia replaces it with George Washington, Rebecca paints a moustache on George "and now you can't tell de difference, all but de snakes." Bridget Lochmuller, infected by Cordelia, approaches the Mulligan menage "with an avalanche of pomposity . . . languid and filled with a sort of On Whov."

Dan can't get the hang of the new place. French and finger bowls perplex him. When McSweeney arrives with a bottle urging him to return to the Alley, the liquor restores his voice and his confidence: "Home rule for me, my wife shall see, I'll wear the trousers, Oh!"

Back in the Alley, Dan is greeted with a welcome-home party, a real "hong cooler" with a "cologne fountain in the entry" for those who seem a bit gamy. Rebecca is staging a "shiverer and tinkettling" for Captain Primrose and his bride. At the wedding ceremony, Primrose complains about the Irish racket: "Can't a man get married without de white population making Jackasses out of demselves?" And Reverend Palestine Puter deviates a bit from the standard marriage text but gets close enough: "And Caroline Melrose, do you of your own untrampled desire and discord take Captain Simpson Primrose for your lawful husband?"

She does, and the festivities conclude with a walkaround, as they all sing "Citron Wedding Cake."

Surprise featured some of Harrigan and Braham's most popular songs: "Never Take the Horseshoe from the Door" and "Whist, the Bogie Man." Dan's troubles began "when the wife that I adore brought in a crowd of her relations and I found the horseshoe laying on the floor." The "Bogie Man" lullaby, sung as an accompaniment to a game of blindman's buff, later achieved extraordinary popularity with English nannies and now would be declared too terrifying for bedtime: "Oh, whist, whist, whist, / Here comes the bogie man! / Oh, whist, whist. / He'll catch ye, if he can."

A "re-altered, re-arranged, and re-constructed" *Picnic* (August 9, 1880) bore no resemblance to the earlier play. Dan, now a "garbage contractor," flies a broom on the mast of his sloop "in memmoration of de day Mulligan swept his relations out of his uptown house." Lochmuller, washed overboard from a ferry and rescued by a German steamer, has spent two months in a Berlin lunatic asylum and now in false whiskers is playing the tuba in August Bimble's band.

Lochmuller is distraught to be "dead by the newspapers" and enraged that his wife Bridget has taken up with the tailor Roderick O'Dwyer. O'Dwyer is so enchanted that he sews buttons on the back of trousers thinking of her. Roderick on his knees to Bridget became a favorite Harrigan scene:

> O'DWYER: Mrs. Lochmuller, look into the eyes of Roderick O'Dwyer.
> BRIDGET: Have you dust in them? It's very windy this morning.
> O'DWYER: Look down deep into me eyes.
> BRIDGET: I could lift it out wid me handkerchief.
> O'DWYER: Nay, nay! No handkerchief could lift the burden that weighs me down and shows its sorrow in me hazel eyes.
> BRIDGET: My boy Gussy had an eye tooth that hurt his left eye, and I had it pulled.

There were other assorted diversions. At the afternoon picnic at Ocean Grove: O'Dwyer gets smashed with a watermelon. A snake wanders across the stage. Dan drives a stick in the ground to make a hat rack: "I was born for a civil engineer." Fagin, another suitor, is transported by the salty atmosphere and Bridget's proximity: "It's a courtin' place. Ain't it baby?" Dan sings and dances to "Locked Out After Nine," the saga of a boardinghouse where everyone's "in bed at eight or. . . ." Fagin and Lochmuller are arrested for fighting and are brought to trial in Squire Jezebel Cohog's grocery store and courtroom. The judge sleeps through the proceedings, awakening only when he hears Fagin mention Tammany Hall. That's evidence enough for Fagin's acquittal. Lochmuller's accent marks him as a German agitator. That offense will cost him ten dollars.

The Mulligan Guard Nominee (November 22, 1880) shifted to serious business in the life of the city: immigrants arriving, Cordelia's female freedom society, and Dan's Tammany adventure. The noise and confusion on the Cunard Wharf reminded many Irishmen of their first day on American soil, when hackmen and runners from the boardinghouses raced about proclaiming enduring love for the "ould country," stretching a helping hand and an open palm, selling bogus tickets for board, room, and transportation, and dispensing misinformation.[4]

Cordelia's F.N.A. (Florence Nightingale Association) meets secretly in the Mulligans' back parlor to sing and sew: "We'll hem and sew, / And bind and tuck, and pray for luck / When freedoms heroes strike the blow." They are making "C.P.s," "E.R.s," and "F.s" (code for chest protectors, ear raps, and flannel shirts) for the Fenians who hope to free Ireland by capturing Canada. This adventure was not a Harrigan invention. Plans for such an invasion had been in the wind as early as 1865, and in June 1866, a hundred thousand strong gathered in Jones's Wood to cheer the thousand sons of Erin who were about to launch their attack.[5] Although the Canadian mission had not brought Britain to her knees, and eight Fenians were killed, Irishmen cheered Cordelia's Nightingales.

Dan's campaign for alderman was loaded with oratory and rousing songs, "Hang the Mulligan Banner Up" and "Mulligan's Promises":

> I promise you employment
> But you must keep it dark
> I'll have you count the sparrows boys,
> Flying in Central Park.

Harrigan loved Dan's politicking. At the rostrum he's transported: "Fellow citizens and friends of the Mulligan champagne, there is no power or oratory or forensic debility in any Dutch Hessian like Lochmuller to defeat me. I arise like the morning sun and I'll never set till the name of Daniel Mulligan is carried from the Fourteenth Ward to Asia, Afghanistan, Parequan, Equidius, Circassian, Balvaria, and the world all over. . . . Why is it that they give us a sidewalk four feet wide in the Fourteenth Ward and Fifth Avenue has a sidewalk twenty feet wide, when feet are larger in the Fourteenth Ward than on Fifth Avenue?" He also assures them there'll be no snow next winter, after he's taken over the "weather Buro."

When a reporter in the play accuses Dan of referring to the "nagur vote," he's astounded: "Did I say nagur? Have you put it down for the newspapers that I said nagur?" He has. Half-sobbing, Dan addresses the Skids: "Be seated gentlemen. I desire the down-trodden African American voters' forgiveness. The Skidmore Guards are friends of mine and I am going to have them incorporated in the National Guard, replacing the Seventh Regiment." (Replacing the Seventh was outrageous campaign talk. This crack New York regiment had just built a fancy new armory at Sixty-Sixth and Lexington.)

As usual there were other bits of nonsense. When Cordelia rifles Dan's pockets, he speaks for all husbands: "That woman's name will live in history. Her heart's like a mountain, her hand is like a shovel. When she dives into your pocket, she leaves nothing but the lining." When Cordelia joins the "Skidmore Masquerade," disguised as Phoebe Brown, Dan is captivated. A calico dress on a quadroon always takes his eye. When Dan slips on Rebecca's dress, trying to infiltrate the Nightingales, Caroline Melrose throws him into the Hudson River.

Everyone's aboard the Albany boat for the finale, to see the governor. Dan is as happy as Christopher Columbus was when he discovered the Battery. Suddenly the boiler explodes. The passengers are dispersed, some toward Albany, others toward New York, and some straight up. As always, Harrigan administered justice with an even hand. When calamity struck, it struck everyone.[6]

The Mulligans' Silver Wedding (February 21, 1881) was the eighth, final, probably the longest—three hours and twenty minutes with no intermission—and some thought the best volume. It was also the final production at the Comique.

There were big scenes at the Criterion Concert Hall—stage and audience both accommodated on the Comique stage, a new Harrigan trick; at the Full Moon Initiation in McSweeney's hayloft, a rigorous ceremony with swords, lanterns, red-hot branding irons, a greasy plank, and a tub of suds; at a clothesline argument in the Alley, between Honora Dublin and Hog-Eye:

> MRS. DUBLIN: You eat your dinner with drum sticks. You have a tail growing out of your head.
> HOG-EYE: No gette madee. Me likee you. Makee welly goodee wifee.
> MRS. DUBLIN: You're a mongrel assiatic. Why don't ye have whiskers on your face like a man. The likes of ye coming to a free country and walking around in petticoats.
> HOG-EYE: Welly nicee ladyee. Come top side of house and smokee one pipe opium. See Ilish heaven soon up quick.[7]

And at the Mulligans, now transformed into a boardinghouse, where Dan's constituents can grasp "the lever [whiskey] that moves the machinery of a great political party."

Cordelia's drunk scene in the parlor highlighted the evening. The Mulligans are about to celebrate "twenty-five years married Achushla, wid never an angry word only what passed between ourselves," according to Dan. He recalls only once when she tried his patience: When he explained to her that the statue of the man on the horse in Union Square was George Washington, "the man that when he was a boy said to his father, 'I cannot tell a lie—I broke the window with a brick,'" and Cordelia inquired, "His father thought some other boy broke it?"

Now, just before the party, Cordelia discovers a "Dear Dan" love letter. She trembles as she reads, and vows to turn the ceremony into a wake. "I'll drink this bottle of poison. I'll put on the dress I was married in that he may see me dead, but not dishonored." The "rat poison" is really a bottle of Calcutta brandy that Dan has relabeled to prevent the "femme de chambre," Caroline Melrose, from "nibbling at it." A neat scene. Dan knows what's in the bottle. The audience knows. Poor Cordelia trusts the label.

When Cordelia in her wedding gown staggers on, announces that she's drunk the poison, and begins to dictate her will—all her dresses and sealskin sack to Caroline Melrose—Caroline urges her to harbor her strength and keep dictating. "My diamond ring and Japanese fan to Caroline." Caroline's greedy eyes glow with anticipation. Cordelia will soon list the house. Unfortunately Dan shatters Caroline's dreams, and when he's told it's too late for a doctor, he winks at the audience, takes a snifter of the poison, and assures Cordelia that they'll die together. "I'll be dead in a minute . . . better measure me for a coffin." Passing the bottle back and forth, they continue their descent to the grave, and when Cousin Dennis (Hart) appears and smells the bottle, he volunteers to die with them. Harrigan, Hart, and Yeamans had a field day! The reviewers were ecstatic. Never had Harrigan's writing and Yeamans' acting been so beautifully joined. No one knew that Annie Yeamans had originated the drunk scene.

During the late seventies, New York ladies cherished the holiday custom of dashing about the city on January 2, sharing a nip with their friends. If one started early and persisted until evening, the results could be comforting. One day when Mrs. Yeamans had been making the rounds, she sent her daughters to the theatre in advance, to be on hand when she arrived. When she met them in her dressing room, which was next to Harrigan's, he heard the daughters sobbing, "Mom's been drinking. Mr. Harrigan will discharge her." Yeamans shouted them down with mushy blubbering: "Don't you fret, my precious ones. Misther Harrigan's all right. I'm all right! Everybody's all right. Where'sh my wig?" Harrigan went to her door, and when he saw her red wig angled across her head and a silly grin on her face, he assured her that he'd carry her through. A few moments later when she came on stage, on cue and sober as a judge, Harrigan almost flubbed his lines. The Yeamans act was too good to be forgotten.[8]

The brandy provided helpful lubrication for the *Silver Wedding*'s concluding extravaganza. Cordelia had misread the letter. It was addressed "Dear Den," not "Dear Dan." That settled, Puter and Primrose wheel in a silvered perambulator. Dan and Cordelia swing the pram around the stage, singing, "Wheel the Baby Out." A theatrical trunk is brought on, filled with shields, togas, and helmets. As they raid the trunk and prepare to render a scene from *The Gladiator,* Dennis leads in his pet monkey, Mungo. Mungo snitches the helmets, the shields, the silver, all available food, and finally the baby. Consternation! Curtain.

The Mulligans' Silver Wedding gave the Comique a triumphant finale before it was torn down to make way for a dry-goods store.[9] Harrigan and Hart had given 514 its best years and given Broadway a new kind of theatre. The "Mulligan series," a *Herald* reporter wrote, "is the 'Pickwick Papers' of a Bowery Dickens. ... To see Harrigan and Hart and their forty followers working double heats, crashing through glass, wiping the stage with each other, destroying their clothing, dancing till they steamed, singing till they howled, fighting till they made friends, to see all this, though it takes three hours, is to understand the devotion and incredible energy put into this business."[10] It had been a glorious time for the Harrigan company—and for their army of friends out front.

12

Tenements, Tammany, and Tweed

The Mulligan years at the Comique had etched the names of Harrigan and Hart, not only among the Broadway stars and New York's most illustrious citizens, but also on the masthead of a weekly tabloid, *Harrigan and Hart's New York Boys*.[1] And in the first issue of "Young America's Favorite Journal," September 18, 1880, Harrigan pronounced his blessing:

> Our ideal of a journal is one that shall contain good, wholesome reading for boys and girls, stories romantic and exciting without being improbable, sketches instructive as well as entertaining, wit and humor without coarseness and vulgarity —in short, a paper which will elevate the minds of its readers, and win not only their approbation but also that of their parents and guardians. . . . Of course Mr. Hart's and my pen are always at your service; and in making your paper the exclusive medium of the publication of my songs, I shall ask you to severely prosecute anyone who infringes on your right in this matter.

A few of the articles attributed to Harrigan and Hart during its first and only year of publication were written by Harrigan, and none by Hart.[2] In "Farewell, Old Theatre Comique!" Harrigan bemoaned the loss of the home of the Mulligans; it had been victimized by progress. "Step by step, year by year, commerce has driven theatres farther and farther uptown, until now theatres are erected where then it would be folly even to have raised the tent of a circus." And on May 28, 1881, Harrigan announced: "Welcome to the New Comique, with all its beauty of decoration and carpeted aisles, its electric lights. Above all, welcome to the successor of the Mulligan Guards, *The Major*, the new comedy with which the theatre will be inaugurated." Harrigan and Hart would be back in the fall, at a new stand, just a few blocks up Broadway.

In addition to the page or two of Harrigan lyrics in each issue, *Harrigan and Hart's New York Boys* offered serialized features loaded with Horatio Alger adverture. The first installment of "Edwin Forrest's Ward; or, Jack Stanley's Career on the Stage by Harrigan and Hart" concludes with "My God! The house is on fire! (To be continued.)" Short stories: "Tom Trix; or, a Young Man about Town by Nick Nipper"; "Hunted Down by a Parisian Detective." Incidental intelligence for boys:

> The following carefully prepared table shows the chances professional men have of catching fish:
> Artists 2 in 50
> Lawyers 3 in 50
> Doctors 7 in 50
> Editors 10 in 50
> Merchants 13 in 50
> Professors and unknown small boys with straw hats and broken suspenders 49 in 50

Selected "comiques": "The Western papers tell of a boy who 'peered fatally in the muzzle of a shotgun.' " "Probably no man so fully realizes the hollowness of life and human ambition as the man who ladles a teaspoonful of new-laid horse radish into his mouth under the impression that it is ice-cream." And, of course, the ads that still fascinate small-fry: "Conjuring or Magic Made Easy," "Bingham's Simple Method of Ventriloquism," "Manual of Etiquette and Art of Making Love."

A serialized piece by Harrigan in the spring of 1881, *Actors on the Road; or, the Adventures of Our Traveling Tour*, promises more than it gives. Mainly it recounts the daily routine of getting baggage on and off trains and the actors' practical jokes. Only one segment, "Fun at Hartford and New Haven," contributes a bit more: When a lanky character on the platform asks Harrigan if the plays really picture New York as it is, if "Mulligans and Becky

Hardrups an' nigger soldiers an' all that in that cussed city live together—sort of thick an' mixed like the innards of a mince pie," Harrigan assures him they're even thicker in real life and with "more spice in 'em." One could wish Harrigan had said more, when he had the chance.

During the Mulligan years, Harrigan was too busy at the Comique, too occupied writing, to write about writing, even in *New York Boys*. His plays spoke for him; he aimed at an evening's fun, three hours plus of Harrigan and Hart turns, a fresh mix of old and new, with characters and scenes straight from the Lower East Side. The game of playwriting was holding the mirror up to nature, and he turned his mirror on the sights he had known when he was growing up, the life still to be seen in his forays around the city. Harrigan never claimed to be a social historian, though he was, or a reformer, which he was not. He reported what he saw and heard, truthfully, with a warm heart, without bitterness or malice, and always with his mirror fixed on the lighter side.

The lower wards of the city, fanning out around Five Points, contained an incredible concentration of humanity and a treasury of human experience to outdistance the most vivid imagination.[3] One historian noted that in 1870 the area along Fifth Avenue from Union Square to Central Park, less than three miles, had about half as many inhabitants as a single block in the Fourth, Fifth, Sixth, or Seventh Ward. Most of the Harrigan country was populated with immigrants and their sons and daughters: Italian-Americans, German-Americans, and—in a clear majority—Irish-Americans. Most took pride in their adopted country, saluting the flag at every opportunity, yet even those who had been stewing in the melting pot for many years continued to be hyphenated Americans; the old-country colors always bled through. And no one, particularly not Harrigan, worried about being American and also Irish. You didn't have to homogenize the population to make a city or a country. *E Pluribus Plura*, as Daniel J. Boorstin has suggested, would make a more accurate motto than *E Pluribus Unum*.[4]

Every schoolboy knows that immigrants flooded into the United States during the nineteenth century; and large numbers of these young scholars, particularly in the cities, learned part of that lesson at home. Scan the school rosters in New York City, even today: most of the names seem more European than American.

From 1820 to 1870, some 8 million immigrants came into the country, 3 million from Ireland. According to the 1870 census, which listed a total population of just over 38 million, almost 2 million were natives of Ireland, 1.5 million plus from Germany, and less than .5 million from England. The figures would have jumped radically if the second generation had been added. The New York City that Harrigan knew when he was writing the Mulligan plays had a population of just under a million, more than 400,000 of whom were foreign born—202,000 Irish and 151,000 German; some 13,000 were listed as colored.

The big Irish influx had followed the potato famine of 1847; in the seven years from then until 1854, 1.5 million arrived. The annual figure peaked in 1851 with 216,000. Most of them stayed where they disembarked. In 1850, 130,000 of New York City's people, a quarter of the population, were Irish-born. In 1855 it was estimated that over a third of the city's voters were Irish.

Not until the sixties did Germans outnumber the Irish entering at Castle Garden: in 1860, 48,000 Irish and 54,000 Germans; in 1880, 71,000 Irish and 84,000 Germans. And not until the eighties did the Italians arrive in significant numbers; in 1880, 12,000.

Even after the immigration patterns began to change, the Irish dominated the New York scene. In 1890, when the population of the city had hit almost 1.5 million, nearly 200,000 were Irish-born, and over 40,000 more were children of Irish immigrants. And if the third and fourth generation were added, the Irish held a clear majority. The predominance of the foreign-born was almost always greater in the cities and particularly in New York. In 1900, when the population of the country had reached 76 million, 10 million were foreign-born and 26 million of foreign parentage.

Harrigan's New York had become one of the most cosmopolitan cities in the world. Jacob Riis, a reporter on the *Tribune* in the late seventies, said that if you made a map of the city with different colors to designate the nationalities, it would resemble a crazy quilt or a zebra, with two gigantic stripes dominating the field: green for the Irish and blue for the Germans. And among the immigrants, Riis found the Irishman the truest and most natural cosmopolite. He shared his lodging with perfect impartiality with Italians, Dutchmen, or whoever else wished to join his neighborhood. And he dominated the social scene.[5] Many contemporary observers, among them James W. Gerard, noted the phenomenon. In a paper read to the New York Historical Society in May 1883, Gerard insisted that "from the number of Irish and their descendants established here, Ireland, instead of England, might now be regarded as the mother country; or, rather, the stepmother country."[6]

Most immigrants did not venture far up the island from Castle Garden. Relatives or runners guided the Irish into the region around Five Points and the Germans to "Kleindeutschland" just a few blocks north, between Canal and Rivington. Five Points, some eight or nine blocks inland from where Harrigan was born, was the most notorious and dangerous single acre on Manhattan, a reputation it held well into the 1870s. In the fifteen-year period before 1850, as the center of the "Bloody Sixth Ward," it had the unenviable distinction of averaging one murder a night.

Although no longer marked by the convergence of five streets, the location can still be spotted: at Columbus Park, midway between Foley Square and Chatham Square, where Baxter, Mulberry, and Park intersect. Known originally as The Collect, after the pond where John Fitch tried out a model of his steamboat in 1796—several years ahead of Fulton—it acquired the name Five Points when the pond was drained, permitting the streets to intersect, and the old brewery that stood on the banks of the pond adopted the name Five Points.

In 1837 the brewery was transformed into a tenement and became home to some one thousand Irish and Negroes, Negroes being consigned to the cellar. Dickens visited Five Points in 1842 and recorded his impressions in *American Notes*: "All that is loathsome, drooping, and decayed is here. . . . From every corner, as you glance about you in these dark retreats, some figure crawls half-awakened, as if the judgement hour were near at hand, and every obscene grave were giving up its dead, where dogs would howl to lie, women, and men, and boys slink off to sleep, forcing the dislodged rats to move away in quest of better lodgings."[7]

Even if the region was less dangerous in Harrigan's time, it was still overcrowded with Irish, Germans, Jews, and a sprinkling of Italians.[8] The *Spirit of the Times* (March 31, 1877) reported that there were chickens in the streets; ducks, pigs, and dogs splashing in mud puddles; five goats on an old wall vainly endeavoring to find a blade of grass; and children everywhere, at least ten to each adult. He heard "Kitty Maloney calling to Pat to be sure he don't forget to call in and see Mrs. O'Flaherty, as she is 'rale sick'. Idle youths lean up against the lamp-posts and smoke cigar ends. There is a class of youths in New York whose chief delight in life seems to be to lean up against posts."[9]

The inhabitants of Five Points, like most of the immigrants on the Lower East Side, and like Harrigan's Mulligan crowd, lived in the four- to six-story tenements jammed together throughout the area. These dreary structures, often built three deep from the street or around an inner yard and reached through dank passageways, "oozing with moisture and covered with unmentionable filth," boasted such picturesque names as Jacob's Ladder, Brickbat Mansion, Bandit's Roost, Gotham Court, and Sweeney's Shambles. After the first tenement on Corlear's Hook was built in 1833 (a four-story structure on Water Street where Corlear's Hook Park is now) and the Five Points Brewery was converted to housing, tenements, or rookeries as they were called later, became home for most immigrants. And in spite of the unhealthy filth and congestion, they offered now-forgotten advantages. A newcomer fresh from the boat could find friends and relatives and get a room for five dollars a month. Old-time residents could earn their keep as superintendents and turn a profit with groceries, liquor, and policy. And absentee landlords realized such magnificent returns on their investments that they tried to perpetuate tenement living.

According to the 1870 census, some 20,000 tenement houses below Eighth Street sheltered 160,000 families, averaging 8 families per building; there were 20 to 30 in some, and one had 200. Nor were tenements decreasing in number when Harrigan was writing about them; even in 1900, some 43,000 rookeries housed over 1.5 million New Yorkers.

One reporter described a typical accommodation of the seventies: the six-story building stood on a lot 50 by 250 feet; the rooms, measuring 12 feet square and with 8-foot ceilings, piled up on either side of an arched-over alleyway, were reached by outside stairways hardly wide enough for two people to pass. Privies and water were available in the courtyard. A family of six occupied two tiny rooms: "The mother, a wrinkled crone at thirty, sits rocking in her arms an infant whose pallid features tell of decay and death. Two older children are in the street. A fourth child, emaciated to a skeleton, rears its feeble frame on a rickety chair."[10]

Harrigan knew the sad side of tenement living, but he chose to write about holiday time, when the clouds lifted, games replaced work and worry, and Irish, Germans, and Negroes discovered a sunny and funny side to their animosities.

Harrigan never dwelt on the heavy weather churned up by Irish and Negroes, such as the draft riots of 1863, when the Irish burned a Negro orphanage.[11] His Germans, though stubborn, dumb, and heavy-footed, were not subjected to serious abuse. When Finley Peter Dunne wrote about the Germans in his *Observations by Mr. Dooley* in 1902, he could have been describing Gustave Lochmuller: "But wanst a German, always Dutch. Ye cudden't make Americans iv them if ye called thim all Perkins an' brought thim up in Worcester."[12]

Harrigan's Irish portraits were more richly detailed than his Negroes and Germans, truer to all facets of the Irishman's character, though he studiously avoided unsavory excesses. His Irish might be vagabonds and rogues, but never bums. Except at rare moments, his Irish didn't fight among themselves. He never drew on the battles that frequently erupted between Orangemen and Roman Catholics in New York.

Most of the attributes commonly ascribed to Irish-Americans appeared at some time in the Harrigan plays, and in a way the plays became a multivolumed biography of the Irish immigrants. Harrigan could not, like G. B. Shaw in *John Bull's Other Island,* ridicule Ireland; Harrigan refused to believe that Shaw was Irish.

He would have been even more skeptical if he had known that Shaw had once said, "Like all Irishmen, I dislike the Irish—on instinct."[13] Harrigan loved the Irish, particularly Irish-Americans.

The Irish that deserted their homeland were mostly peasants who had rejected the land or been rejected by it; they had no urge to return to farming in America. They crowded into the cities, and most of them became common laborers. An 1876 survey reported that the Irish held more than 50 percent of the "common drudgery" jobs in New York. Although these were the only tasks for which they were qualified, many reports suggested a lack of industry, ambition, or efficiency, the same laziness as one observer had noted on Irish farms: "They scratch, pick, dawdle, stare, gape, and do anything but strive and wrestle with the task. The most ludicrous of all human objects is an Irishman ploughing."[14]

If there were questions about their industry, there were none about their sociability. Nature had endowed them with geniality, generosity, and an exuberance for sharing their pleasures with friends. Thomas Macaulay once said they were "distinguished by qualities which tend to make men interesting rather than prosperous, . . . an ardent and impetuous race, easily moved to tears or laughter, to fury or to love."[15] They gave their own style to life in the tenements, refusing to be subdued by dreary surroundings. Their spirit had not been broken by their struggles with the English. Why should they now be broken by physical discomfort? They became nineteenth-century playboys of the Western world.

No other Americans, hyphenated or native, could surpass them in talk, in conviviality, in drinking, in fighting, in singing, or match them in the pleasure derived from these enterprises. Most were worthy descendants of Cormac Carthy, the Lord of Blarney, whom Queen Elizabeth accused of putting her off with "fair words and soft speech . . . all Blarney. What he says he never means."[16] They prided themselves on their fancy talk, on their jabs at the highfalutin, even when they slipped into belligerent contempt for their intellectual superiors.

The Irishman's search for companionship, his eagerness to stand high with friends, led him to the neighborhood saloon. He was rarely a solitary boozer; but he had an easy tolerance for "a good man's weakness."[17] When social historians later began to probe the psyche of their subjects, many argued that the New York Irish had been trapped by their stereotype. They were obliged to be friendly, witty, generous, pugnacious, and partial to drink to perpetuate the image story writers had created for them. That the Irish did more than their fair share of heavy drinking was at least partly documented in the 1940s: among white Bowery bums, more than 44 percent were Irish. A record of admissions for alcoholic psychosis to New York State institutions showed that the Irish led the ethnic groups with 25.6 percent; and the Scandinavians ran a poor second at 7.6 percent.[18]

Drinking led to dancing, singing, raucous arguments, and frequently to fights, which then led them into the paddy wagons, named in their honor. One of Harrigan's contemporaries observed that an Irishman always got into more trouble than the English, the Americans, or the Germans because he was "more impulsive, more mercurial, more excitable; he [would] publish his indiscretion on the highway and [would] himself identify his nationality with his folly."[19] He was what he was openly and for all the world to see. Long before Notre Dame's "Fighting Irish" played football under Eastern European aliases, the Irish were known as expert fighters. They gained that reputation in the Civil War, in the Mexican War, and in New York's saloons. And many of the later urban folk heroes—Maggie and Jiggs, Moon Mullins, Dick Tracy in the comic strips, James Cagney in the motion pictures—were depicted as pugnacious Irishmen.

In New York, as on the "ould sod," the Irish had three social centers: home, church, and saloon, two of which became headquarters for Harrigan's crowd. Except for a few incidental references, he allowed his dramatis personae privacy in their communion with church and God. He concentrated on domesticity, on communion with neighbors, and on politics.

As soon as a son of Erin arrived on Manhattan Island, he discovered his political identity. He was an Irish-Catholic-Democrat, and he was enrolled with the party in the local saloon. Political activity came naturally, and he had reason for his affiliation with the Democrats.[20] Jefferson and his followers had been sympathetic to France, while Hamilton, Jay, and the Federalists had been Anglophiles. More immediately, in Harrigan's time, the Irishman discovered that local politics bore similarities to the informal popular sovereignty he had known at home where local leaders saw that the unjust laws of the absentee legitimate government were properly subverted. He was already familiar with being herded to the polls "to be voted."

Some admirable aspects of New York politics were new. Here was the first great city of the world that was ruled by men of the people, and many of the cogs in the political machine had come from Ireland.[21] From the top boss to the district leaders to the block captains, order, not tyranny, was the watchword. And the new arrival soon discovered that Irish-style city politics was personalized. His alderman provided food, housing, medicine, and domestic guidance; he was on hand for christenings, weddings, and wakes; and he controlled the city jobs for which the Irish were eminently qualified. In 1863 a correspondent of the London *Times* visiting New York said that there was "scarcely a situation of honour or distinction, from chief magistrate down to police, that was not filled by an Irishman or one of his descendants."[22] In the seventies more than half the police force was Irish.

The New York Irish discovered long before John F. Kennedy that public office "beats chasing a dollar," that industry, goodwill, and natural conviviality counted more there than money and education—a fact that would be demonstrated more clearly later by Al Smith, James J. Walker, and Jim Farley. Smith and Walker became leaders in the New York legislature while still in their thirties, and Smith became the political folk hero of the city as Lincoln had been for the frontier. Franklin D. Roosevelt's right-hand man, Jim Farley, who knew politics as well as anyone, reported that "I never in my life met a humble Irishman; it just doesn't run in the strain. The fact is that I have met few who were not their own figurative secretaries of state. Whatever else they may lack it isn't opinions or willingness to fight for them."[23]

New York was governed by Tammany Hall, an organization that reflected the rise of the Irish in politics. Originally rejected by the pseudo-Indian Tammany sachems, the Irish gradually penetrated the sacrosanct wigwam and finally in 1880 even elected one of their own as mayor, William R. Grace of the shipping line. Tammany never had such devoted Indians as the Irish, if the stories can be trusted. At a Fourth of July gathering, one Irishman asked why Mr. Murphy had not joined the singing of the "Star Spangled Banner": "Probably because he didn't want to commit himself before checking with Tammany." When a block captain confided to his district leader that he was about to be married, the leader inquired if he had been given the go-ahead from the Grand Sachem.[24]

Organized in 1789, shortly after Washington's inauguration, Tammany was named after the legendary chief of the Delawares. Members ranked as hunters and warriors, were ruled by twelve sachems and a grand sachem—only native born Americans were eligible for these posts—and their headquarters was called The Wigwam. On the Fourth of July and on Tammany Day (May 12), the braves painted their faces, dressed in full Indian regalia, and paraded about the city carrying bows, arrows, and tomahawks.

In the early years Tammany rejected all foreigners, but the Irish gradually inched in, notably in the Jackson campaign of 1828. In the 1830s they manned the Tammany machine in the Sixth Ward, and with the great migrations of the forties and fifties they took a firm hold on city politics.[25]

The Tammany leader whose name was still on the minds of New Yorkers when Harrigan sent Dan Mulligan into politics was William Marcy Tweed. In fact, whenever politics was mentioned in the last half of the nineteenth century, one automatically heard "Tweed" or "Tweed Ring." A great hulk of a man, over six feet tall and weighing nearly three hundred pounds, Tweed was destined to command. He was born in New York of Scotch-Irish parentage in 1823. In 1850 he was elected to the Common Council, then popularly known as "The Forty Thieves." In 1863, as grand sachem of the Tammany Society, he became president of the Board of Supervisors, where he perfected his system of plunder with the help of his ring: Peter B. Sweeny, city chamberlain and "the brains"; Richard D. Connolly, comptroller, "Slippery Dick"; George G. Barnard, Albert Cardozo, John H. McCunn, the "ring judges"; and Mayor Oakey Hall, his "front man." One newspaper commented that New York City "is governed by Oakey Hall, Tammany Hall, and Alcohol."[26]

Although Tweed's notoriety rested principally on his financial dealings, his power was demonstrated in other areas. He made naturalization easy. A faithful Irish Democrat could go to the saloon in his neighborhood, get a red ticket reading "Please Naturalize the Bearer," and proceed to court where judges frequently naturalized batches of one hundred fifty at a time with the aid of a half-dozen Bibles strategically spotted around the room. In 1868 over forty-one thousand aliens became citizens, four times the previous annual average. On November 2, 1868, Horace Greeley's *Tribune* praised the tireless patriotism of Judge Mc-Cunn: "It is rumored that he has issued an order naturalizing all the lower counties of Ireland, beginning at Tipperary and running down to Cork. Judge Barnard will arrange for the northern counties at the next sitting of the chambers."[27]

Tweed was a chairmaker who "quickly learned the art of living without work." In 1861, after he had tried a term in Congress, he was bankrupt. Ten years later, after dedicating himself to New York, his fortune was estimated at $15 to $20 million, accumulated by his untiring efforts to discover the needs of the city and by his willingness to keep several projects working simultaneously. He formed a furniture factory to supply the city. He bought the *Transcript* and had it declared the official paper of the city and used its auxiliary printing company to provide stationery for city offices and schools—the 1870 bill, $2.8 million. He bought carloads of condemned breech-loading rifles from the United States Army, then sneaked a bill through the legislature requiring all state militiamen to be armed with the rifles. His big windfalls came from cooperating with contractors, a sure source of revenue, as many later politicians have discovered.

The courthouse in the rear of City Hall was Tweed's most rewarding venture. When it was begun in 1862, $250,000 was authorized for the work; the next year an additional $1 million was requested and approved. Similar appropriations were added every year until, in 1872, with the building still unfinished, the price tag, including interest, stood at $14 million. The subcontractors helped immeasurably in swelling the costs and accommodating Tweed. Carpeting came to just under $5 million; plastering, $3.5 million; and plumbing, $1.5 million.

Through the efforts of the *New York Times* (which the ring had tried to buy when Henry R. Raymond died) and *Harper's Weekly,* particularly Thomas Nast's cartoons, the ring was smashed in 1871. Tweed was indicted on 120 counts, ranging from grand larceny to conspiracy, sent to jail in 1873, released in 1875, and rearrested. He escaped to Cuba and then to Spain but in November 1876 was returned to jail, where he died on April 12, 1878. He was the only member of his ring who suffered. The others skipped the country.

In spite of his conviction, Tammany loyalists revered his memory, and hundreds marched past his coffin. They preferred to recall his $50,000 contributions to charity, the free coal he provided in winter, the free beer in summer. And though Tweed may have tarnished the Tammany name, the shame did not endure.

In 1880 Harrigan's New Jersey judge in *The Mulligan Guard Picnic* automatically released all prisoners who uttered the magic name Tammany. And whenever Dan Mulligan swung into a new campaign for alderman or for coroner, he marched to the podium waving the Tammany flag.

13

The New Comique

The new theatre was on the east side of Broadway at Waverly Place, a ten-minute walk uptown from the old Comique. Directly across the street from the New York Hotel and backed against the La Grange Terrace, where John Jacob Astor lived, it was in a busy part of town in 1881. The area is less busy now, but theatre activity still thrives there. Joseph Papp's Public Theatre, a block away, occupies the same relative location on Lafayette as the Comique did on Broadway.

The address 728 Broadway was not new to Harrigan. He made his first New York appearance there when it was called the Globe. Like so many theatres, then and now, it was perpetually searching a new name. Originally the Church of the Messiah, it was transformed into Lucy Rushton's Theatre in 1865, then became the New York, Fifth Avenue, Metropolitan, Fox's Broadway, Globe, National, American, Manhattan, Wood's Broadway, Bryant's Opera House, and finally, in its last and most lustrous years, Harrigan and Hart's Theatre Comique.

Owned by the Stewart estate, the theatre was just two blocks south of A. T. Stewart's famous eight-story "Iron Palace," the largest iron building of its day when it was built in 1862 and still in 1881 the largest retail store in the world. Stewart funds provided a new facade for the theatre, of Philadelphia pressed brick; Harrigan and Hart spruced up the interior in bronze, ivory, and buff, brought up two figures from the old Comique for the proscenium niches, added bird and animal friezes, installed a prismatic chandelier, upholstered the parquet seats in raw silk, and installed iron staircases, a safety innovation.[1]

The partners invested heavily; they loved the theatre and hoped to call it home, permanently. The stage was a good size, with a thirty-two-foot proscenium opening; Harrigan often said that he liked a stage small enough to allow the actor a quick exit: "Let the talk go flip-flap for a minute and then out of sight. The effect is fifty times stronger." He also wanted to be near the audience: "When performers are almost surrounded by the audience, the actors can do much better."[2] With an oval-shaped parquet only fifty feet deep and seventy feet wide, actors and audience resided in cozy proximity. Still, the house was big enough to be profitable and to accommodate all classes: some twelve hundred seats were divided equally between the main floor, balcony, and gallery. The move uptown brought in the fashionables, and for them Harrigan laid a red velvet carpet from curb to lobby. They were welcome as long as they did not inhibit the "shirt sleeve brigade."[3] Harrigan had deep affection for the pugnacious gallery gods. He had been one. They might smell of horses, beer, and boiled cabbage; they might rock and stamp, shout too lustily, but they let an actor and a playwright know where he stood.

There were other inviting features. He and Hart had comfortable quarters in the parson's study. Braham and his twelve musicians (three violins, viola, cello, bass, flute, clarinet, two cornets, trombone, timpani) could breathe parquet air instead of being squeezed in under the stage. The lobby was spacious and opened onto Broadway through two large arches. And the theatre's location was excellent. The Sinclair House at Eighth and Broadway was handy for a nightcap, and Scott and Earl's at the corner of Sixth Avenue and Eighth for an oyster supper—and both were on the way to the new Harrigan home at 14 Perry, just four blocks from the theatre.

Harrigan ignored expense to assure a first-class operation. Most of the actors, twenty-seven men and eight women, who moved up from 514 had been promised a boost in pay. One report said Wild was to get $151 per week and Yeamans $150, Wild insisting on being the higher paid; another equally reliable report repeated the figures but switched the names. The executive department boasted three Harrigans: Ned as stage director, his father treasurer, and his half brother Warren assistant treasurer. Witham continued as scenic artist and G. L. Stout as prompter. There were a master machinist, a property man, an engineer of gas and steam effects, and a publicity agent. The chiefs were augmented by thirty-six "attachés," doorkeepers, ushers, watchmen, et al. The box office would be open nine to four, matinee performances were at two on Tuesday and Friday, evenings except Sunday at eight, and tickets cost twenty-five cents to a dollar.[4]

On opening night, August 29, 1881, the house was crowded to the doors, according to the *Spirit of the Times,* "a thoroughly American audience in our first thoroughly American theatre, giving the Comique a genuine Knickerbocker house-warming."[5] The place was a gem of mechanical art, and the acoustics were perfect. The partners well deserved the warmth and affection they received because they had "striven constantly to give a certain character and tone to their entertainments," though the *Times* man found some unnecessary gaudiness in the decorations.

The Major demanded the full strength of the company and extraordinary skill from the machinists, and it introduced Major Gilfeather, one of Harrigan's happiest rogues. Gilfeather had acquired his title from an obscure British regiment, his chest of medals for equally obscure heroics, his white and red coat, blue trousers, and fancy gaiters from indulgent merchants, and his gift of gab from Harrigan and Old Lavender. He could have served as a model for W. C. Fields's fancy talkers and for the expansive Major Hoople in Eugene Ahern's "Our Boarding House," a favorite comic strip of the 1930s (which still survives today).

Again Harrigan assembled his eccentrics in familiar locales: on the dock with a fresh load of immigrants; in Caleb Jenkins's policy office; at Coney Island, "the poor man's Saratoga"; and on the roof of Percival Pop's fireworks factory. On the dock a bewildered young Irishman wanders around struggling with his precious cargo, "eighteen shovels full of County Connaught" he's going to plant in his "backyard in America and walk over every morning for luck." In the policy shop, Gilfeather proclaims the glories of the numbers game; it offers better odds than stocks and bonds. A

Negro chorus echoes his sentiments with "4—11—44," so boisterously that Jenkins implores them to quiet down: "too much hilarity breeds contempt"; they also draw the police. Miranda Briggs (Yeamans), an enchanting boardinghouse madame, is pursued by Gilfeather and Percival Pop, who pleads for "one spark of love to inflame the powder magazine in my heart and blow me into the valley of joy and happiness." She prefers the major. She wouldn't put *Pop* on a tombstone, thought *Pop* would be cheaper to inscribe than *Gilfeather*.

Pop's risky occupation was put to good use. While Negroes are sunning themselves on the roof, surveying Manhattan—"de big building am de Tribune, from de top of it you can see all de young men dat went west"—Pop and the major are in the office below drinking and philosophizing. When the major lights his cigar, Pop reminds him that "one spark of fire and you and I can guess the conundrum!" Their dreamy speculations and long pulls at the bottle slowly obscure the hazard and the major pitches his butt into a pile of shavings. "Explosion. Business of roof effect. Smoke seen ascending through roof. Fireworks then seen through windows of factory. A large battery is then exploded and the omnes [the Negroes on the roof] each of whom are attached to wires are seen by audience to ascend until hid from view by sky borders. The roof splits in pieces. The front of the factory sinks through the stage, and the debris of roof crashes and falls to the stage amidst smoke and fire. Heads, limbs, and bodies of omnes seen by audience descending from sky."

It was a grand explosion, one of the best. In 1895, when the play was repeated, one critic wrote: "As I tottered away I felt as if Ali Baba and his forty thugs had clubbed me with Chicago sandbags, and all the wild mustangs in all the stables had run over me, and all the stableboys had caressed me with currycombs, and Wagner had been sung in a boiler factory."[6]

The casualty list was announced in the next scene: Caleb slid down a telegraph pole; "Bottles jumped on a carpet two niggers were shaking in de street." Some sunbathers were jarred, others boxed, and "de dead are so mixed up you can't tell wedder you're burying a relation or a friend." Jule Garman's head got on Delameter's body; somebody found a glass eye belonging to Mister Callowell, but it turned out to be an agate some boy lost; and a wooden leg for Misses Grass wouldn't fit; it was a baseball bat.

The new Comique was off to a rousing start. Gilfeather and friends staged a one hundredth performance celebration in November and continued until January, 152 performances, just one shy of *The Ball* record.

If Tony Hart felt shortchanged with the part of the cockney Henry Higgins, Harrigan made it up to him with Widow Nolan in *Squatter Sovereignty* (January 9, 1882), the play that filled the rest of the season and outdistanced *The Major* with 168 performances. If other managers could have spotted another Harrigan, another Harrigan and Hart company, they would have rushed them into service. Fortunately for the Comique, there were no duplicates or near duplicates.

The new offering reverted to Irish-German unfriendliness, to a female role for Hart, but had location scenes in new parts of town: the Widow Nolan's shanty; Captain Kline's Fifth Avenue drawing room; and the hillside around the shanty. Many critics declared that the captain's quarters were more gorgeous than Augustin Daly's upholstered parlors. Daly, one of the leading producers of the day, may not have gone that far, but he was impressed. He wrote to Harrigan a week after the opening:

> You can charge to my account an afternoon of fresh and unalloyed enjoyment. I think your epic of Shantyville is something all by itself. It is, I think, your best. Mr. Hart surpasses himself as the Widow Nolan. I have no leading woman who could touch the hem of his petticoat in the part, and as for yourself, you're a living chromo, where on earth did you pick up that walk and those trousers?[7]

Much of the play was drawn from life. In the 1880s, squatters had transformed old boxes, barrels, and sheets of tin into shanties in Central Park, on the west side of the park in the sixties; and along the upper stretches of Fifth Avenue, they occupied so much of the rocky hills that their settlement became known as Shantytown.[8] According to the reporters, Harrigan and Witham had caught the authentic flavor of the village, an observation that delighted Harrigan because he had written the play the previous summer at Schroon Lake before he had seen Shantytown and had simply relied on newspaper descriptions and his imagination.

Felix McIntyre (Harrigan), loquacious royal astronomer to the Duchess of Connaught—his "heavenly penetrator" can show you "Uranus, Venus, Mars, and Jew Peter" for a dime—has pledged his son Terrence, so fresh from Ireland that "he don't know what ice cream is yet," to Nellie Nolan, only daughter of Widow Rosey, queen of Shantytown.[9] The widow's clan from County Clare and the McIntyres from Templemore attest the contract and the dowries: bedstead and slats, iron skillets, a pair of India rubber boots, and three white geese and a drake from Felix. From the widow: a down feather bed, a cradle she lay in herself, a Morning Glory number nine stove, and her precious pet goat. Her Billy can butt with the best, but he also has his gentle side; he breakfasts with the family, and "if a child in the neighborhood took on a crooping, he'd halt and he'd gaze like a man."

The betrothal creates havoc. Billy, the first to break the bargain, seeks a fuller life on Fifth Avenue, invades the pickled onions and eats the lace curtains in the Kline mansion, is captured, then rescued by the assault forces—Maguires, McIntyres, and the widow—and returned to Shantytown. Their triumph quickly turns sour. Nellie has eloped with the Kline boy. McIntyres and Maguires battle over the dowry, and just as County Clare and Templemore are about to annihilate each other, Kline and his brewers arrive. The Irish close ranks and destroy the Dutch. Fences are shattered, bodies tumble down the hill, the jackass Napoleon escapes from his stable, the geese from their pen, and when the police arrive, "General Consternation!" Harrigan had discovered an uptown word! At the first performance, the geese were given too much rope and, imbued with opening night enthusiasm, landed on some of New York's smartest bonnets. A few nights later, Napoleon missed his footing and dropped through a stage trap.[10] Animals made unreliable actors, but Harrigan continued to cast them.

Many thought Harrigan's latest documentary his best and the new songs—"Paddy Duffy's Cart" and "Miss Brady's Piano For-Tay"—as catchy as any in the Harrigan-Braham album.

Prosperity seemed now a settled fact of life for Harrigan and Hart—more reassuring to the Harrigans than to Hart. Solvency never troubled Hart. As long as the day's pleasures could be accommodated, tomorrow must look out for itself. The Harrigans proceeded more cautiously, though never as penny-pinching worriers. With the move uptown and the expense of refurbishing the theatre, they gambled on the success of the new Comique: not only did they split away from the Brahams and acquire their own home on Perry Street, between Waverly Place and Greenwich Avenue, where Seventh Avenue now cuts through, but Mrs. Harrigan invested in a house on Madison Avenue, uptown of Shantytown, which brought her a rental of $1,200 a year.[11]

During the summer of 1881, while Harrigan was on a short tour of the Midwest, she was busy with their new quarters. She wrote to him in Saint Louis urging him not to stay out late at night —"you know it won't do you any good"—and to hurry home to see the wonders. Every room, on all three floors, was furnished in fine style, the fireplaces worked, his study at the rear of the second floor was ready for the writer: glassed-in bookcases, a walnut bust of Shakespeare, and his desk settled where he could look out on the backyard and the lilacs. And *"there'll be no creditors to dun you"*; everything had been paid in full. Annie had guarded the Comique profits and now put them to good use. If he worried about her wandering around the place by herself, he needn't. Her sister Addie had been staying at night with her and Eddie; her Aunt Mary had come in regularly, and the Brahams were close by.[12]

The move to Perry did not separate the families. Harrigan and Braham were always together at the theatre. Mrs. Braham was frequently in charge of the children, and she constantly watched her daughter's health. When the Harrigans went to Schroon Lake in late July, leaving Eddie with his grandparents, Mrs. Braham sent daily warnings to Annie about colds, about keeping her breast warm—Annie was then pregnant with Anthony.

The few weeks' vacation at Taylors-on-Schroon (later known as Schroon Manor) was not the only testimony to Harrigan's new affluence. Grandfather Joseph Braham in London wrote that he was just about eighty and having trouble with his breathing. The doctor said he needed sea air. He was delighted that Annie had acquired a good husband; he would like to see a picture of him. Apparently Harrigan responded. A month later, the old man wrote thanking Edward for the picture and the money. It was a godsend; a month at the shore might restore his breathing, though his doctor now advised two months as a safer investment.[13]

Having not speculated on a vacation before, Annie and Ned were surprised at how easily they adapted to the new luxury, and after a second summer on the Taylor porch, they decided to build their own summer home. Ned found 125 acres on Schroon's southern shore, with an apple orchard and a brook, and hired a carpenter to begin construction the next year. His instructions were simple: "Build it big, very big; we are going to have a lot of children."[14] Late in the summer of 1883, with Mrs. Harrigan supervising, the construction began; the following summer they moved in, and for the next seventy-five years some Harrigans were there every summer, at The Boulders, The Maples as Annie called it, or The Big House as it was known in the neighborhood. Frequently Schroon visitors mistook it for a hotel. (A primitive painting of the house now hangs in the Logan living room. The original artist set the place on a barren hill; Joshua Logan added appropriate summer foliage.)

The builder took Harrigan literally, constructing twenty rooms on two floors; a third-story attic; a wing with kitchen, laundry, and servant's quarters; and a double-deck porch encircling the building, convenient for children spying on guests and for Harrigan to write. The place was meant for children and guests, and both responded. Adelaide recalled that, in the early nineties, her mother often carved a roast for twenty to thirty, and rarely did the table count drop below a dozen.

When the house was going up, Harrigan was already back in New York, but Annie reported the progress. The finishing lumber had arrived. She had selected basins, sinks, and bathtubs; running water would be piped into the tubs and marble basins, not into the sleeping rooms. There would be open fireplaces in the dining room and library. She dispensed with a gas machine and electric lights "as I think it is a little too much J. K. Emmett." (Emmett had made a fortune as a minstrel performer and had just purchased the

Van Rensselaer estate on the Hudson River.) Her duties had been aggravated by a cold—"don't tell Mama"—by Tony's whooping cough, by Eddie's racing about—"I can hardly keep sight of him" —and with all the activity she still weighed 153 pounds. He could help her by ordering pipe in New York for the reservoir, sending her a basket of peaches and two or three bottles of Tokay wine.[15]

Once the house was finished, life was no less complicated. Servants from the city, whether Scandinavian, Irish, or Negro, were a problem. Some were "hoisters" and had to be dismissed. One Irish lass took off before breakfast one morning because she'd heard a banshee at her window, and most wearied of country living by mid-August. The plumbing that Annie had chosen so carefully did not corroborate its claims and had to be protected by a sign, on display more often than not, "Under no circumstances use the toilet."[16] (An emergency three-holer was available outside.) Just as the servants played out in August, so did Annie. Usually her collapse began with an aching tooth, when the Saratoga racing season was announced. One day her pain would become unbearable. She then packed her prettiest frocks and, with her newest straw hat and her parasol, took the buggy to Riverside, twelve miles away, for the fifty-mile train trip to Saratoga Springs. When she returned, she talked little of the dentist, a good deal about the Grand Union Hotel and about sitting with Lillian Russell in her box at the track.

Adelaide, like the other children, had happy memories of Schroon: Mr. Pritchard, who drove the butcher cart and wore golden hoops in his ears, which he said protected his kidneys. The fancy Abercrombie and Fitch garments and equipment her father ignored. He preferred to set out for an afternoon's fishing in old pants and shirt and a farmer's haying hat, carrying a bamboo pole and a can of worms. He would return waving a couple of sticks that might be mistaken for fish until he tied up at the dock. Harrigan once described his pleasure in fishing: "I like to ponder upon what they think when they poise perfectly still for two hours in front of my hook without moving either toward or away from me."[17] One day, through some miscalculation, he returned with a five-pound bass and, to commemorate the catch, one of the boys traced its outline on the porch with a jackknife, preserving the record for posterity. And no one could ever forget the sad, final days at the end of the season when the shutters were nailed, the rowboats—*Old Lavender, Waddy Googan,* and *Pete*—stashed in the barn, and the family took the train to Albany and the night boat to the city.

With Mrs. Braham's constant concern for her daughter, her increasing responsibilities for grandchildren, and David's continuing collaboration on new songs, and as Harrigan began writing and even rehearsing at Schroon, the Brahams decided to find a summer place of their own in the vicinity. They came up alone late one spring, and David wrote his daughter that they had discovered a cottage that "delighted your Ma." They would retain the dining room and kitchen and invest a thousand dollars in a handsome front building, "so it will be a credit to you and Ned."[18] As Harrigan's fortunes expanded, David's could not keep pace, but if the Brahams ever thought of themselves as poor relations, the thought caused no trouble. Harrigans and Brahams were never separated by more than a short walk in Greenwich Village, at Schroon, or later on Manhattan's Upper West Side.

14

Cordelia's Aspirations and *Dan's Tribulations*

The second season at the uptown Comique gave strong support to Harrigan's domestic expansion, though it took four plays. The first was a non-Harrigan play, a "picturesque Irish drama" by G. L. Stout called *The Blackbird* (August 26, 1882). Even with a whirlpool sensation devised by Witham—"the heroine whirls terribly, sometimes creakingly from ledge to ledge like the gentleman in Poe's story," waiting for Harrigan to save her—it did not catch on.[1] The reviewers advised Stout to return to prompting and Harrigan to his own plays.

Mordecai Lyons (October 26, 1882), a Jewish melodrama about a faithless daughter and an orphan threatened by incest, was still not in the Harrigan mainstream. In spite of a sprinkling of clichés about Jewish thrift—"don't vast de bread by dropping de crumbs," dunk it in coffee; buy beer without froth—most reporters thought Mordecai's middle name must be Mulligan. And the play could not be saved by the new scenes in Harrigan's photographic history of the city: the pawnshop loaded with junk, the garden of a Hudson River mansion, and the Victoria Shades beer parlor, an actors' hangout where gossip is mixed with song. A stage doorman recalls "A fellow named Tubbs who played a wave in the *Lonely Man of the Ocean* and got round shouldered holding the ocean up." Mendoza (Hart) sings about his frustration in mashing a girl at Macy's emporium. Her only response is "Cash! Cash! Cash!"

Even though Harrigan's friends tolerated his histrionic vanity in tackling the role, they urged him to abandon the sterile clap-trap and return to the Mulligans. One critic even volunteered a plot: Dan should run for Congress against a millionaire and his son Tommy return from Kalamazoo to join the campaign.[2] Harrigan enjoyed playing Mordecai, credited Henry Irving's Shylock with giving him the idea, and was overjoyed when Edwin Booth said it was the best part he had ever played,[3] but Harrigan, Irving, and Booth were insignificant voices compared with the public.

After a month he returned to politics, the Babylonian tenements, and fresh on-the-spot views of city life, described in one of the songs "McNally's Row of Flats":

> It's Ireland and Italy, Jerusalem and Germany,
> Oh Chinamen and Nagers, and a paradise for cats
> All jumbled up togather in the snow or rainy weather,
> They represent the tenants in McNally's row of flats.

McSorley's Inflation (November 27, 1882) expanded Harrigan's album: Washington Market, a crew of masculine-looking females manning the stalls and hawking their wares in "The Market on Saturday Night": "Pickles and chow chow and dogs that go bow wow; / Parsnips and crosses and little babies dresses." A real *Herald* wagon. A horsecar drawn by a real horse. A Salvation Army band beating off rum with a drum:

> Ol' Jonah he lived away down in a whale,
> In a little backroom very close to the tail;
> Don't give it away, for he's out on bail
> And he sings in the Salvation Army, Oh.

A Negro senator from South Carolina and his private army marching to "The Charleston Blues," and McSorley bellowing "I Never Drink behind the Bar." The famous McSorley's Saloon, just off Cooper Square and now called "McSorley's Old Ale House," one of New York's oldest landmarks, was already a landmark in Harrigan's time and very handy to the Comique.

Peter McSorley, campaigning for coroner, views with "great alarm the progressive movement of the Italian element," and the Chinaman who "would put his lepress hands upon the anglo-saxon circassion and drive us into the whirlpool of the Pacific

Ocean." He's the staunch friend of the Irish and the colored people:

> When I am elected I will take the bald-headed eagle down from City Hall and put up the four-leaved Shamrock. I will move the reservoir to the Eighth Ward for a free bath house for colored people. I will paint every telegraph pole red white and blue for the colored barbers of this city; I will fill West Point with colored cadets.

McSorley's campaign meets stronger opposition at home. A new twist. He pleads with Bridget to sell her stall: huckstering lowers his standing; she should dress herself in silk bloomers and "walk out wid me to make a stagnation upon the pedestrians. . . . It makes a difference in the harmony where there's an aesthetic taste in de husband and an everyday bowl-of-coffee taste in de wife."

Dan Mulligan had been rechristened Peter McSorley to honor the saloon and to take account of Yeamans' absence from the company. Cordelia was her part, and with Tony Hart now playing Harrigan's wife, a new name was required.

Everyone was delighted to see Harrigan again in familiar surroundings. Some missed Yeamans—she had signed for the season with *The Lights o' London,* a melodramatic thriller. More missed Billy Gray, who had died during the run of *Mordecai Lyons.* One reporter said he could hear Gray's ghost in the wings cautioning his replacement to be more quiet and more unctuous; "make your points without working so hard. Remember me and observe the modesty of nature."[4] Friends of the Comique guarded the histrionic purity of Harrigan's company.

The second season was filled out with *The Muddy Day* (April 2, 1883; on one manuscript, titled *Bunch o' Berries*), a Harrigan extravaganza that had not yet become a play. (It would later be incorporated into *The Last of the Hogans.*) McNab and Schoonover (Harrigan and Fisher), rival garbage scow captains, are courting Widow O'Leary (Hart) and also competing for the best New York mud. McNab has cornered Mulberry and Mott, a mess that's "too impregnated wid oyster shells, hoopskirts, and eperdemics." He's striking for Broadway; it's softer and juicier. The Negroes have also moved to the river and prepared their "Floating Bethel" church for carnival time with flags and banners, a wench dressed as the Goddess of Liberty, another as the Spirit of Cuba, a pan marked "baked beans," games of chance, kisses for a dollar, and a crooked dice game. "You can't have a church fair widout gambling" nor show a profit without white brothers, though you can't tell one white man from the other: "Dey're so far apart you can't tell 'em alike." A new Harrigan melee interrupts the festivities: the barge is rammed by a mud scow, the congregation is immersed, swims ashore—one sister paddles the pulpit—and is greeted on the dock by the "hootey, tootey, Kleiner Deutscher Pets—the Turnverein Cadets," the juvenile 69th reincarnated.

With such astounding effects, "unsurpassed by any theatre in New York," the Comique was "filled with deputations from the uptown clubs, rows of ladies from Murray Hill laughing as loud as the newsboys in the gallery, and Irish Aldermen in the front rows out-applauding the Italians in the boxes."[5] Harrigan at his second best provided a joyous evening.

Repeatedly Harrigan had insisted that he would never allow anyone else to play his pieces, but with Schroon demanding more cash, he decided to enlarge his empire and send his plays on the road under a new banner, The Hanley Combination, with the Harrigan parts played by Eugene Rourke. Rourke had been chief of supers at the old Comique, took minor parts in the Mulligan plays, and from time to time had served as Harrigan's amanuensis. The scheme worked, first with *Squatter Sovereignty*, then *McSorley's Inflation*, and in the 1884–1885 season with *Dan's Tribulations*. After seeing a matinee of *McSorley* in Philadelphia (September, 1883), Harrigan wrote to Annie that he was amazed by her uncle Martin Hanley's magic touch. Their half of the Philadelphia week came to $700, $500 of which was already on the way to Schroon.

Even with the official Hanley Combination on the road, play pirates were still on the prowl. On the Boston programs for *Dan's Tribulations* Hanley announced that all parties presenting any Harrigan plays would be prosecuted, local managers would be held equally responsible with traveling companies, no subterfuges would be tolerated, offenders would be penalized $100 for the first and $50 for each subsequent infringement.[6]

Harrigan's expansion alerted Braham to the wider world. He

advertised in the newspapers and distributed cards announcing that Braham's Comique Orchestra could be engaged for concerts, balls, and parties. Inquiries to the theatre or to 175 W. Tenth Street would receive immediate attention.[7]

When Harrigan opened the new season, refreshing the public's memory with a month of *The Ball* and another of *The Picnic*, both "revised and remodelled," Annie wrote from Schroon: "How does the people take the play now? I hope they laugh." Harrigan replied with the *New York Mirror* notice: "The Comique was packed. Ed King's xylophone solo was rapturously encored. Mrs. Yeamans, back from her season's absence, received an ovation, a basket of flowers across the footlights, and corsages thrown from the boxes. The actor-manager's appearance was also the signal for tumult. The comedy ran along to its end with an accompaniment of incessant laughter. . . . From Harrigan down, the company acted with vim and kept the ball rolling briskly. Miss Granville was the true embodiment of the frisky, slangy downtown girl (Kitty Lochmuller), and her flesh-colored Jersey in the ballroom scene created a sensation. Witham's scenery was capital, and the march of the Skidmores produced the old-time delight, and the old songs were relished with a will."[8]

Gertie Granville, a newcomer, had been praised by earlier reporters, though not so lavishly. She had joined the company at the new Comique, played Hart's (Higgins's) girl friend in *The Major,* his (Widow Nolan's) daughter in *Squatter Sovereignty,* and became Mrs. Tony Hart in the summer of 1882, when their paths crossed in London. She did not yet feel comfortable with the Mulligans, with the Harrigan clan, but Tony assured her that would come later. He was a full-fledged member of the family, at home and in the theatre, and she would be too. He was wrong; instead of drawing her into the circle, she drew him away.

After the Mulligan warm-up, *Cordelia's Aspirations* (November 5, 1883) kept the principals in their familiar roles, expanded well-tested madness, and hit a new record, 176 performances. Cordelia's lace-curtain aspirations, the invasion by her relatives, and her futile attempts to housebreak Dan create the chief disturbances, and her generous draughts from the mislabeled roach poison —"roach" not "rat" on Madison Avenue—the loudest cheers.

George C. D. Odell, the venerable historian of the New York
stage, reported that the "old boys" were still chattering about
Yeamans' drunk scene fifty years later.[9]

Cordelia and Rebecca, back from the Grand Tour, have picked
up a smattering of French and a "fat red-headed brother and three
bird-seed sisters" who've deserted Ireland "where the cow would
never rise its head for fear of losing its cud." The relatives are
proposing to share their rich sister's life of milk and honey. Puter
and Primrose are on the dock at Castle Garden, "whar Columbus
landed," to welcome Rebecca. Puter got thrown out of his pulpit
for "some irreverent remarks when his bunion formented," took
two dollars from the collection plate, played it on 4–11–44, hit
four dollars, bought a catering business, and hired Primrose as his
"facto factotum" and decked him out in a magnificent white uniform that overpowers Rebecca: "I feel like ice cream running
down a paper collar." Additional dockside rejoicing is supplied by
a returning Uncle Tom Combination. (Young Harrigans frequently got their theatrical baptism in this group.)

When Cordelia breaks the news that they're moving uptown and
auctions off the furniture, Dan grabs the one precious item that
can't be sold, "that trifle that held his wee bite . . . that emblem of
labor that hung in a corner beyant on a nail. . . . My Dad's Dinner
Pail." It was one of the best-loved songs and one of Harrigan's
biggest production numbers. Grocer, butcher, barber, et al. "focus
on Dan upstage as he exits—then curtain back up—repeat of
chorus. Chorus lady takes a slipper from her foot and throws it up
to Dan so that he catches it. Omnes appear sad as Dan is about to
leave Mulligan's Alley."

On Madison Avenue, Dan is again confounded: he drinks from
the fish tank, smooths his hair with the crumb brush, and to capture a remote piece of meat climbs on the table and stabs with his
knife.

Cordelia's drunk scene is slightly altered. Her brother McFudd
has persuaded one of his sisters to write a love letter to Dan.
When Cordelia reads the letter and begins sipping the poison,
McFudd gets her to deed the house to him. She agrees, though she
has difficulty in poking the pen into the ink bottle. The poison has

ruined her aim. The next morning at breakfast, when she asks
Rebecca if she has heard about her indisposition, Rebecca answers
honestly: "No. Only everybody knew you were loaded."

After the relatives deliver their daily laundry to Dan and join
Cordelia for their morning ride in the park, Dan begins his journey to rebellion:

> Be careful if you marry
> A Julia, Kate, or Fran.
> Don't shoulder her relations
> Like Daniel Mulligan
>
> I've her father and her mother
> Wid her sisters and her brother
> A lazy idling loafer a big Corkonian
> Her uncles and her cousins
> And aunties by the dozen
> All living on the earnings
> Of Daniel Mulligan.
>
> There's her second cousin's brother
> Her consumptive ould stepmother
> Coming in the steerage, a hungry ragged clan
> Wid their boxes and their bedding
> On my carpets they'll be treading
> And they live upon the earnings
> Of Daniel Mulligan.

(Similar sentiments had been heard in Gilbert and Sullivan's
Pinafore in 1879!)

Honora Dublin and Walsingham McSweeney lend moral support and a pitcher of beer to Dan's rebellion. When Cordelia returns, he serenades her with "I'll Wear the Trousers," and then
pronounces his ultimatum: "I'm tired of this sham delusion. If you
haven't sense I'll teach you. This is my property." With the help
of a sneaky lawyer, he's tricked McFudd. Cordelia's ragged signa-
ture has assigned the property to him.[10] But nothing can disturb
Dan's sweet memories of their early life in Tipperary "where we
both carried turf to the same school house," or untrack his love
"for me own bonnie wee little wife." And for the ladies out front
who might not possess Cordelia's redeeming charm, he has some

advice: "All ye women that are looking for royal loyal husbands when you get them don't turn round on the bridge that carries you over."

The extraordinary success of *Cordelia's Aspirations* was not accidental. The company was in top form. There were no falling bodies nor broken skylights; the new nonsense made sense. For two hours and forty minutes everything was propelled by Dan, Cordelia, and friends, who they were and where they were. And Annie Yeamans pulling at her poison and weaving her way to the grave was funnier than ever. Discussing the play years later, Harrigan said that Cordelia's aspirations "gain what value they have because they are couched in the dialect of the poor emigrant and flavored with the aroma of want. A cultured, refined, and beautiful millionaire Cordelia, aspiring to be numbered among the billionaires, talking faultless English, would excite not the shadow of a smile, but simply pity and disgust." Human nature may be the same the world over, but it is "most virile and aggressive, most humorous and odd among those who know only poverty and ignorance."[11] Harrigan knew what he was doing.

And he knew that strong aspirations often lead to tribulations, in this case *Dan's Tribulations* (April 7, 1884), the sequel, a heady mixture of old and new: Fat men in the loft. Fire in the cellar. Hog-Eye romancing Rebecca. And Cordelia, still on Madison Avenue, hounded by creditors and operating an Academie Française for debutantes. Dan, dispensing groceries and grog in the Alley. Kitty and Tommy, returned from Michigan, disguised in veil and whiskers—their first appearance since *The Ball*—to pay off Cordelia's creditors and reunite the Mulligans.

Both Dan and Cordelia are beset with tribulations. When a policeman informs Dan that he can't dispense liquor unless he's licensed as a hotel, he quickly moves cots into Rebecca's flat and McSweeney recruits two Italians to sleep in them.

When Cordelia's creditors are about to seize her furniture and then the house, Dan's lawyer advises him to strike a deal with a friend and pretend to sell the house for a dollar. Mrs. Lochmuller, now employed as Cordelia's cook, willingly cooperates, but she does not stick to the bargain. When Tommy and Kitty appear and Cordelia shouts into the speaking tube, ordering food and drink to celebrate the reunion, Bridget rebels. It's her night off, and she's having her own party in the kitchen. Cordelia discharges her. Bridget reminds her that that's impossible. The house belongs to her. Tommy comes to the rescue. He examines the dollar that Bridget gave Dan as payment for the house. It's counterfeit. The deal's illegal.

With happiness and solvency restored, Cordelia presents her French scholars in a drill with sticks and brooms and a rendering of their theme song, "Une Leçon de Chant Française," with alternate verses sung in English translation.

The springtime lark—great fun for Hart quick-changing from Rebecca to Tommy—may not have matched *Cordelia's Aspirations,* but Broadway's enthusiasm was not diminished. One critic wrote, "Harrigan and Hart have created a new order of entertainment. It is an American order. Nothing like it exists anywhere in the world."[12] Another detected "a man of ideas at work who parades no purpose except to entertain." Harrigan thrived on the tributes but reminded one interviewer that success at the Comique was not accidental: "I suppose a great many people think this business of mine is all velvet. They think that I am surrounded by a company that does not cost much. Why bless you, these people of mine cost a great deal more than the usual actors. They are all specialists who are the best paid in their lines. Sometimes in the street mobs you see on my stage every man is an actor capable of getting a laugh. You cannot play my pieces with one star and a lot of sticks."[13]

As if to illustrate his magnanimity, Harrigan engaged a company of thirty-eight plus extras for *Investigation* (September 1, 1884), the new attraction in the fall. And everyone had a fresh role in a completely new play. Unmistakable Harrigan nonsense, characters tailored for Harrigan actors, but with sharper darts aimed at new targets: romantic fiction, cooking schools, amateur theatricals, pollution in the city, and political peccadilloes in New York and Albany. Assemblyman Theodore Roosevelt and his Committee on Cities had just discovered appalling political corruption in New York.

Among the fresh eccentrics: DeArcy Flynn (Harrigan), "a modern New York Irishman." Bernard McKenna (Hart), a dealer

in glue, a suspected polluter. Mrs. Belinda Tuggs (Yeamans), who
has inherited a candle factory and planted a gigantic $1000
marble candle on her husband's grave and thinks of him whenever
she smells grease. Her daughter Sarah runs a cooking school, and
her daughter Julia is infatuated with dime novels and tries to write
them. The Italian-Chinese couple, the Hop-Sings—she's a fortune-
teller, and he runs an opium joint. And Oscar Onderdonk, Ezra
Wheatfield, and Orion Overhoe, country-bumpkin legislators in-
vestigating the wicked city. The big scenes: Graduation at the cooking school; Hop-Sing's opium parlor; amateur night at the Comique.

Mrs. Tuggs welcomes the legislators to the graduation ceremony. They immediately assume their legislative postures: feet on
the table. She's honored to have them in the city. Not only can
they share the graduation pudding, they'll have an opportunity to
see for themselves the pollution that rises from McKenna's glue
factory. Everyone knows that boiling goats, dogs, and horses for
glue produces worse smoke than boiling mutton fat to make
candles.

The girls march in with their prize concoction, singing "The
Plum Pudding." (No doubt they were recruited from Cordelia's
French choir.) Everyone samples the pudding, including DeArcy
Flynn, who is scheduled to play Romeo to Mrs. Tuggs's Juliet at
the Comique that evening. Mrs. Tuggs informs Flynn that she's
engaged a real minister to play Friar Lawrence. He'll marry them
for real. Flynn is enraptured at the prospect: "Ah, Belinda, I am
happy only when I look down into a pair of mellow soft and
dreamy eyes, there the springs of nature throw their burning jets
of lovelight over a cold bleak and barren world inhabited by the
brute man." The passion overpowers him. His legs stiffen with a
cramp. "The leader of the orchestra draws his bow over a string
making a doleful sound." The pain shoots into his arm, to his
stomach, over his entire body. The violinist enlarges his accompaniment as the pain spreads. When a doctor arrives with a
stomach pump, the cooking-school girls admit that they've acci-
dentally poured glue into the pudding.

The long, dark climb to Hop-Sing's den (modeled on a joint in
Pell Street) was documented from life: "A distillery on the ground

floor, Hogan, McGreevy, and Donnizetti families on the second floor, the tailor Lowasky and the Cuban cigar maker with Burns the lamplighter and four other Scandinavian families on the third floor. On the fourth the German dying wid consumption and the Negro family's christening party." The traffic in Hop-Sing's parlor resembles that in Grand Central Station: Mrs. Tuggs; her daughters; a writer who's eager "to hit a pipe and dream of plots for a new melodrama"; a cowboy actor from Death Valley who shouts, "Stand clar thar," as he fires cigarettes from his trick revolver; and the legislators singing "The Boodle," a hymn to the "little green note that keeps us afloat."

While the assemblymen wait in the hall, Flynn sneaks in three Negro wenches, turns out the lights, summons the lawmakers, and tells them to feel for girls. If they're lucky, they're entitled to a kiss. When the lights are switched on, legislators and wenches are intertwined, and the girls' Negro boy friends are glowering in the doorway. "*Consternation*! 'My girl hugging a white man.' " Flynn calms his victims with opium and when they've collapsed announces: "The Legislature has the floor." Overhoe is not completely subdued. He raises his head and mumbles, "The member votes nay. Votes nay. I'm with the corporations all the time." Then he's on his feet shouting, "I'm going to jump off the Brooklyn bridge. [The bridge had just opened.] Cut down the trees in the Adirondacks. The nation wants shingles." He gradually returns to snoring. Standing up! It was one of Harrigan's funniest scenes.

For the entertainment at the Comique, Flynn and Belinda struggle with the balcony scene. It runs smoothly, long enough to show that Harrigan and Yeamans could handle Shakespeare, then Romeo jabs a thorn in his finger, his sword gets caught between his legs, the balcony sags, and finally, on "There lies more peril in thine eye than twenty of their . . . twenty of their . . . of their," he's stuck. The stage manager throws, "Swords," then the carpenter, "Swords"; Romeo misses the prompt and stomps the floor, pleading, "Gallagher, the word!" A head appears through a trap door, "Swords." Finally the orchestra leader shouts, "Swooards, swooards." Romeo shouts back, "Play! Play for Caesar's sake." That signals the marching music for *Julius Caesar*. Supers parade on. The orchestra leader climbs on stage, fights with Romeo, and finally smashes his violin on Romeo's head. "Dare goes a hundred and fifty dollar Cremona."

On November 26, the play hit the 100 performance mark. On December 4, Harrigan and Yeamans joined Henry Irving and Ellen Terry in a benefit for the Actors' Fund at the Academy of Music, Romeo and Juliet plus Shylock and Portia. And on December 22, 1884, after 129 performances, *Investigation* abruptly terminated its engagement. The Comique burned down!

15

Fire and Separation

After the evening's performance, Harrigan had called a rehearsal of *McAllister's Legacy*. It was behind schedule for its opening just two weeks off. At 1:30 A.M. the actors were exhausted. Harrigan agreed to quit for the night and turned the theatre over to the night watchman, Austin Heffern, Tony Hart's brother-in-law. Everything seemed safe and secure, as it did when Heffern departed in the morning, just before 7:00. Normally he stayed on duty until the carpenters arrived at 8:30. The morning of the twenty-third, nothing was happening. Nothing ever did. And on the twenty-third his breakfast hunger struck earlier than usual.

At 7:30 A.M., a German scrubwoman arrived, went to the balcony toilet with her coat and hat, smelled smoke, opened the balcony door, and saw the stage blazing like a bonfire.[1] She ran out of the building screaming. She searched for a firebox, but when she couldn't find one she raced to the Harrigans' house on Perry. A porter in the New York Hotel across the street saw the blaze at about the same time, ran to the box at Washington Place and Broadway, couldn't make the key fit, and went on to the engine house on Great Jones Street. He kicked at the door and then saw the men already in action. A policeman had had better luck with an alarm box, and his alert reached the firemen over the wires at 7:45.

When they arrived just four minutes later, the front of the building was flaming. In twenty minutes the roof caved in. By this time, as gas meters began to explode and timbers were crashing into the blaze, thirteen steamers[2] and four hook-and-ladder trucks were at the scene. The Harrigans had also arrived. Annie recalled that they had dodged among the morning milk cans on their journey. Some two hundred guests were running wildly in and out of the Colonnade Hotel next-door, many still in their nightgowns. The New York Hotel was overflowing with spectators in the entrance and at the windows. Every few minutes someone announced that the fire had eaten into the Colonnade. Fortunately all were false alarms. By 9:00 A.M. the chief declared the fire under control but ordered two steamers to stand on duty for the day and the next night to watch the smoking pit. All that remained of the Comique were the massive walls of the old church.

Although Harrigan grieved more than most of his friends ever knew over the loss of his "jewel," he began immediately to look for a new home, and to all the gloomy sympathizers who marched through the parlor on Perry later in the day he proclaimed, "That's all over; let's talk about the future."[3] His dear friend and father-in-law had been the first to raise the gloom while they stood on the street in front of the building watching the blaze complete its destruction and David learned that his scores and his violins were destroyed. He put his arm around Ned and said, "No sense in grieving over the ashes; I still have music in my head and you have plays, let's hunt for another shop."[4]

They speculated first on the Star Theatre, like the Comique in size and where Ristori was about to give up her struggle, but they finally came to terms with Hyde and Behman for the lease of the Park on Thirty-fifth, just west of Broadway. The Park had recently been an aquarium, museum, and menagerie and now, some said, was a white elephant. Just two days after the fire, Harrigan announced that the company was back at work and would be ready to open in January, though the scenery might be sketchier: "If we paint a window now it probably won't have any ivy around it."[5] He knew his friends would be tolerant. Rehearsals were back in the swing; in the afternoon at Tony Pastor's and in the evening at the Academy of Music. Then as now, those in the profession accepted act-of-God disasters as mutual responsibilities.

Estimates of the loss appeared in the newspapers even while the soggy remnants were still smoldering. The *Herald*, though regretting the loss and sympathizing with the partners, noted that Harrigan and Hart had begun with "nothing but their heads and heels and had now for several seasons made more money more steadily than any other management and are very rich."⁶ Rich was a bit strong. Harrigan was closer to the truth when he reported that "our all" was in that building, over $100,000 plus the $16,000 rent they had paid for the season.⁷ Most estimates figured the total between $150,000 and $200,000, with varying breakdowns but most commonly: Harrigan and Hart's $60,000 investment in the interior; Judge Henry Hilton's building, $50,000; scenery $30,000; costumes $8,300; actors' personal properties and costumes $8,000; new scenery for *McAllister's Legacy*, $10,000; Braham's violins, $1,000; and box-office cash, $1,150. Only a few damp items were recovered—some charred stacks of music and two of Johnny Wild's wigs. There was no insurance!⁸

For the next weeks, reporters kept the story alive with fresh details. No one had a solid explanation of the fire's origin. The paint room seemed to be the most likely location. Harrigan and Hart were said to have argued about insurance, Hart insisting that it was a waste of money, and he had won. Another account, apparently true, placed the blame on Harrigan's father. William had neglected to pay the premium. The argument provided columns of copy, setting Harrigans against Harts. William's lapse had to be balanced against Tony's brother-in-law's early departure. A sentry must never leave his post. Someone searched out Fire Chief Bresnan, who had inspected the building in 1881. He had found it extraordinarily safe, compared with other theatres, though he had recommended a 1,200-gallon tank on the roof, a larger fire hose backstage, and wire baskets around all gas jets. He was uncertain if his suggestions had been followed.⁹

The Actors' Fund, to which Harrigan had given office space on the second floor, apparently had all its records in a fireproof safe. It lost only some dilapidated furniture. Harrigan had been one of the incorporators of the fund in 1882, along with Booth, Jefferson, Wallack, and Barnum, and served on the board and executive committee until 1885. (His daughter Nedda is now president of the Actors' Fund.)

The move uptown into strange quarters with new scenery was achieved more rapidly than anyone could have guessed, and on January 5, 1885, *McAllister's Legacy* replaced the animals and fish at the Park. Like *Investigation,* the new play explored new territory, if with less distinction and less success. The program synopsis defines the territory:

I. Interior of Molly McGouldrick's Farmhouse and Baldy O'Brien's Smithy. The Reading of the Will.

II. 1 Waiting Room in the Van Dusen Mansion. The Sale of the Land.

2 Hallway in the Rookery in Africa on Thompson St. Viva la Liberté.

3 The Levee at the Colored Brokers. How Money is Made by the Millionaires. The Legacy Explained.

III. Interior of the New York Stock Exchange. A Warm Day from Trinity to the Ferry. General Unravelling.

Again novel eccentrics and novel scenes: A horse doctor who treats humans while off duty, a French communist who plants bombs in clocks, and a refugee from Bloomingdale's Asylum who went mad in Philadelphia over a milliner and now stands in front of Macy's staring at the wax manikins. Harrigan's brokers "A, B, C, and D" shout orders, whisper that Vanderbilt's sick, the market will drop, and finally break into a brokers' ballet. One reporter declared that Harrigan didn't know Wall Street; his New York Stock Exchange "suggests the ravages of a more protracted financial panic than has yet been known."[10]

Friends who transferred to the Park were more anxious to welcome Harrigan and Hart than to judge *McAllister's Legacy.* According to the *Spirit of the Times,* opening night was overflowing, four deep at the back: club men, officials, politicians, stock exchange men, lawyers, and ordinary old friends. At Harrigan's entrance, the house cheered and wouldn't stop until he made a speech. At the end of the act, Braham was called to the stage and given a new violin. Life at the Park looked promising.[11] In January, the Seventh Regiment bought out the house, other clubs settled for blocks of seats, and after a month Hanley reported they were grossing more than $12,000 a week.[12]

Behind the scenes, the future looked less rosy. When Harrigan tried to negotiate a contract for the next season, Hyde and Behman demanded $30,000. With the dilapidated condition of the Park— the seats and interior decorations salvaged from Booth's Theatre the only vestiges of elegance—Harrigan was unwilling to go higher than $15,000. The owners overplayed their hand and refused to compromise, and Harrigan moved to the Fourteenth Street Theatre on his terms and with a tentative option to extend the lease for ten years.[13]

McAllister's Legacy, at the new stand on March 3, did not get off to a strong start. Some attributed the slim showing to the early summer weather—it was "wicked to laugh in the heat." Others thought that too many New Yorkers had gone to Washington for the inauguration. Still, as one reporter noted, there were enough old friends on hand to compel Harrigan to demonstrate the Irish walk and Tony "to execute his salaam and give a pull to his front curl."[14]

Legacy held on for two weeks, was replaced by *The Major* for a month, then *Cordelia's Aspirations* for three weeks, and on Saturday, May 9, 1885, Harrigan and Hart appeared together on Broadway for the last time.

Rumors of a split had been circulating along the theatrical grapevine all spring. There were reports that the partners were not on speaking terms at the time of the fire, that after the fire the families argued about who was to blame. Some said Tony's wife Gertie had hounded him to strike out on his own, saying he wasn't getting a fair deal in the partnership.

On April 30, the *New York Times* found "ample indication that the whole story has not come out." There were too many conflicting reports that had come to their attention: A week before, Harrigan's half brother had predicted that Hart would retire from the firm. A few days previous, Harrigan himself had claimed that the partners had extended their lease on the Fourteenth Street Theatre, although they did not regard that as the best possible location. And both of the partners had been repeatedly avowing their undying friendship, insisting that nothing personal was involved in their differences.[15]

On May 5, the *Times* uncovered more details: Tony had given Harrigan a note on the second of May saying that he was quitting on the tenth. With that note in hand, Harrigan had immediately set out to renegotiate the touring contracts for Brooklyn, Jersey City, Newark, Philadelphia, and Boston, excluding Hart from the company.[16]

Colonel Sinn at the Park Theatre in Brooklyn refused to renegotiate. He announced that he would sue them if Hart failed to appear. Apparently neither of the partners wanted to challenge Sinn and risk exposing their differences in court.[17] Harrigan and Hart were reunited in Brooklyn for a week of *The Major* and a week of *Investigation* and, on June 13, took their anticlimactic final farewell.

The real finale for them and for their Broadway world had come a month earlier on May 9, a difficult night for both and by a freak of fortune doubly difficult for Harrigan. Baby George Harrigan had died at 9:30 that morning of acute bronchitis. Just two months old, he had been born the day the partners had moved to the Fourteenth Street, and "last night," the *Times* reported, "Harrigan was forced to leave the dead body of his child to caper before the public and furnish food for its laughter."[18]

Tony got the first tribute from the final night's crowd, and they refused to listen to Rebecca until Tony came forward to acknowledge their greeting: "Ladies and gentlemen, I thank you for this kind reception. I hope I shall always retain your favor and that I shall always receive as kindly a reception from you in the future."[19] When he returned to the scene, he looked like a winning horse, decked out in a floral horseshoe that had been passed over the footlights. The welcome for Ned was louder and longer. Several times he tried to back off, but finally he had to submit to the continuing applause and the basket of flowers swinging at the footlights. He avoided Hart's finality in his remarks: "All I have to say, ladies and gentlemen, is that I think New York wants a little more work, and I'll insure your lives on Monday next." He'd given Hanley a short farce, *Are You Insured?* to occupy the company for the rest of the season.[20]

After the final curtain, Rebecca and Dan took their calls together, then separately, and finally together again. They stood at the footlights, their hands joined, until well after midnight. Such a wave of sadness engulfed the theatre that the *Times* concluded only a spirit of "Long Live the King" could finally relieve the grief: "Harrigan will bury his child today and appear in Jersey City tomorrow night."[21]

New York was shaken. At Christmas the disastrous conflagration; four months without a proper home to call their own; and now this shattering blow. Although they had played only five seasons at the first Comique, only three and a half at the second, it seemed as if Harrigan and Hart had always been a part of Broadway. Both were besieged by friends who wanted to mediate, if mediation were possible. Mayor William R. Grace talked with each of them, without success. The cheeriest Pollyannas could discover no bright lining in the cloud. Sadness ruled everywhere, as it did even a year later when the *Chicago Herald* grieved: "A pair of scissors burst asunder, a turtle dove bereft of its mate, Damon without Pythias—none of these examples of ruptured union serve adequately to express the state of desolation and comparative helplessness which has fallen upon these two artists since fate tore them apart."[22]

The search for explanations continued: quarrels about the fire, over insurance and the delinquent watchman. Hart had been pushed into the background in business affairs. Cliques had developed backstage among the women. Neither of the Annies, Braham or Harrigan, liked Gertie. She was too fancy, too scheming. Harrigan had detected signs of illness in Hart, had urged him to go away for a rest, and he had refused.

The most tantalizing speculation appeared in the *New York Times* two years later (August 7, 1887): "But for a death that occurred in Second Avenue nearly a half dozen years ago Harrigan and Hart might be together yet. That event led ultimately to the discovery that, with all his cleverness as a comedian, his true goodness to his parents (his running away from home not counting against him long), thoughtful care of other relatives, lavish generosity to acquaintances who were going down hill, Tony lacked the mental stamina to resist his natural impulsiveness when to yield to it seemed to be imprudent, and with that discovery the social tie between the two old associates began to crack."[23] The secret of the death on Second Avenue has never been revealed.

Understanding the separation was not much more difficult than explaining their union. Except for the extraordinary way in which their talents joined onstage, they were worlds apart. Hart was a rosy, happy man without any of Harrigan's vein of seriousness. Harrigan headed home after a performance; he needed sleep to be fresh for the morning rehearsals. On matinee days he ate lunch in his dressing room, and after the matinee his dresser, "Eighty-forty," administered an alcohol rub to assure a solid showing in the evening. He kept at work constantly.[24] Tony was geared to sociability. He never turned down an invitation, and he was smothered with them. He stayed out late, was late for rehearsals, loved the high life with all its flash and glitter. One night Tony and Gertie arrived at the theatre in a fancy, new coupé with the door emblazoned "G.G. and T.H.," a coachman in scarlet livery, and the harness studded with silver. Harrigan did not cheer. He was passionately committed to walking and to horsecars.[25]

Gertrude Granville slipped into the villainous role unwittingly when she joined the company at the new Comique, married Tony the following summer, discovered that Harrigan roles were not tailored for her as they were for Tony, and that even after she and Tony had adopted Billy Gray's orphaned son, Harts were radically outnumbered by Harrigans and Brahams. She must have sensed the initial family skepticism. They regarded Tony as a member of the family. She was an interloper. Gertie had been married twice before, to Charles E. Blanchard, an early associate of Charles Frohman, and to William J. Fleming, a minor actor; and during the first season at the Comique it was clear to everyone that she concentrated more on Tony than on her acting. After the marriage, according to some, she became ambitious and conniving for herself and for Tony. At one rehearsal she appeared "magnificently arrayed in seal-skin, satin, laces, and diamonds" and demanded a part in the new play, or Tony wouldn't go on.[26] The Brahams and Annie were all for settling their differences once and for all. Ned could not tolerate a showdown. He had to protect Tony, keep the peace as long as he could; he'd write a part for her. Somehow Harrigan always avoided, or at least postponed, unpleasantness. No actor ever complained of harsh words, harsh deeds, or a hasty rebuke from Harrigan, and even after their break, and to the end, Harrigan spoke kindly of Tony, and Tony of him.

While Hart was a freewheeling bachelor he had always been a regular in the Harrigan-Braham home. When he married, Gertie took command and kept him to herself in their own home, a brownstone on Forty-sixth just east of Park Avenue.[27] They shared their quarters with a short-haired Saint Bernard named Gluck, a feeble English bulldog, Fleas—according to Annie Yeamans, Fleas had a sealskin coat to match Gertie's—assorted parrots and canaries, and a marmoset monkey named Pat Rooney.[28] During the last season of the partnership, Gertie spent more time with her domesticated friends than she wished. She had not had a role since *Cordelia's Aspirations,* and after the fire she seemed to be totally excluded from the family business councils.

Certainly if the Harrigan and Hart partnership had become unbearable, or even difficult, this was the propitious moment for separation. Their joint investment had gone up in smoke; their financial fortunes were no longer intertwined. When reporters hounded them about their plans for the future, Hart said he had none. An honest answer. Harrigan said that he'd conclude the contracted tour, go to Schroon to rework *Old Lavender* for fall, and after that he only knew that he'd continue to work in New York onstage and off. "There's a branch of human nature here to be worked up into plays that cannot be found anywhere else in the world."[29] He had a mass of notes and ideas that hadn't yet taken shape.

16

Saddle, Gig, and Horse

Saddened as he was by the separation, Harrigan could not suppress his industry and ambition. He returned to the Park, brought Hanley back from the road as manager, and opened *Old Lavender* on August 31, 1885, to a healthy reincarnation of over one hundred performances. He continued there for four full seasons—a slightly longer term than the partners had had together at the Comique—producing six new plays plus *Investigation, Cordelia's Aspirations,* and *The Lorgaire,* then undertook a full year's cross-country tour, and on December 29, 1890, opened his new Harrigan Theatre, just across Broadway from the Park.

At forty-one, Harrigan was in his prime, still enjoying a sixteen-to-eighteen-hour day. He made the best of his new circumstances, without complaint and with remarkable success. The Park was a shabby facility. The house and stage were too large; it took an immense amount of coal to heat the place, and on cold nights it simply could not be made comfortable. And he had to be landlord as well as tenant. Hyde and Behman limited their activity to collecting the rent, though Hanley had persuaded them to accept a percentage rather than the exorbitant $30,000 they had originally demanded. Harrigan freshened the interior with crimson upholstery, installed a new Witham act drop, a vignette of the Battery and the Produce Exchange, expanded the company, and raised Wild and Yeamans to $250 per week. He paid for quality, perhaps even more willingly now without Hart. But he kept the same scale,

$.25 to $1.00, and the larger house was crowded regularly—one reporter said "his clientele would follow him to Harlem or Riverside Park"[1]—and he, as well as Hyde and Behman, were well rewarded. According to Hanley, the owners realized $30,000 to $40,000 per year, "three times what the morgue was worth," and after the first two seasons Harrigan had accumulated an astonishing $100,000, to be invested in solid securities.[2]

In spite of Hart's absence, he did not face the new venture alone. Hanley and Braham were still with him, and each in his way was as much a part of his theatrical life as Hart had been. From the beginning he and Hanley saw eye to eye on business, and he and Dave had evolved a system for making songs that always seemed to work.

When a play was finished, Harrigan passed Braham the lyrics, one verse and the chorus for each song. Braham scanned them, usually getting a rough idea of time and style for each, and piled them on the piano, or more often stuffed them in his pocket with some blank pieces of music paper. Some of his speediest composing was done on the horsecars and the elevated trains. He worked one line at a time, covering the rest with his music paper and humming the words until a tune evolved. When it suited him, it was transcribed. If the notes didn't come quickly, he passed to the next line and then worked back. Sometimes it took a month to find all the tunes for a new show; more often they came at the first attempt. One horsecar ride produced "Babies on Our Block." Five minutes on the elevated gave him "Maggie Murphy's Home," the song that just missed being Al Smith's theme song.

In the early days when the Brahams and Harrigans occupied the same house on King Street, the collaboration involved the whole family and all hours of the day and night. Braham recalled struggling over "Mary Kelly's Beau" for *The Mulligan Guard Picnic*. One night he woke up with a tune in his head, lit the gas, sat down at his table, and went straight along to the last two bars. He tried three endings before he hit the right one. As he often said, "You must be very particular to get the right snap at the end to make the tune go." He woke Ned and hummed it for him. Ned thought it just the thing. After quickly scratching out a rough score, he roused his daughter Rose to play it, and with the family gathered round the piano Harrigan sang. Annie predicted it would catch on more than any other tune in the play. She was right.

Braham escaped the indecision that troubles most composers because he fixed his own ground rules early in the game: never two songs in the same time (meter) in the same play. Tunes must fit the voices of the actors, and he knew the notes they could handle. Tony's voice had to be nursed very carefully. Sweet as the spring air in his falsetto range; if pitched too low it became frosty and harsh. Johnny Wild required the simplest tunes, simple as for a child. The public clamored for a new hit song in every play, but Braham knew the odds against him: "There are only a few notes available, comparatively few combinations, and no really new themes." Now and then his study of classical music helped with musical ideas, but he couldn't honestly say where his tunes came from. Writing music was like writing poetry or prose: "It is simple enough if you only have the knack for it."

In 1891 a reporter asked Braham how many songs he'd composed and which were his favorites.[3] Probably around one hundred eighty had been published, another twenty were still in manuscript, and he had the most recent ones in his pocket. The public seemed to favor "Babies on Our Block," "Widow Dunn," "The Mulligan Guard," and "Charleston Blues." He would never dispute them, although he was proudest of "Mollie, My Crumpled Horn Cow."

The season at the Park began strong with an embellished *Old Lavender*, then struck bottom with *The Grip* (November 30, 1885), Harrigan's feeblest play. There was only one joyous night, when the Seventh Regiment bought out the house, decorated it with flags, bunting, and wreaths and themselves with an "expanse of linen in shirt collars alone that was something immense." They called Ned back for a German dialect recitation after the play and joined him in singing "Get Up Jack; John Sit Down."[4]

The Grip had a special attraction for the military. While on the field of battle, two Civil War buddies have promised their baby son and daughter in marriage. When the soldiers meet twenty years later to execute the bargain, Harrigan makes it difficult for them to recognize each other. The colonel, in whose home they meet, has exchanged costumes with his servant Patrick Reilly (Harrigan), and his daughter with her maid Rosanna Reilly (Yeamans). Reilly, of course, makes the most of his newly acquired authority. He sends the servants (colonel and daughter) on ridiculous errands and marches them about the house "a la Mulligan."

The farcical festivities are augmented with an assortment of city types who drop in to see the colonel: Handsome Grogan, who has learned his elegant manners serving as a floorwalker at Macy's. A choir of politicians who sing of their achievements in "The Aldermanic Board." Finally, the two old comrades recognize each other by the regimental handshake.

Harrigan was apparently fascinated with the idea of the grip. He later reused the story in a vaudeville sketch called *Sergeant Hickey.*

The season's next entry, *The Leather Patch* (February 15, 1886) was more in the Harrigan line. Most of the characters had appeared in *Christmas Joys and Sorrows,* but here their lives become more complicated. Dennis McCarthy has retired and married a second time. He has turned over his undertaking establishment to his son Jeremiah (Harrigan). His new wife, Madeline (Yeamans), has quickly lost her bridal innocence and cultivated a strong arm. She confides to her fellow feminists: What's the use of soft talk? Married people survive more peacefully with a bit of quarreling. Dennis is fed up with her abuse. He recovered from the griddle on his head yesterday morning, but the bed slat last night almost broke his back. He tells his son Jeremiah that he's going to pretend to die. He's written a codicil to his will leaving all his money to him. Jeremiah should poke holes in the coffin so he can breathe and prepare the cockloft (attic) for his resurrection. He's coming back to haunt Madeline.

Jeremiah disposes of his father as directed and then hides the codicil underneath a leather patch on a pair of riding pants.

Madeline appears with Roderick McQuade, her favorite undertaker, the competitor from across the street whose window is always neatly decorated with white and black caskets. She wonders why her stepson cannot exhibit similar good taste. McQuade is about to bury an Italian for twelve dollars. If Jeremiah had not blackballed him for membership in the Association of Undertakers, he could charge twenty-five. Madeline could help him get even with Jeremiah by giving him a pair of Jeremiah's trousers to put on the Italian's corpse. She obliges. With the leather-patched pants.

With his customary generosity, Harrigan tossed in bonus characters. When Jeremiah tries to track the Italian's corpse to retrieve his pants, he's too late. They've been removed by Jefferson Putnam, a body snatcher—"What you put down we take up."

Pursuit of the pants brings Jeremiah to the Five Points. It was the first time Harrigan had used the exact location. As Jeremiah canvasses the used-clothing dealers in the area, he encounters Caroline Hyer looking longingly into the saloon where McCafferty "dales out the rum that swells the mortality." He buys her a drink. Caroline downs it in one gulp, coughs, and inquires if it was a "five or a ten." She's perplexed because "the ten always burns a little but 'de five carves its way down."

A hack arrives, drawn by a real horse. It stops center stage, the door opens, and "at least nine, and preferably thirteen 'omnes' dismount" bound for the undertakers' masquerade ball. As the hack moves off, Dennis in his ghost getup is discovered hanging on the back. One critic praised this triumph of realism and congratulated Harrigan for drawing the line at horse and hack. He could have secured real coffins and borrowed real corpses from the morgue.[5]

Dennis reappears regularly throughout the play, shining his lantern on his ghostly face. Finally to Madeline and McQuade when they are about to be married by Jeremiah, who is disguised in the whiskers and spectacles of a Judge Doebler. Doebler speaks with a German accent, gets started on the wrong page—"ashes to ashes"—and when he asks if anybody objects "if she takes dis thing," the ghostly Dennis appears and threatens to "decompose" Madeline unless she swears never to hit him again with a griddle or a bed slat.

Even without the Mulligans, *Leather Patch* was one of Harrigan's funniest plays. Hart's absence had not altered Harrigan's formula. He continued to draw on his stock of surefire scenes and routines, brightening and updating them with fresh inventions.

Again in the fall of 1886, his second solo season, he opened with a revival, a month and a half of *Investigation,* before introducing the new plays: *The O'Reagans* (October 11, 1886) and *McNooney's Visit* (January 31, 1887).

The O'Reagan's, returning to familiar scenes and familiar characters, was essentially an evening of variety turns set against a New York panorama: Bernard O'Reagan's (Harrigan's) waterfront saloon, Gilligan's Court, on the beach at Sheepshead Bay, and on the Cunard dock with a "practical" steamer. Gilligan's Court expanded on Mulligan's Alley: Barbershop with working chairs. A stable, hayloft, cellar, a flour and feed store. Hop Yet's Laundry with three Chinamen ironing. Dougherty's Distillery and Naturalization Center.

Each scene was supplied with an appropriate song. In the saloon: "A B C's" and "The Little Hedge School," memories of growing up in Ireland. From Gilligan's Court it was only a stone's throw to "Mulberry Springs." Let the fashionables go to Saratoga, Long Branch, or Newport—the boarders at Mulberry Springs, though poor, "could be aloof on the tenement roof." At Sheepshead, "Strolling on the Sands." At the Cunard dock, "The U.S. Black Marines." The marines are embarking for Egypt to serve the country and protect the flag. Too many politicians have "grabbed all de stars out of it and are now wearing de stripes."

There is a political campaign between Killhealy and Krouse battling for the Negro vote. A secret female society, the Wives Mutual Protective Association, which has contributed $1,000 to the fund for Home Rule. The small thread of plot hangs on the $1,000 bill that inadvertently gets stuck to a mustard plaster and finally ends up on a Negro prize fighter.

There were variations on old themes and some new routines. O'Reagan exhorts the politicians: "The foreign population rules this town; the Dutch rule the west of it, the Niggers the east of it, the Italians the south of it, and the Irish the whole of it." And Annie Yeamans and her daughter Emily create a unique comic sensation impersonating Miss Hop Yet and Miss Chow Chow. Miss Hop Yet snuggles up to every man in Gilligan's Court to ask, "Ilishman scratchee my backee?" It's the Chinese way of making love.

McNooney's Visit offered a full evening's light entertainment only mildly disrupted by a story. The scenes at the Tombs and in court had been used earlier in *O'Brien, Counselor-at-Law* and *The Doyle Brothers*, though a Black Maria loaded with prisoners was new, as was a revolving stage: "Actors remove two chairs from behind railing off door L.H. upstage and all books and everything movable so as to avoid revolving scene from catching." Two locations were new to Harrigan's crowd: Norah Gilmartin's Welcome Hour Nursery and Dr. Hilarious Spoonful's Health Emporium.

The flimsy and sometimes confusing plot deals with a young man who will inherit a fortune if he keeps his marriage secret until he's twenty-one. He does. The other thread, laced by Harrigan and Yeamans, is livelier and easier to follow. Martin McNooney, a rustic Irishman in the city to be married, has become incapacitated because that mission has coincided with his annual St. Patrick's Day drunk. He's been picked up by a country detective as a suspect in a Yonkers robbery. Norah Gilmartin, his wife-to-be, eases his troubles as best she can, though she has more demanding obligations, keeping goat's milk supplied to her babies. She operates the Welcome Hour Nursery. Her cradles are all occupied, but she worries about how long her good fortune will hold. She's just raised her daily fee to fifteen cents to meet her inflated overhead.

Most of the Harrigan hilarities were saved for the final act in Dr. Hilarious Spoonful's health parlor. The place is well supplied with dumbbells, Indian clubs, striking machines, pulling machines, rubbing tables, crutches, and a vapor bath. Martin McNooney appears here in full marching regalia. He's just ducked out of the St. Patrick's Day parade for a quick massage. The fife and drum corps can still be heard offstage. As he's examining the equipment, he's startled by a pair of strong female hands on his shoulders. Dr. Spoonful apologizes for her abrupt approach: "I have so much practice my hands go out unconsciously to rub, even before I know if I'm rubbin for rheumatism, gout, neuralgia, lumbago, or obesity." This hefty masculine female was a novel creation. Perhaps Harrigan had read Henrich Oscar Von Karlstein's account of the strange creatures at the New York Liberal Club: "Strong armed women with short hair and puny men with manes down to their shoulders." (Von Karlstein's *Gotham and Gothamites* had just been published.)

Harrigan's fun in the parlor is shared with others: A young

couple singing, "Of all the days that's in the week / I dearly love but one day; / And that's the day that comes between / a Saturday and Sunday." Two patients are being chased by an invalid wielding a slap stick. Martin joins the chase with a baby carriage. The invalid tumbles in the buggy and is wheeled out. And, during the confusion, if anyone is listening, the threads of the plot are tied together.

Harrigan had used a nursery and a rubbing parlor in an earlier unproduced sketch, "Nugent the Rubber," which contained one good line not used here: "He died in an upright position. He was hung."

Early in the run, Harrigan discarded the Tombs scene and substituted the policy shop scene from *The Major*. It was later expanded, and *McNooney's* was retitled *4–11–44*. According to one critic, "this grimy, bare, dimly-lighted policy room populated with tattered and wildly grotesque Negroes clutching slips of paper showed, as no other scene ever had, the Hogarthian side of Harrigan's talent."[6] Policy (numbers) was not new to Harrigan. His Negroes in other plays had invariably devoted their spare time to the numbers, but here they are completely absorbed and render a song outlining the game's fatal fascination; "What am it keeps de darkies poor? / Four 'Leven Forty-four."

Policy originated in the London lottery shops early in the eighteenth century to provide for the players who could not afford a regular lottery ticket.[7] Picking a number on a lottery was called insuring a number, and the slip on which the number was written, an "insurance policy." Thus, *numbers* and *policy*. The game was introduced to New York as early as 1800. In 1818 one office reported a profit of $31,000 in three days. By 1820 there were sixty establishments in the city; in the seventies and eighties, from five hundred to seven hundred. These "exchanges," as they were sometimes called, ranged from dirty dens on Cherry or Thompson to the elegant, spacious exchange on Broadway near Saint Paul's Church; yet all had a similar layout: an outer reception area and a long, narrow inner room, so dark that gas jets burned throughout the day. In Harrigan's time, the lucky numbers were based on the state lotteries or on the Royal Havana Lottery. In recent years the winners have been taken from bank clearings, pari-mutuel totals, baseball scores, and custom-house receipts. (New Jersey has now added policy to the state lottery, removing it from gangster control and giving the state treasury the profits.)

Most of the jargon and lore of Harrigan's time still persists: "Day number, Saddle, Gig, and Horse" indicate the combinations:

Day number: a single number; 5 to 1 (the usual odds)
Saddle: two numbers; 44 to 1
Gig: three numbers; 300 to 1
Horse: four numbers; 640 to 1

Gig was the favorite with Negroes and the favorite gig, 4–11–44, was frequently called the "magic gig" or the "washwoman's gig." The fascination, then and now, derives from the small initial investment—commonly twenty-five cents—and the occult systems employed to select a winner.

Dreams were always a part of policy, and such how-to volumes as *Old Aunt Dinah's Policy Dream Book* (1830) were still in vogue in Harrigan's time. A dream about an elephant with cat's eyes and fiery teeth was checked in the book before one headed for the policy office. Some dreams were known to everyone without the aid of the book. A dead horse meant luck. An anxious sweetheart meant a winning "gig": the day of the month, her age, and yours. Other sure signs: a deam about a man, 1; a woman, 5; two women, 15; a Dutchman, 14; a Negro, 14. Some shops retained professional dreamers who dreamed while you waited, for a price. One of the famous seers was Aunty Green, a thin, wiry Negress who looked like an Indian.

In Caleb Jenkins's shop, Harrigan used the standard layout and all the business of slips, numbers on the board, jumping, shouting, and a police raid to hale everyone into court for the next scene. Policy raids were common in the seventies and eighties. Although they normally interrupted business for only a day, that created a rough day for the regulars.

Why Harrigan turned to variety concoctions passed off as plays he never explained. Certainly his imagination had not dried up, with such sparkling inventions as the massage parlor and the Welcome Home Nursery. Perhaps, as someone said, he turned to outlandish scenes because he had not found a new formula for Dan

Collyer, Hart's replacement. Collyer had been a variety man with Josh Hart in the late seventies, with Tony Pastor as singer and comedian in the afterpieces—in the *Patience* burlesque with Lillian Russell—yet he could match neither Hart's "uproarious comicality" nor his skill at juggling an audience as if the laughs were bouncing on the ends of his fingers. Some thought him Hart's superior "in the more delicate phases of his art."[8] But Harrigan did not tailor parts for his "delicate phases." He sent him on as Rebecca Allup or in new wench roles that seemed still designed for Hart.

Tony would have welcomed a part written by his old partner. After two futile years of barnstorming, even Gertie may have realized that wifely ambition had clouded her judgment, that Hart needed Harrigan's plays, Harrigan's business at rehearsal, and Braham's songs. Tony had not felt so alone on stage since his "Master Antonio" days. In the fall after the separation, he tried a play called *Buttons*. It opened in Burlington, Vermont, had a few nights in Boston, struggled around the Midwest, and finally expired in Saint Paul, because Gertie was not well.

The Harts retired to Worcester, keeping up appearances in the social life of the community. On January 1, 1886, when they attended the Washington Ball, a reporter noted that Gertie was neatly gowned in pink satin with a white lace overdress and that she was remarkably decorated with diamond ornaments.[9]

Hart tried a New York comeback in *Toy Pistols* (February 20, 1886). As Isaac Roast, editor of the *Toy Pistol,* he enlivened the second act by impersonating an Italian, a young Hebrew, an Irishwoman, and a Chinaman. The attempt to duplicate a Harrigan tour de force lasted five weeks. When he appeared for two weeks with Lillian Russell in Charles Hoyt's *The Maid and the Moonshiner* (August 16, 1886), *The Theatre* detected "indifference in the stalls and rebellion in the gallery." He had lost the "touch-and-go . . . the free, breezy, unquenched vitality. . . . He strives to be humorous; he is not; he strives to be interesting; he is uninteresting because he is forced."[10]

When he tried again with a week of *Donnybrook* (December 13, 1886), *The Theatre* was even more depressed: "He looks pale, haggard, and thin. Only a little while ago he and his partner 'owned the town.' Tony was the cunningest little fellow that walked the streets. He was so very wholesome; he possessed one of those rare, magnetic smiles that win one's sympathy so completely—'a smile that would coax the birds off the trees.' Now his rosy chubbiness has vanished, and the smile is destroyed by a moustache. I advise Tony to get back with Mr. Harrigan if it is a possible thing."[11]

Donnybrook was like an early Harrigan concoction: melodramatic heroics mixed with fun by Con O'Grady (Hart), a warmhearted, wholesome little fellow who sings and dances at the Donnybrook Fair. With feeble encouragement in New York, the Harts hit the road again. They began with a pitiful week at Hooley's in Chicago (January 17, 1887), got snowbound en route to Lafayette, Indiana, struggled through a week in St. Louis, a worse week in Cincinnati—total gross $700. Providence, Lowell, Lynn, and Worcester were no more generous in late February and March, and after two weeks in Brooklyn and Williamsburgh, Hart closed *Donnybrook* and his career with an engagement in Boston.

If the partnership had not seemed so indestructible, the partners so bound to each other, if their theatrical fortunes had not risen in tandem, the change after 1885 might have appeared less astounding. Perhaps Harrigan was not riding as high as he had with Hart, but his success at the box office had not diminished. His views on the theatre, on playwriting, on acting were being taken as gospel, and the serious critics of literature and the theatre were enrolling him in the permanent record of his time, while Hart was sliding into his pathetic final days.

17

Harrigan's Mirror

Among the big critical guns of the late nineteenth century, none
carried heavier ammunition or took surer aim on his targets than
the "chill and conservative"[1] William Dean Howells. In the "Editor's Study" (*Harper's,* July 1886), after Harrigan's first season
alone, Howells wrote:

> Mr. Harrigan accurately realized in his scenes what he
> realizes in his persons; that is, the actual life of this city . . .
> Irish-American phases in their rich and amusing variety, and
> some of its African and Teutonic phases. It is what we call low
> life, though whether it is essentially lower than fashionable life
> is another question. . . . In his own province we think he can-
> not be surpassed. The art that sets before us all sorts and
> conditions of New York Irishmen, from the laborers in the
> street to the most powerful of the ward politicians and the
> genteelest of the ladies of that interesting race, is the art of
> Goldoni—the joyous yet conscientious art of the true dramatist
> in all times who loves the life he observes. . . . Mr. Harrigan is
> himself a player of the utmost naturalness, delicate, restrained,
> infallibly sympathetic; and we have seen no one on his stage
> who did not seem to have been trained to his part. In certain
> moments the illusion is so perfect that you lose the sense of
> being in the theatre; you are out of that world of conventions
> and traditions, and in the presence of the facts. . . . Consciously
> or unconsciously, he is part of the great tendency toward the
> faithful representation of life which is now animating fiction.[2]

Howells compared Harrigan with Goldoni; other critics noted his similarities to Hogarth, to Balzac, and to Dickens. George Edgar Montgomery detected a "distinct Zolaesque realism, a similar logical sequence."[3] Harrigan had been acclaimed first by the newsboys, then adopted by the Bowery B'hoys, the East Side shop girls, and the common people of his neighborhood; the uptowners followed, and finally the dramatic critics and literary men recognized his genius. His audience expanded because Harrigan's ambition did not "stop short at the climaxes of broken heads, horseplay, and copious dust."[4] He probed the low life of the town with humorous accuracy, never deviating from the truth, though exercising a friendly freedom with facts.

Richard Harding Davis speculated that there were only a few hundred people in New York who did not know and love Edward Harrigan, and for good reason: he had been reproducing and delineating characters from the life of the city, authentic living men and women, giving New Yorkers a mirror of their times. "As a historian of the war of the races Mr. Harrigan makes no mistakes" and has no equals.[5]

With the door opened by Howells, reporters solicited Harrigan's thoughts on the theatre, on his writing, his formula for success, and editors tempted him with cash and a conspicuous by-line if he would oblige with an essay. With interviewers he was generous and frank. Writing about his writing was less inviting, and he undertook it infrequently: In a symposium, "American Playwrights on the American Drama," in *Harper's Weekly* (February 2, 1889) he joined Augustin Daly, Bronson Howard, and William Gillette. For *Pearson's Magazine* (November 1903) in an article called "Holding the Mirror up to Nature." And in three newspaper pieces: "The Play's the Thing," "The Playwright's Art," and an untitled article in which he responded to A. M. Palmer.

A. M. Palmer, manager of the Madison Square Theatre, had apparently taken issue with Howells, insisting that Harrigan's plays were unworthy of serious attention. They did not truly represent American society, dealt only with types, and were simply prolongations of sketches. To the first charge Harrigan replied: "Whoever votes the Republican or Democratic ticket in the United States must be an American, no matter what may be his mother tongue or color. So I class my works as American, and the greatest compliment paid to my plays by foreigners is that they do not understand them. . . . The phrase, a prolongation of sketches, coined by Mr. A. M. Palmer, is not well put regarding my plays. I would say a continuity of incidents, with some simple reason for their dovetailing, and each link on the string sustained by some natural motive that calls for the building of the entire stage structure. In this principle of playmaking, or sketch-prolonging, we find reason for the character-drawing which should be the one great aim of the dramatist. . . . Laughter and tears should be the component parts. The sunshine is not appreciated without the shade."[6]

Some Harrigan ideas stand out conspicuously in his essays and in the interviews: His writing hand was never guided by some mysterious super power; he always knew what he was doing, conscious of the effect he wished to achieve. His theatre was designed for entertainment, for laughs, for brushing away the blues. "Life is too short to take allopathic doses of woe when we can avoid them."[7] Spectators want to see something of themselves on the stage. Holding the mirror up to nature is as applicable to the "swarming myriads of New York as to the Greek warriors before Priam's city or the lords and nobles who surrounded the Tudors."[8] In each of his plays he unfolds an album of scenes from life in the Empire City.

No playwright worthy of the name preaches morality; neither does he gild vice and sin and glorify immorality. He knows that "the majority who control the machine are right-doing and filled with kindness and good nature."[9] Although many of his types have rough going, he felt no need to show the mire that surrounded them. Perhaps he had, as one critic claimed, disinfected his slums, but you don't get laughs by "blowing chaff in the face of the audience."[10] On another occasion he said, "Nothing can ever be heard or seen in my theatre that I would blush to have my wife or mother see or hear."[11]

If a spectator feels compelled to think, he must proceed on his own. Harrigan's characters do not specialize in thinking. They are men of action, and, as everyone knew, they came directly from New York's lower wards, many from the Corlear's district where, in a dozen tenement blocks, one could find a greater concentration and diversity of nationalities than anywhere else on the globe, where "after eight o'clock the United States language is a hard find, where vice in rags holds high carnival all night long."[12] These lowly citizens were more richly endowed with humanity than their uptown brothers, and humanity always came first with him. He added race and nationality for ornamentation.

He sought types because they activated immediate and gratifying identification. Irish and Negroes were favored because "they form about the most salient features of Gotham humanity, and they are the two races who care most for song and dance."[13] There were still (in 1889) at least three hundred organizations in New York like the Mulligan Guards and probably fifty like the Skids.[14] Being Irish himself he had an advantage in sensing the finer gradations and contrasts that might otherwise have escaped him.

He studied the Negroes by talking with them, attending their balls and parties, observing the "luxuriant side of their natures, their riotously funny simplicity."[15] He knew their Southern relations well enough to know that the New York Negro who kept a poolroom, owned horses, and delighted in affluence, particularly if it could be displayed on his person, was a different type. The New York Negro had developed his own fancy talk, more colorful and ingenious than that of his white brother.[16]

A playwright should not thrash about trying to discover something brand new. Aesop and Shakespeare had covered most everything, but anyone could put old wine into new bottles and without the "stain of appropriation."[17] Genius was not required. "Unrelenting drudgery, athletic bounding spirits and the hide of a pachyderm" were. A dramatist had "best adopt the methodical, systematic routine of the mercantile man."[18] Harrigan stuck to writing from late morning until six o'clock every day except matinee days, varying the routine only for emergencies. Sometimes a play was well along before it reached his desk. He once said, "I'm writing another play. When it's written, I'll put it on paper."[19] He worked with large notebook pads and a pencil, though he regretted that his handwriting had become less legible.[20]

First he insisted that the characters justify their existence, give a decent reason for showing themselves; then he would scald them with hot water from all sides. He enjoyed pushing them into trouble, took less pleasure in getting them out. A few loose ends never disturbed him. Finding a string to hang the people on was his most difficult chore. Plots were nightmares! Through the first stage of writing, he calculated everything to the demands of the stage: how the scenery could be shifted—models helped; how long the scenes would play. In the second step, as he added wit and humor to the dialogue, more fun and nonsense to the climaxes, he always saw the actor's face and heard him speak, usually actors he knew as well as he knew himself. The third phase, staging and rehearsing, was invariably the longest and for him the most exciting.[21]

Unfortunately no one ever detailed an eyewitness account of this third phase. Actors said he was great at rehearsals, and Harrigan said he enjoyed bringing a play to life. No one described the transformation of "Business" and "Business at rehearsal" into knockdown and slambang routines that sometimes ran as long as five minutes. If someone had written a "Harrigan at Rehearsal," or an antiquarian had preserved some of Harrigan's models, the persistent stage directions in his manuscripts—"Business," "Business at rehearsal," "See Model"—would be less tantalizing.

His plays demanded the right actors. He reminded anyone who questioned that fact that "you can buy a copy of *Hamlet* for fifteen cents, but you must look long and far for your Hamlet."[22] And dealing in types as he did, he required actors whose physical peculiarities came close to their real-life counterparts and actors who didn't lose their naturalness when they mounted the stage. He never tried to disguise a young man with a beard and gray wig; cosmetics did not create age. Nor did he ever let personal considerations distort his judgment. As he once said, "John may be a good actor, an honest fellow with a family to support, but if he doesn't suit my character I won't try to use him."[23] When he needed a new type, he went to the small and obscure theatres, the variety halls, never to the major theatres. He had great confidence in his ability to cast correctly. He once said that he could put together the best company ever seen in *Hamlet*, with himself cast as a grave digger.[24]

All his actors shared his concern about how they looked. Harrigan garments weren't built. They had evolved in the distant past, having adapted their shape to the body and spirit of their host. Finding costumes became the off-duty task of all Harrigan employees. Immigrants fresh off the boat, workers and watchers at construction sites, and dockside vagabonds were good sources. Harrigan once explained that, for the revival of *Old Lavender*, Dan Collyer's hat had come from a shop on the back streets of Syracuse, the coat from a Baxter Street pawnshop, the pants from a beggar on Sixth Avenue, the limed shoes from a mason who welcomed a new pair in exchange. "In the old days Tony and I spent more time hunting for costumes than anything else. Until the fire we probably had the finest collection of character costumes in the world. Often clothes from immigrants and bums were a hazard to health and were taken to the roof to be boiled and spread out to dry."[25]

Before rehearsals Harrigan always reexamined his text. If some lines seemed too familiar or "chestnutty," or slowed the action, he removed them, always working for a fast pace and strong contrasts; that's what the audience expected. They also expected spontaneous explosions, and such spontaneity could only be achieved by meticulous rehearsals and precise cues. Effects might have seemed haphazard. Their preparation was not. Supers were called for the initial rehearsals and rehearsed as carefully as the principals. When the critics proclaimed that Harrigan's theatre had the best-drilled supers in New York, they could not have found sweeter words for Harrigan.

In the late eighties he outlined his stage director's credo, a credo that most directors even today would heartily endorse:

> The only possible way to produce plays truthfully and valuably is to have one intelligent and observant mind control everything down to the least detail. Following any other rule must end in imperfect presentation. . . . A good play must be placed before the public by a man who knows the value and use of every constituent connected with a theatre. . . . The cheapest super must be looked out for and taught. Every light that is thrown must be gauged by one dictator. His power must be as supreme as the general of an army, and he must dare to exert the same authority and have everything done to suit him. If he gets an actor on his stage who insists upon being arbitrary,

he must either discharge the actor or resign himself. . . . I could give the best play I ever wrote to some man who did not understand me or had not the ability to make people do as he wished and my play would fail miserably. . . . It is the exertion of this one man power that secures the best results. It is in stage directorship our theatres are often deficient. A capitalist, a carpenter, a business manager cannot produce plays.[26]

Of all the staging he had seen in New York, he thought Henry Irving's the best: "He's the king of us all as a director."[27] Harrigan did not sympathize with the efforts to isolate the American stage from foreigners. In 1888 the newspapers were filled with xenophobic talk, much directed against Irving; and a group calling itself the Actors Order of Friendship had hired Robert Ingersoll to help it repel the intruders. Harrigan shared the *New York Post*'s view that this was an infantile cry that the public simply interpreted as an acknowledgment of American actors' hopeless inferiority. Harrigan was an artistic free trader. He once told a reporter, "I will accept English methods, French methods, or Chinese methods if they teach me something I do not know."[28]

Still, he admitted to a touch of provincialism, if that's what it was. He believed that plays should be written for the New York stage and not for touring. Railroading had an unhealthy influence, forcing a dramatist to formulate his scenes to conform to a baggage car and the exigencies of one-night stands. Could not each of the major cities develop its own drama and its own companies and let the road combinations fade away?[29]

Undoubtedly these thoughts were on his mind as he headed for California in the summer of 1887, even though the company was traveling in high style with a private coach and Pullman. The forty-five members of the troupe plus assorted wives and dogs lived in what passed for luxury, with the aisles taken over daily for a kind of street parade, featuring arguments between actors and between wives, dogfights, and much singing.

According to Harrigan's daughter Adelaide, the departure from Jersey City was disrupted when she and her brother Tony came to say goodbye. Tony screamed and grabbed his father's pants with a bulldog grip, refusing to spend his summer at Schroon while San Francisco was still a possibility. He won, shared the berth with brother Eddie, and Adelaide found accommodations in her parents' drawing room. With this hasty change of plans, their wardrobe was as limited as the two changes of Rebecca Allup's husband, "on and off."

At ages six (Tony) and five (Adelaide), such deprivations quickly faded in the face of the daily excitement of early morning arrivals in strange towns, watching Uncle Martin and Louis Farber, the property man, dispatch the trunks to the hotel and the wooden chests of props and canvas-covered wardrobe hampers to the theatre. Hotel rooms promised new adventure until they revealed the same shabbiness, brass beds, and brass chandeliers dotted with the same fly specks as the room from which they had just departed. Not until they reached the Baldwin in San Francisco did hotel and town match Adelaide's expectations. The hotel was elegant. The town was filled with wonders: cable cars, fresh fruit she'd never seen before, and Chinamen who were not laundrymen, whom one wouldn't dare call, "Chinky-chinky Chinaman, chop, chop, chop." She remembered spending much of her time in Chinatown with her mother and Aunt Marietta (Ravel) Hanley buying cups and saucers and teapots.

The tour was profitable everywhere except Chicago, where they competed with hot weather as well as with Daly's and Palmer's touring companies. In San Francisco Harrigan was welcomed home as was Annie Yeamans, and the Alcazar Theatre was crowded nightly with friends who knew he could do no wrong, though on this occasion he did. Harrigan admitted later that he had made one mistake he would never repeat.[30] He localized *Investigation,* using a committee from the Sacramento legislature visiting an opium den on the Tar Flats. After the change had been set, he discovered that the audience wanted to see New York and hear about Albany and Mulberry Bend. Ordinarily Annie would have visited with the Rowe family; she had begun her career with Rowe's circus in Australia and during recent years had been sending them money under the impression that they were destitute. Now she was summoned to meet with their lawyer. They had both died and left their San Francisco property to her.[31]

18

Tuberoses Spell
"Partner"

Back home on Perry Street, Harrigan talked with a reporter about his plans for fall.[1] Although he was opening the season later than usual, he was still going to begin with revivals of *Leather Patch* and *Cordelia's Aspirations*. When the company was warmed up, he would introduce *Pete*, a new kind of play. His friends should understand that he had shifted ground because he did not want to wear out his welcome with local dramas. Next summer he even planned to go to Ireland, where he would write a play full of heroic speeches against England—"cull my people and my story right from the sod, just as from the slums of New York." The play from the sod never got written. When the time came for going abroad, he backed down. "What's the use of going to Europe to see the people of foreign nations," he told his friends, "when you can see them all in a walk from Union Square to the Battery?"[2]

Reporters always enjoyed interviewing Harrigan at home, where he was relaxed, unhurried, and "looking more like a well-groomed and intellectual member of the clergy than like an actor"; and with Annie and the children sharing the limelight, he revealed more of himself than he did in the theatre. Harrigan had only two lives in these years: at the Park and at 14 Perry. His friends pestered him to endorse innumerable St. Patrick's associations. He refused them all. Contributing to the Irish cause with his stage characters was enough. He participated in benefits for the sufferers from conflagrations and malarial infestations, the annual benefits for the

Roman Catholic Orphan Asylum, and, of course, for the Actors'
Fund, but he became a joiner only once. He was among the
twenty-one original members of the Players Club.[3]

Harrigan news flowed easily, from him, from Annie, from the
children, occasionally a snippet from Margaret, the Irish nurse on
loan from the Brahams, from Harrigan's valet "Eighty-forty."
Eighty-forty—that was his lucky number—could have told more
than he ever had a chance to tell. For parties he engineered
stretching the striped awning from the door to the street, checked
the French caterers, settled the musicians behind the ferns to keep
them out of the creamed oysters and chicken salad. He fancied
gin, particularly on party nights, and frequently his sight deterior-
ated and his tongue grew heavy. One night Annie Harrigan fooled
him in her Carmen costume, and he announced her as a visiting
beauty from Spain.

Everyone commented on Annie's Spanish look, her gypsy
beauty, her laughing black eyes. But her breezy cheerfulness, her
perpetual smile were unmistakably Irish. One friend was sure that
she smiled in her sleep. Her hyperactivity was native American,
derived from the demands of young Ned, Adelaide, Tony, and then
William. She was either listening to Ned's newest creation, pasting
a poultice on Tony's black eye—he was a fighter—or inspecting
Addie's latest attempt to pass as a teenager. Addie loved to dress
up, and whenever she did, she seemed to look more and more like
her mother. Annie's duties were endless. The lace curtains in the
parlor were invariably decorated with notes to herself: "Tony—
music lesson; Ned—dentist; Bank—Mtge." Adelaide reported that
she wondered for years why "Bank—Mitchie" required such
constant attention.

The children's preserve was in the attic, though their quarters
were frequently crowded with hampers, with seamstresses, or with
a shaggy black Labrador retriever performing his inspection duties.
Young Ned had already begun to test his talents with attic theatricals, written and managed by him. Once he tried to persuade
"Betsey," the dressmaker's model, to execute an acrobatic pas de
deux, which sent her crashing through a window.

The attic was subdued when visitors were in the house. The
children were in the parlor, scooting across the tiger-skin rug,

circling the grand piano, dodging the Japanese urns, or they were on the glassed-in verandah at the back of the house. Here the obstacles were suits of armor and a grandfather's clock. Fortunately the theatrical portraits of Edwin Forrest, Billy Gray, and others that covered the walls were out of reach.

At home Harrigan shed his theatre manners, "completely cloaking his identity under the sweet countenance of a calm-faced citizen." He settled into his chair, looking too "well-built and well-nourished" for an actor. He winked, cocked his head, then with his dark eyes sparkling, his face lit with a smile, "happy as a poet," and his sharp chin elevated just enough to command center stage, he rolled out the sweetest brogue to be heard this side of heaven. He loved to talk, as an Irishman should, and as he talked he cuddled a young Harrigan or two, or three, on his lap. Visitors to Perry Street always spoke of his way with the children. They treated him more like a brother than like a father. And he was "as tender as a woman when he speaks to or touches one of them."[4]

Most of Adelaide's memories were of her father. She recalled the "roundsman" (policeman) making his circuit and swinging his nightstick on a scarlet cord, the errands to the baker and butcher with Eddie and Tony. Mostly she remembered the morning walks with her father down Perry and across Greenwich Avenue to Brant's drugstore. He went to Brant's for his daily ration of three Havana cigars. One he lit from the jet on the counter, and he stuffed the others in his vest. From there they went to Mrs. King's candy store for licorice or coconut taffy, then to the Fourth Street Park to enjoy the cigar before starting the day's work. And along the way, someone would call, "Sing us a song, Ned." Someone was always shouting, "Sing us a song, Ned." It was the happiest time of the day, though most times of the day were happy in the house on Perry.

Harrigan's friends at home were matched by a loyal crowd in the theatre who followed him from the Comique, to the new Comique, to the Park. A letter signed "Little Em'ly" recounting a visit to a matinee of *Cordelia's Aspirations* suggests that the old gang was on hand at the Park: "My gracious, I never ran across a noisier audience. There was a man right back of us continually eating peanuts and scattering the shells right and left. I found one in my bonnet when I got home. Every other minute, he'd shriek ouuuu . . . look at Harrigan! Oh, lor' he takes the cake, he do!— and then a peanut shell would lodge in his windpipe and he'd set up such a dreadful coughing that we couldn't hear a word that was said on the stage. And the babies! They must all have been teething that afternoon!"[5]

When *Pete* opened on November 20, 1887, the Harrigan faithful were taken on a sentimental journey to new locations: a Southern plantation, the verandah of the Blossom Hotel, and a Florida dock where a practical steamboat moves out into the stream. As it moves, its "wheel revolves picking up clean rice to represent water."

In *Pete*, Harrigan returned to the melodramatic entanglements of his early plays. Colonel Coolidge has inadvertently married twice. His first wife has given him a child unbeknownst to him. His second wife is after his fortune. He's called up to join his regiment, is killed, and when the second wife tries to claim the plantation, she's foiled by his child Mary Morgan with the assistance of Old Pete. The telltale document is the original wedding license. The witnesses' names have been shot away, but Pete has retrieved the wad from the bullet, with the names! It took three hours and ten minutes to ravel and unravel the story, explore related subplots, exhibit both threatening and entertaining spectacles, and introduce slavery songs and spirituals.

Among the spectacles: A cruel beating of Pete with a snake whip and then his recovery as little Mary bathes his bleeding cuts. As a reward for her charity, the villain tosses her in a millpond, and she's rescued by Pete.

For fun: A wedding in the bush by moonlight, to be conducted by a circuit rider. Pete thinks he's a circus rider. Before the itinerant preacher arrives, the Negro couple petition Pete to marry them. Pete insists that he's not qualified: "My geological position don't give me de license to tie niggars in de marriage state. I'm only a mower in de vineyard. I got de facility to dip sinners in de creek but I haven't got de mancipation from de church to stigmatize de marriage."

Through most of the play, Pete strums the heartstrings as a traditional Uncle Tom but with Harrigan comedy touches added.

Pete's proud of his education, though he admits that "he gets tied-up" after the "A.B.C's."

The critics praised Harrigan for giving Pete "a true African quality without constantly suggesting the white man beneath the burnt cork."[6] Some thought the play too long, too remote from Five Points, but audiences loved the new creation. They crowded the theatre even during the famous March blizzard, sending *Pete* to a record 176 performances.[7]

One night, sometime in January 1888, Harrigan spotted Tony Hart in a box. No one in the audience recognized him. After the performance he came back, with his brother John Cannon, and the old partners embraced and talked of old times. Hart looked puffy but said that he was feeling much better every day, that he had no plans for the future, though he was eager to return to the stage, probably next year. It was a warm reunion, their first since the separation, and their last. They never met again.[8]

After Hart had closed *Donnybrook* in Boston, the newspapers had kept up with him, even with no theatre news to record. On August 7, 1887, the *New York Times* said that "Mr. Hart's over-taxed nervous system has left him well-nigh shattered . . . seriously an invalid." A month later the newspaper reported that the talk of insanity was not true. Hart's physician, Dr. T. S. Robertson, said that he was suffering from paralysis of the muscle of the mouth and tongue and would soon be completely recovered.[9]

On December 15, the *New York Herald* published the rumors that had been floating through the city for several months: "THE TELLTALE LISP / TONY HART'S TROUBLE BEGINS LIKE THAT OF JOHN MCCULLOUGH / ALL THE SYMPTOMS OF PARESIS / Why Ned Harrigan's Former Partner Has Been Forced To Leave the Stage." The odd fattening of his tongue that caused him to lisp and stutter had doomed him to worse than sudden death. For some time other symptoms had also been apparent: the enlargement of the pupils of the eyes, omitting letters when he wrote, and most pitiful, "in excesses of fury he has struck his wife and had no memory of his rage." In earlier medical examinations Hart had been led to believe his trouble lay in the muscles of his cheeks, damaged by the use of burnt cork for so many years.

The Hippocratic oath apparently did not restrain his physicians. The *Herald* reporter called on Dr. Robertson. He was unavailable, but his partner, Dr. Trent, was familiar with the case and quite willing to tell what he knew. Robertson had consulted with Dr. Hammond and Dr. Harrison; all agreed that Hart had paresis, that the prognosis was not promising.[10]

Hart's friends were outraged, and Mrs. Stephen Fiske spoke for them in denouncing "such mean and contemptible journalism." Mary Fiske, better known as "Giddy Gusher," usually entertained readers of the *New York Dramatic Mirror* with polite essays: "Life in a Flat," "Prevalent Perfumes," "Inequality of the Sexes." Now she pleaded for pity and justice for Hart. Being in constant communication with Tony, she could report that his control over his speech and facial muscles had been improving remarkably. How could the newspapers be so cruel? "The man has sat and brushed the fast-gathering tears as he read the heartless summing-up of his life's work. His fortunes were so welded with those of Ned Harrigan that when they parted every fibre of Tony's anatomy felt the wrench (as I believe Harrigan's did also). . . . Financial disasters came in a sort of torchlight procession, sickness and death—he has buried mother and sisters in one season. . . . If he can continue improving and still read the newspapers he must be more than human. . . . For Heaven's sake, daily journals, forbear."[11] If reporters must have someone to abuse, they should attack her. She recently had trouble getting her hat on, a sure sign, the doctors would say, that Mary Fiske has hydrocephalus.

Early in January, Hart's friends realized that the *Herald* story came near the truth, that Tony needed help. In February, Nat Goodwin announced a "monster benefit" to be held at the Academy of Music on March 15, sponsored by the Masons, Elks, W. J. Florence, A. M. Palmer, et al., and featuring an act or two of *Julius Caesar* that should be "the funniest thing seen on the American stage."[12] Hart's dear friend Goodwin was the prime mover—some said he as well as Gertie had urged Hart to break with Harrigan—and on March 8, he came up from Philadelphia where he was playing to auction tickets for "one of the best little men who ever played in New York." Box A sold for $175 to L. C. Behman of Hyde and Behman, owners of the Park. (Some said that Harrigan was the real purchaser.) Other boxes went to Tony Pastor, the Boston Elks, the Theatrical Mechanics' Association, to Tyson the ticket speculator; A. M. Palmer offered twenty dollars apiece for any unsold seats.[13]

Although the performance was delayed for a week because too many actors were to be out of town on the fifteenth and also because the sponsors still hoped to persuade Henry Irving to appear, at 1:00 P.M. on Thursday, March 22, 1888, the curtain went up on the "monster entertainment" (without Irving): sixteen acts, plus Maggie Mitchell and her company, Frank Mayo and company and the pièce de résistance, scenes from *Julius Caesar*.[14] Hart slipped on stage as a super, and when he was recognized, the house rose en masse and cheered, Caesar's entourage joining in the tribute. A reporter who visited Hart backstage after the performance said he was "just as neat and precise about the fit of his trousers, the shine on his patent leather shoes, and the neat fitting gloves as he ever was."[15] His face might seem a little puffier, but that made him look more like his hero Napoleon. (In Hart's scrapbook someone wrote under the picture of Napoleon, "The man that Tony loved.") It was a profitable tribute. Fourteen thousand dollars were turned over to Hart, with the understanding that if any money remained in his estate it should pass to the Actors' Fund.

On June 24, Dr. J. G. Park, superintendent of the State Lunatic Hospital at Worcester, announced that Hart had been admitted as a private patient, "incurably ill of paresis, or softening of the brain."[16] A friend who visited him that summer found him happy, much thinner, and enjoying his daily walks about the grounds. In December, his old champion the "Giddy Gusher" said he was improving, that next summer Harrigan should send Mrs. Harrigan to Long Branch or Saratoga, and he and Hanley should take Hart to the Adirondacks for a summer of fishing, hunting, and loafing. She knew that there was still a deep love between them. A year earlier when she had ridden up Broadway with Hart, they had spied Harrigan, and Tony had turned to her and said, "That dear boy Ned; it was his spirit that gave me courage in a great many tight places." At that moment and many since, "I'd have given the hair off my head to have joined their hands, as I believe their hearts have always been joined in loving sympathy."[17] This was her final note on Hart. She died two months later.[18]

In the spring Hart was released to his father and sisters, hoping to go back on the stage, but as one reporter noted, it was "simply preposterous to suppose that Tony Hart will ever act again. Most of his time is spent in crying, and he is hardly able to articulate a single word with any understanding."[19] Although she was in failing health, Gertie did attempt a return to Broadway, in March for two weeks in *The Paymaster,* in September a final week in *McKenna's Flirtation.* Before the end of the year, Tony was back in the institution, and on March 16, 1890, he was last seen in public, at his wife's funeral. Accompanied by a hospital attendant, he was a shadow of his former self, and when he followed Gertie's casket down the aisle he sobbed like a child.[20]

In May some of Tony's friends attempted to break Gertie's will, claiming that, because of an excessive use of stimulants, she was of unsound mind when she gave Tony's jewels to any friend who admired them and when she deeded the house on Forty-sixth Street to her brother John Monahan. Monahan was a barkeeper in Waterbury, a worthless fellow, and not really her brother.[21] The legal maneuvering to determine if his friends could act in his behalf carried on too long to help Tony.[22]

On August 11, 1890, a "Half an hour talk with the unfortunate comedian by telegraph to the *Herald*" revealed that he was broken in mind and body and slowly dying. Old friends would not recognize the pale, white-haired man with sunken eyes and cheeks who lives in a ten-foot-square room, scrupulously clean but furnished only with an iron bed and a camp chair. When the reporter talked with him on the grounds, he seemed in a happy frame of mind. To the question, "You have relatives here?" he gave a rambling reply: "Oh yes. Forty thousand. The Donneybrook Fair scenery, that's all right. I used to make $450 a night. Harrigan's all right. He's going to write a play for me. We never had any trouble. He knows all about it. Pretty girls—too bad!"

Tony died at 2:30 A.M. on Wednesday, November 4, 1891, three months past his thirty-sixth birthday. The *Worcester Gazette* reported that he spent his last days in a big armchair at a window looking out on Lake Quinsigamond, unconscious of everything around him and never opening his lips.[23] The funeral on November 6 began at the residence of his niece, Mrs. P. H. Murphy, followed by a solemn high requiem mass at St. John's Church and burial in St. John's Cemetery. Among the mourners were his aged father Anthony Cannon, David Braham, Martin Hanley, and Mrs. Edward Harrigan with Eddie and Tony, and surrounding the casket were flowers from "Brother," "Little Tony to Uncle Tony," a harp of blossoms with a broken string from Hanley, and a large pillow surmounted with a cross, fringed with ferns, in a border of orchids and a field of white carnations, and with bride roses and tuberoses spelling "Partner."[24]

Harrigan was performing a new play in his new theatre and could not attend. He told an interviewer that it was really Tony's big heart that had put him in the grave, that his habits and character had changed before the break, that he had known of Tony's dread disease a year before their separation; still he insisted, as they always had, that only business considerations had forced them apart. If the partners shared secrets, they remained secret.[25]

During Tony's last sad years, Harrigan was concluding his term at the Park, discovering parts of the city he'd missed before, and toying with plans for a theatre of his own.

When he returned from two months' vacation at Schroon, he told a *Times* man who turned up at the first rehearsal that he would forestall criticism "by promising that the keynote of *Waddy Googan* is fun with the usual slight semblance of the drama."[26] What he did not reveal was that it was mainly a tour de force for Harrigan accompanied by a glance at some unsavory Italian crooks. More Italians had arrived in New York to disturb the natural battle lines. Now Germans and Irish first had to subdue Italians before they could attack each other.

Harrigan played Waddy Googan, a hackman who ranges over the city from Red Hook to the Willow Garden, to a Canal Street dump under the wharf, to the old Spring Street Market. (It is not surprising that Harrigan's original title was *The Metropolis*.)[27] He also appeared as Joe Cornello, a demented sailor who has joined Mother Donnetti's gang. Harrigan changed costumes a half-dozen times, often walking off as Waddy and entering almost immediately as Cornello. His Italian disguise was so convincing, his dialect so authentic, that many spectators refused to believe that Harrigan played both parts. And more astounding, particularly to the critic from the *Times,* he managed to make the "Dago" sympathetic and pathetic when everyone knew that "the Italian immigrant is a disagreeable character!"[28]

Even Zola could not have done better with the chippies, gamblers, politicians, and swells at Willow Garden, and as usual the audience delighted in the latest Harrigan observations: When a Dutchman is desperate he commits hari-kari by blowing out the gas; an Irishman gets drunk for ten days. The Googans worry about sending their daughter away to school at Mount St. Vincent.[29] When they survey the harbor through a spyglass, Mary Googan fears the garbage fleet will choke the channel and kill the fish, and Waddy marvels at the Statue of Liberty: it looks like a big cigar sign for the country! (The statue had been unveiled two years earlier.)

Harrigan's performance aroused more attention than the play. Even the famous French actor Coquelin was impressed. When he and his host, Brander Matthews, the Columbia professor and playwright, went backstage, he was also impressed by Harrigan's command of French.[30]

On October 26, 1888, after the second act of *Waddy Googan,* Frank E. Aiken, candidate for sheriff, suddenly appeared on stage, turned to Harrigan, and announced: "This is your birthday and your employees have asked me to present you with this silver water service as a mark of their esteem and affection." When the audience rose, Harrigan's face "bore an expression of blank amazement as he spoke: I tell you ladies and gentlemen I'm stuck—clean knocked off my pins, but I can assure you that this beautiful token will urge me on to make harmony the keynote among the attachés of my theatre, as it has been in the past."[31] When he retreated, Annie Yeamans entertained the audience with two minutes of "impromptu remarks on the efficacy of cold water."[32]

Waddy was followed by a revival of *The Lorgaire* and a spring season of *Pete, O'Reagans, 4-11-44,* and *The Grip.* And then in June 1889, with a company of fifty and with *Old Lavender* and

Squatter Sovereignty added to the repertoire, Harrigan headed for San Francisco and a full season on the road—fifty-two weeks without a break.

In spite of the absence of two old-timers—Mrs. Yeamans and Johnny Wild stayed in New York—the company got a rousing welcome everywhere. During eight weeks at Murphy's Alcazar Theatre in San Francisco, Harrigan's and Murphy's smiles of contentment brightened as every week "swelled their plethoric purses."[33] For the first time the Harrigan family was drawn into the company. In Leadville, Colorado, on the way out, Annie Harrigan went on for an ailing actress—her one and only appearance onstage. Eddie's and Tony's careers endured longer. They played peasants in *The Lorgaire* and Topsy (Eddie) and Eva (Tony) in the "Uncle Tom Combination" in *Cordelia's Aspirations.*

Eddie had also begun imitating his father, jotting down sketches and songs for a juvenile theatrical team, Edward Harrigan, Jr., and David Braham, Jr. The enterprise never progressed beyond a few pages and such lyrics as "You'd never say your grace / If you looked at her face," and

> For I love my Bessie
> And Bessie she loves me
> We always on Sunday night together take our tea
> At eleven I depart and it almost breaks my heart
> To leave my little Bessie all alone.

A scene he wrote for a comic pair called Pete and Eliza sounds like a Harriagan melee: "By this time Eliza has got upon the board that is laying across the box and table and Pete by jumping on the other end of the board over-weight and the board springs up knocking Pete down and throwing Liza in the barrel. The barrel breaks and they get up and do song and dance. P.S. On account of an encore do another song and dance." Inside the cover young Eddie wrote a prophetic inscription: "Please return so the son of an actor manager can keep it till the curtain calls on Eddie Harrigan."[34]

In San Francisco and along the return route—San Jose, Oakland, Stockton, Sacramento, Reno, Virginia City, Salt Lake City, Denver, Kansas City, and Chicago—Harrigan was interviewed about his plans for the future. He was not going back to the Park.

He had already spent over $12,000 improving the place, and he refused to pour more money into another man's property.[35] If he couldn't locate a theatre to his liking, he might build a small place of his own somewhere above Fourteenth Street. He enjoyed the traveling, found it refreshing mentally and physically, it might even stimulate a new play. His future plays might change, though he'd stick with human nature, and he was sure there was still a market for plays about New York life, though the Negro business and straight horseplay had probably seen their day. "The audience doesn't want the blowing-eyebrows-off-and-sticking-pins-in-bald-heads drama any more."[36]

Finally, back in New York in January 1890, he rested for two months, in March revived *Old Lavender* in Brooklyn and Williamsburgh, in May and June added *Squatter Sovereignty* and *Cordelia's Aspirations* for six weeks in Washington, Philadelphia, and Boston, before retreating to Schroon for the summer.

Comique, *Silver Wedding*

Credit: Harvard Theatre Collection

Hart in *The Major*

Squatter Sovereignty

Witham's Sketch for *Squatter Sovereignty*

FINALE OF LAST ACT OF "SQUATTER SOVEREIGNTY."

Squatter Sovereignty

THE SQUATTERS OF NEW YORK—SCENE NEAR CENTRAL PARK.—[SKETCHED BY D. E. WYAND.]

Squatters in Central Park

Schroon Lake

Witham's Sketch for *McSorley's Inflation*

Dan's Tribulations

Dan's Tribulations

Credit: Nedda Harrigan Logan

Hanley's *McSorley's Inflation*

Anne Yeamans in
Cordelia's Aspirations

Gertie Granville Hart

Harrigan in
Cordelia's Aspirations

Anne Yeamans in *Cordelia's Aspirations*

Witham's Sketch of Baxter Street, *The Leather Patch*

Credit: Museum of the City of New York

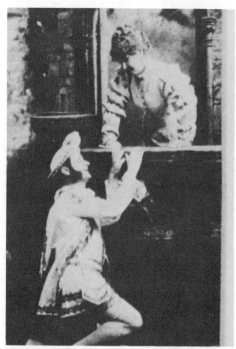

Harrigan and Yeamans in *Investigation*

Annie Yeamans in *The Leather Patch*

Last picture of Hart

MR. HARRIGAN AS THE MAJOR.

MR. HARRIGAN AND MRS. YEAMANS AS DAN AND CORDELIA MULLIGAN.

MR. HARRIGAN AS WADDY GOOGAN.

MR. HARRIGAN AS WILY REILLY.

MISS ADA LEWIS AS KITTIE LYNCH, "THE TOUGH GIRL."

MRS. ANNIE YEAMANS.

MR. JOHN WILD.

MISS ADA LEWIS.

Harrigan Company, 1891

Harrigan in *Reilly and the 400*

Harrigan's Theatre

Harrigan's Theatre

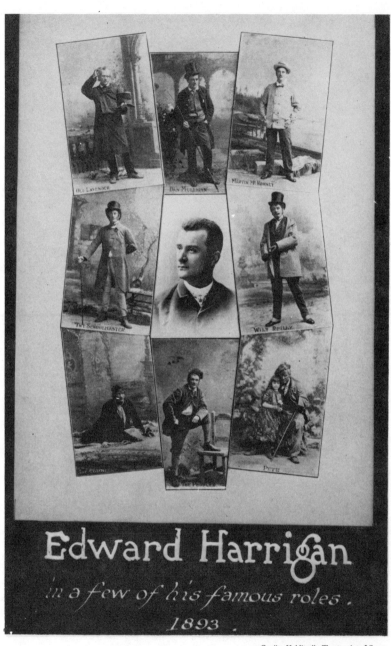

Harrigan's famous roles, 1893

Eddie Harrigan

Bray and Harrigan in
Under Cover

Harrigan, last photo, 1908

Annie Braham Harrigan

Annie Harrigan and Eddie Harrigan

Family at Schroon Lake

William Harrigan as the Captain in *Mister Roberts*

The Harrigan family (*top row, l. to r.: Nolan, Adelaide, Phillip; middle row: Anthony, Annie Braham Harrigan, William; bottom: Nedda*).

Harrigan in *The Lorgaire*

Nedda Harrigan Logan

19

Harrigan's on
Herald Square

Schroon provided little rest that summer. There were too many trips to the city, and in early September Harrigan was back in town straw-bossing the finishing touches on his new theatre, his and Annie's. Without her careful accumulative instinct they would not have had $90,000 to swing the deal. Even that was not enough to buy the land and erect the building. Additional funds came from a mortgage and from Austin Corbin, president of the Philadelphia and Reading Railroad.[1]

Talk of a new theatre had appeared in the press as early as February 1889.[2] Mr. Kimball was to design a sixteen-hundred-seat house at some yet-to-be-determined site, to be constructed of red brick, with a white and gold interior, and to be equipped with a mechanically perfect stage. In April, after finding a suitable location just a few blocks uptown and then discovering that too much blasting was required, Harrigan abandoned the project. For the time being he would settle for a lease on the Standard Theatre.[3] When that deal was snagged by the owner's refusal to refurbish the interior, Harrigan thought again about building and for a while toyed with leasing the Herald Square island, bounded on one side by Sixth Avenue, on the other by Broadway. He could secure a ninety-nine-year lease on good terms, but he finally buckled at the thought of not owning the land. The African Methodist Church came to his rescue. It was abandoning its quarters on Thirty-Fifth Street, next to the northeast corner of Sixth Avenue, just across

Broadway and across Sixth from his present location at the Park.

Francis H. Kimball—supervisor of the Comique reconstruction and architect for the famous Madison Square Theatre—was instructed to duplicate the Comique, except in combustibility. As a result the New Harrigan Theatre outclassed all its competitors in fire prevention. An abundance of emergency exits. A sprinkler system and a large tank on the roof. Iron partitions and wide staircases constructed of iron and slate. Dressing rooms and main curtain thoroughly fireproofed. And the heating boiler installed outside the main building.

The facade was laid up in cream colored brick decorated with white Italian Renaissance terra cotta. (John Golden, the theatrical producer who built his own Broadway theatre in 1926, once said that if any bricks dropped on a critic the disaster should be credited to him. He had been an apprentice with Horgan and Slattery and had helped build the front wall.)[4] A small balcony and two side windows with plaster figures of Dan Mulligan and Pete overlooked the entry, and mounted above the Spanish tile roof were two flags: the Stars and Stripes and a "HARRIGAN" theatre banner.

The lobby floor was mosaic. The walls and ceiling were covered with ornamental plaster. At each end of the lobby, staircases led to the balcony. The side walls of the auditorium were light red, the ceiling pale blue, the carpets brown, and the chairs light blue. The six boxes—four adjoining the parquet and two at the balcony level —were decorated in ivory and gold. A central chandelier with forty-nine lights supplied most of the illumination. With comfortably wide seats, the theatre accommodated only 915 (parquet 375, $1.50; balcony 265, $.75–$1.00; gallery 275, $.25). The limited capacity provided the kind of snug congregation Harrigan preferred.[5]

Throughout its life as the Harrigan, the Garrick under Richard Mansfield, guest house for the famous Jacques Copeau company from Paris, and finally as the first home of the Theatre Guild, the theatre was praised for its simple charm, its unobstructed sightlines, and its remarkable acoustics. For more than twenty years, it was known as the best house on Broadway.

The Harrigan opening was announced for December 15, 1890,

shifted to the twenty-seventh, then to the twenty-ninth. On the eighteenth an auction of opening night tickets was held at the Madison Square Theatre and brought in $2,240. Front proscenium boxes went for $115 and most orchestra seats for $14.[6]

The promise of the advance sale was borne out on the twenty-ninth. By five o'clock the lineup for the gallery extended to Fifth Avenue. Seven minutes after the house opened at seven, the gallery was filled to capacity, and two eel-like youngsters snaked through the rows selling songbooks. A detail of police patrolled along Thirty-fifth and on Sixth Avenue. A black cat strayed in the stage door and was warmly welcomed.[7] Ushering the "high and low, great and small, classes and masses" into place until every seat and all standing room were occupied and getting all in order backstage took longer than announced, but when the musicians appeared just after nine and Braham entered the pit, the shouts and cheers bounced through the house. Even Ed King's xylophone solo got more than its usual applause.

The big tumult was, of course, reserved for the principals. Hands and throats were exhausted in welcoming Harrigan, in welcoming back Yeamans and Wild, and the long evening was regularly interrupted with spirited observations from the gallery. In the garden scene one of the "Gods" from the upper reaches announced that the champagne was "d' genuine boney fidey article, bein' cracked for luck on d' first night."[8] Bedtime was forgotten. The curtain did not go down until 12:30, and everyone stayed until Harrigan took his final curtain call.

Harrigan had hit the peak of his career with *Reilly and the Four Hundred,* with the Harrigan Theatre—"now the most American thing in America."[9] Few could have guessed that the play would outdistance all others with 200 performances in its first season, 136 in its second, that it would be his final big success, and that he would occupy his own theatre for only four seasons. It was a triumphant climax to his march from Corlear's Hook to Herald Square.

Harrigan's Irishmen had invaded lace-curtain country in earlier plays—where they had fruit in the house when no one was sick (Fred Allen's definition)—but Cordelia and friends had not mingled with the authentic swells, the social aristocracy of Ward McAllister's "Four Hundred." Four hundred, according to McAllister, because Delmonico's ballroom at Twenty-Sixth Street and Fifth Avenue accommodated that many.[10] Delmonico's was New York's bureau of social standards. McAllister reported regularly on the adventures of the "Four Hundred," and in *Society as I Have Found It,* which hit the bookstores just before the *Reilly* opening, he announced, "If you want to be fashionable, be always in the company of fashionable people."[11] Harrigan had selected a timely title.

He had also advanced his odds on success by bringing Annie Yeamans and Johnny Wild back into the fold, writing rich parts for everyone, and devising a new role for himself, Wily Reilly the pawnbroker. Harrigan had originally intended to make the character a Jewish pawnbroker named Cohen, but Annie vetoed the idea: "You've got to play the thing they think you are; and besides you can't open in my theatre as a Jew; don't forget I own it."[12] It was a persuasive argument. The theatre was in her name, even had her initials carved on the front of the building.

Wily Reilly (Harrigan) knows that there's "a wide margin between pawning a railroad and an eight-day clock," that there's something about his trade that "prevents a man from feeling easy in high society." Still, like so many immigrants, he has pushed his son Ned into the uptown world, sent him to law school, set him up in a Murray Hill apartment, and now poses as his uncle, Sir William Reilly, the baronet from Ballymacfuddy in the County Dow, to help him get the girl he loves. Reilly also wants to beat out Herman Smeltz (Fisher), who is also pursuing the girl. Smeltz is a former ship's butcher who was court-martialed and tattooed with a pig's snout for having stolen a pig. He now controls a sausage trust and moves in high society.

Reilly added two spectacular scenes to Harrigan's album: the Saloon Deck at the Lee Shore and Casey's Hall. Commodore Toby Tow, like the real-life rich eccentrics at Newport, has transformed his mansion into a ship. He says he got the idea from one of his friends who stripped his Newport cottage to make it look like a Seventh Regiment barracks. Toby's servants dress like sailors, race about ringing ship's bells and polishing brass, and one of

them, Salvator Maginis (Wild), a Negro from an Italian neighborhood, is so conditioned to life at sea that he can't sleep unless
someone's sloshing in the tub.

At the "Great Four-Hundred Ball" in the saloon, Reilly's house-
keeper (Yeamans) strides in posing as Lady Isabel Reilly, her
chest and neck encrusted with jewels. Herman Smeltz is decked
out in stiffly starched, full-dress clothes, but he has forgotten to
take off his overshoes. Sir William Reilly outclasses everyone. He's
garbed in a red sack coat, white silk vest, and lavender trousers,
and his fingers are blazing with diamonds. Harrigan had never
looked fancier. The costume does not, however, suppress Reilly's
pawnbroker instincts. He carefully fingers a lady's tiara and pronounces it eighteen carat. It could bring a good price.

The Coachman's Union dance at Casey's Hall explores another
facet of New York's social life, the downtown "Four Hundred" at
play: Firemen, sailors, coachmen, chippies, and toughs. A slumming party from uptown. A Negro band in gaudy uniforms. A
visitor from Troy who sings of his Gotham adventures in "Taking
in the Town." A bit of melee for the old-timers: Two beauties
battle over Salvator. One gets tossed through a window, the other
through the roof of a fruit stand. The pugnacious Billy Lynch, who
struts about in skintight pants bragging about his "tree knockouts
and a traw." He's eager to slap down anybody friendly enough to
ask his name. And, heading the list of the downtown celebrities,
Maggie Murphy and Kitty Lynch.

The revelation of low life was so startling, so true to life that
many crowded into Harrigan's theatre, not only to gape at the
upper crust at play, but to observe the toughs at close range without risking assault.[13]

Reilly probably would have caught on even without Harrigan's
newest sensations, the teenage chippies Maggie Murphy and Kitty
Lynch, played by Emma Pollock, age sixteen, and Ada Lewis,
seventeen. Emma's Maggie Murphy blew into Casey's "like a sweet
breath of air from over a meadow," and as she "stood ready to do
her jig dance surrounded by roughs, toughs, and fallen women, she
made you think of a little violet dropped among the weeds."[14]
Reporters could not control themselves. She was "like a little
bobolink fluttering down from a rose into a frog pond." Her prize

jig led into "Maggie Murphy's Home," Al Smith's favorite song, the favorite of all Irishmen who knew that "an organ in the parlor" *did* "give the house a tone."[15]

In the pawnshop Kitty Lynch drew more applause than Harrigan with much less to do and say. He never objected. He and Annie had discovered Ada Lewis among the supers in San Francisco. One night Annie had heard her backstage imitation of a "hoodlum girl." The next night Harrigan caught her improvised act and agreed that they should take her to New York.

He gave Broadway no advance notice of his treasure. When Kitty appeared at Reilly's pawnshop to retrieve the shoes her brother had pawned—dressed in a tight little jersey jacket, a long, shabby, patched skirt with frayed edges, a shapeless black hat pulled over her stringy hair, and her feet pushing out of torn shoes, stooping because she felt too tall for the part—shoved out her hand "with the peculiar tough-girl gesture," and whined, "Say, Reilly gimme me shoes!" cheers broke across the gallery, then descended to the balcony and orchestra. As the shouts continued, Harrigan sauntered to the wings and whispered to Annie, "The money's safe."[16]

One story of the opening night has been engraved in Harrigan folklore. With the ovation for her act-one bit, everyone backstage knew that the audience would demand Kitty's reappearance at the act-three ball. During the intermission Harrigan quickly wrote a few new lines. Annie Harrigan and Marietta Hanley found a gown and stripped themselves of their opening night jewelry.[17] The story can not be entirely apocryphal. The prompt scripts call for Kitty's entrance in a ballroom costume.

Kitty's sensation was not accidental. Harrigan had studied the tough girl in her native habitat: She lives in a tenement close to the dump; her parents are foreigners—Italians, Irish, or Hebrews. She has learned her speech from them, and like them has great difficulty with past tenses: "He brung it and when he bringed it I was sorry dat he brang it." Her peculiar "tough-girl gesture" gave the audience "an immediate flashlight picture of the entire characterization."[18]

With the double triumph, a new hit play in a new theatre, interviewers besieged Harrigan, asking him to update his thoughts on the theatre. As usual, he obliged. The reporters found him amazingly boyish offstage, his face smooth-shaven and sunburned, his "clear, blue eyes of Kilarney" always twinkling, his mouth twisting easily into a smile, and his slight twinge of a brogue turning the vowels to music.[19] He recognized that tastes in the theatre had changed, and he had tried to keep up but without bowing to the fad for exhibiting human flesh. Kitty might seem brazen, expose her ankles, and parts of her costume might fit snugly, but she kept her clothes on and in place. He had more respect for the public's demand for vim and vigor, touch and go, brisk crisp dialogue, and true-to-life acting. He abhorred the highfalutin affectation that prevailed among so many society actors. To demonstrate his point for one reporter, he got up and sat down stiffly on the edge of the chair, one hand on his knee and the other on his hip with the elbow pointing like an arrow. He held the ramrod pose for a moment and then said, "Now that's no way to do it. Nobody sits down like that."[20] He then plumped in the chair, dropped his arms, and leaned back as if to savor every ounce of comfort the chair provided. With so many artificial actors now on the stage, he said, he spent most of his rehearsal time trying to get people to act natural.

He admitted to one reporter that he gave the lion's share of a play to himself. After all, the public paid to see him, expected to see more of him than of the others. At the same time, he did not hesitate to put another man forward, as long as he didn't think he owned the show. He was sure that the success of *Reilly* did not depend entirely on the play. Theatregoers enjoyed comfortable chairs, good music, a well-dressed company, and the general luxury of a well-appointed theatre. The new Harrigan provided an abundance of comfort and luxury, plus extraordinary protection from fire.[21]

He advised young playwrights to read widely in Shakespeare, Molière, and Sheridan, but they must be careful not to plagiarize. The critics would be waiting for them if they did. When asked why he did not experiment with different kinds of plays, he explained that theatre experiments were too costly. No manager could ignore payday, and experiments did not pay salaries. He cherished the box office as his most trustworthy adviser.[22]

Hanley's box office glowed brightly straight through the season, and with the promise of renewed life for *Reilly* in the fall of 1891, the Harrigans took another step uptown to 236 West Forty-Fourth Street. The new place may have seemed dull and drab compared with the Perry house, but Ned and Eddie could walk to the theatre and Adelaide to Miss Bragg's School at the Broadway corner.

There were no additions to the family at the new address. After William's birth three years earlier, Annie had suffered such a severe case of childbed fever that the doctor had advised a lengthy recess from childbearing. He told Harrigan that Annie was like a young apple tree that had borne too much fruit. The Harrigans respected the doctor's admonition until they moved again three years later to 46 West Sixty-Eighth Street. Philip arrived at this new address so unexpectedly one evening that Annie had to excuse herself from a dinner party to accommodate him, and a year and a half after Philip, Nolan was born.[23] The Harrigan family was then completed, or so they both thought. Too much sadness then hung over the house to wish for more children.

Harrigan gave *Reilly* a clear field in the new season, holding off *The Last of the Hogans* until December 22. *Hogans* was the last of the old-time Harrigan plays. Its big scenes expanded on earlier extravaganzas.

Part of the Mystic Star initiation (a burlesque of the Knights Templars, Mystic Shriners, and Sons of Malta) had been used in *The Mulligans' Silver Wedding.* The "Floating Bethel" and the barge collision were borrowed from *Muddy Day.* The story that propels the play revolves around Hughey Hogan, a bricklayer. He's foxed his widow and relatives by sealing the Hogan pedigree and other family assets in a church cornerstone before he disappears, presumably to sea. In the final scene, he confounds everyone when he returns as a wild man from the Dime Museum dressed in "brown tights, brown knit undershirt, a short skirt with ball trimmings, big shoes with bead trimmings, red wig and red whiskers." Harrigan had an eye for odd sights.

The Knights of the Mystic Star are elegantly costumed for their initiation ceremony in blue jackets trimmed with spangles and stars; blue, knit kneebreeches; long, blue stockings; Zouave caps with tassels; and white, low-cut patent leather shoes. Before the ceremony they exchange derogatory observations on the Bleecker Street Italians and their secret society, the Mafia. Fortunately their razors are more lethal than stilettos, and, as their "most wise and sawed-off prophet" reminds them, Italians are "Rats," "Stars spelled backwards." At one moment when their lookout spots a police inspector, they all pick up tracts, sing a spiritual, "On de Rainbow Road," and assure the officer that they're holding a prayer meeting.

As they prepare for their victim, they march around the stage waving lanterns like Indian clubs and at regular intervals form the letters "S.T.A.R." Harrigan's prompt script supplied three pages of instructions for their maneuvers. Their initiation victim is Essau Coldstream's girl friend Augie, a "femme du chamber," ahead of her time: "I sweep tapestry, dust velvet, and polish de ivories of de piano. I *scrub* nuffin'!" She's led over rubber balloons, rolled in a tub until she's seasick, marched over the backs of the Knights, and just as she's being lifted to the throne and declared a member of "de side degree of de silver garter," the Floating Bethel is rammed by the Mohawk, sending bodies in the air, splashing in the river, and bouncing on the deck.[24]

The new melee hung on until April 16, when *Reilly* returned for a final stand. Two plays had filled the season and filled the theatre. It was Harrigan's last solid season. During the next year, good fortune began to slip away. For the first time since he began the Mulligan saga, there was no new Harrigan play, and the old favorites—*Squatter Sovereignty, Mulligan Guard Ball, Cordelia's Aspirations,* and *Reilly*—had to be shifted in and out in quick order to keep the theatre open. Even the weather and the civic watchdogs were uncooperative.

When he revived *Dan's Tribulations* (August 28, 1893), he was assaulted by the heat and attacked by the Society for the Prevention of Cruelty to Children. The *Evening Sun* reported that the humidity did not favor burnt cork. Before Johnny Wild had got through the funeral scene, he had almost turned white again, and the complexion of Reverend Palestine Puter's bride was not blessed with fast colors either. "Before the wedding was consummated the bride's white garments and wedding veil had taken on an ebony edge."[25] Harrigan observed the bleaching and with his "old familiar bow and scrape of the foot, the familiar side-long swing of his left arm, stepped forward and said, 'I thank you for this warm reception.' "26

Harrigan had crossed swords with the Society for the Prevention of Cruelty to Animals in the past, and with Henry Bergh, its founder and president. Bergh had objected to horses, donkeys, and geese being corrupted by the stage, and he particularly objected to the cats in the Mulligan Guard's chowder pot who invariably got singed by the footlights. He had not pressed his objections, partly because he knew that Harrigan was born within a block of his father's old shipyard, and he himself had laughed too uproariously the night a horse had fallen through the stage and had to be hoisted out with a derrick. Commodore Elbridge Thomas Gerry, grandson of Vice-President Elbridge Gerry, who had joined Bergh in founding the Society for the Prevention of Cruelty to Children in 1874, was less generous. He tried to prohibit Harrigan from using his son Willie in *Dan's Tribulations.* When Harrigan explained to Acting Mayor George McClellan that the youngster was only on stage for three minutes with no words to say and that he was home in bed by nine, he got a permit, augmented with cease and desist orders for Gerry. The *Spirit of the Times* advised the commodore to stick to his business, the America's Cup Race, and figure out how to beat Lord Dunraven.27

When a new play, *The Woollen Stocking,* finally appeared in October, 1893, Harrigan's friends detected little of the old Harrigan and quickly let it expire. Stalking the ownership certificate for the "Woollen Stocking," a Pennsylvania coal mine, did not arouse much excitement, and only the authenticity of the Jewish colony in Hester Street, Harrigan's stevedore boss, and Wild's fish peddler received favorable notice. (Only part of the manuscript, in Harrigan's deteriorating handwriting, has survived.)

Just before Christmas Harrigan revived *Old Lavender,* in January *The Leather Patch,* and after a final week of *The Woollen Stocking,* he closed the Harrigan Theatre and took to the road: to Bridgeport, Boston, Philadelphia, and in April, a two-week stand at an off-Broadway outpost, the Harlem Opera House on One Hundred Twenty-Fifth Street.

The Harrigan Theatre was leased for the spring months to

Pauline Hall's Opera Company, with Pauline struggling to conceal her shapely figure. She appeared as Prince Raphel in Offenbach's *The Princess of Trebizonde*. In the fall only one tenant could be found for the Harrigan, *Man without a Country* by James W. Harkins, Jr., and that for only a single week.

20

Flat Broke in Tacoma

The financial panic of 1893, with banks closed and railroads going bankrupt, as well as the failure of *Woollen Stocking,* drove Harrigan to the provinces and kept him away from the city until December 1894. Sometime in the spring, while he was on tour, he apparently speculated on going to England or Australia, but he never got beyond speculating. According to one reporter, "sensible Harrigan has changed his mind about going abroad."[1] In the summer he returned to San Francisco—this time at the California Theatre—with *Reilly, Cordelia's Aspirations, Old Lavender,* and *The Mulligan Guard Ball,* and with the family supporting him offstage and on. Adelaide retained vivid memories of this visit, of the Sunday mornings when she attended mass with Aunt Marietta and stared at the painted ladies on Dupont Street (now Grant). She invariably got whacked with a prayer book and advised to keep her eyes to herself. She remembered the backstage battles with the property man over the doughnuts reserved for use in Pop's waterfront cafe and the night she went onstage as an alley urchin in *Cordelia's Aspirations.* After the "Dad's Dinner Pail" number she took off her slipper, spat on the sole, and threw it at Dan. She had seen the business often enough to know exactly what she was supposed to do. Her father picked up the shoe, picked her up, and bowing to the audience, whispered in her ear, "Turn your face front, darling, smile a little and throw a kiss with your fingers."[2]

Taking a bow did not come naturally to her. She retired from the stage after her debut performance.

Eddie had begun appearing fairly regularly. He had been in *Reilly* the previous spring in Boston and with some success, according to his own report. He had written to his mother that he'd made a hit, and it was not just because the "suit looked great."[3] In San Francisco Harrigan had begun a new play, *Notoriety,* and was writing a rah-rah college boy part especially for Eddie. He said that if Eddie, or any of the children, wanted to follow in his footsteps, he would give all the help he could, providing he saw a glimmer of talent. Sure the stage was a tough life, but as he told one reporter, "the people connected with the theatre are liberal, generous to a fault, and kind-hearted, and on the whole it's a pleasant life even with the ups and downs."[4] Eddie seemed drawn to the stage, just as he himself had been at Eddie's age. He was not going to push him away, though he did try to slip him some advice via a newspaper story. Harrigan told a reporter that he would like to see Eddie out front. "He'd make a great theatre business man."[5]

Eddie must have taken the advice without abandoning his role as an actor. When *Notoriety* was tried out in Philadelphia in November, prior to New York—an innovation for Harrigan— Eddie wrote to his mother that he and Pop had been figuring how they could bring expenses down to $2,500 or maybe even $100 less than that. Costs had to be cut.[6] As it turned out, *Notoriety* needed more than economy. When it reached New York, it survived at the Harrigan for only sixty-four performances.

At the opening night on December 10, 1894, Harrigan was welcomed back to Broadway with the strongest ovation he had ever had and with so many flowers that the theatre looked like Covent Garden. Florists must have sold out their entire stock. During the first two acts, ushers raced up and down the aisles carrying baskets as big as themselves, and when Harrigan stepped through the display to offer his thanks, he looked "as bright as ever, frisky as a youngster, and brimming with good humor."[7] It was a happy night for everyone.

The next day a few critics dampened the opening night euphoria. The *New York Times* thought that Harrigan had exhausted his old material without conquering any new field. Another reported that Ned had lost his old confidence; the prompter had to throw him his own words.[8] But most were friendly, delighting in the old Harrigan touches and discovering some new pleasures. Eddie, Jr., taller and handsomer than his father and an excellent young lover, executes some astonishing fancy dancing when he joins his Yale and Harvard chums after the game at the Burnt Rag. He is a "dancing fool." There are other diversions in the dingy Tenderloin barroom: David Braham, Jr., as a Negro wench named Linda Linseed. Wild as Mealy Moon, a pugilist trainer and bodyguard for the German millionaire Fred Hoffman (Fisher), who has been threatened by a mythical mob of anarchists. Some turns are deliciously vulgar: The saucy girls with their "swaggering airs." The drunken crones from Cherry Hill reeling through the slums with sunshine in their hearts and maudlin tears dripping from their eyes as they sing about their mothers.

As in *Reilly,* New York low life gives way to gaudier and classier scenes. This time at Barney (Harrigan) Dolan's Road House and Molly Malone's lawn at Saratoga. Molly (Yeamans), grown rich selling junk and playing the horses, has sunk her fortune into stocks and a Saratoga racing stable. (Molly was modeled on the wealthy eccentric Hetty Green, then known as the richest woman in America and as the "witch of Wall Street." Although Hetty's fortune was said to have hit $100 million ten years before her death in 1916, she wore old, ragged clothes, carried odd bits of food in pockets hidden around her skirt, lived in a run-down boardinghouse, and went to a charity clinic for medical care.)[9]

Again, as in *Investigation,* Harrigan's favorite pair turned to Shakespeare. Molly's Saratoga lawn became the Forest of Arden for Harrigan's Touchstone and Yeaman's Audrey, but even their most ardent admirers admitted that their *As You Like It* did not match their burlesque of *Romeo and Juliet.* It was difficult to burlesque Touchstone and Audrey. Shakespeare himself had carried them too far in that direction.

Except for the Comique fire, good fortune seemed to have guarded Harrigan's career at every turn. Now Lady Luck seemed to be veering away, and on February 17, 1895, while he was appearing again as Major Gilfeather, she deserted him completely.

Eddie, Jr., not yet eighteen, died of peritonitis. According to an often repeated family story, the news of his death reached the theatre during the interval before the third act, and the audience departed quietly, unwilling to face Harrigan when he came back on.

On an earlier night in February, Eddie had returned from the theatre—he was appearing as Granville Bright in *The Major*—complaining of a chill and a pain in his right side. Adelaide was ordered to crank the iron gadget on the wall to summon a Western Union boy to be sent for the doctor. The doctor diagnosed Eddie's sickness as an aftermath of the typhoid fever he had had when he was nine and prescribed hot flaxseed poultices. For three days Annie heated the flaxseed in a small tin pot over an alcohol lamp for the hourly applications. When the illness persisted, two consultants were called, and Annie, exhausted by her nursing and watching Eddie fade with pain, screamed, "My God! My God! Save my son! Save my son!"[10] It was too late. The hot poultices had aggravated the infection. He died within a few hours of a perforated appendix and peritonitis.

The story about the theatre audience, though not true—Eddie died on a Sunday—reflects the devotion of Harrigan's friends and the love they knew he held for his son. Ned and Annie had suffered through infant mortality, accepting that burden as the inescapable curse of parenthood. Losing a seventeen year old, the light of his father's life, his professional heir apparent, tore a wound into their hearts that never completely healed. Among the many friends who comforted them, none shared their loss more completely than Annie Yeamans. Not only had she loved Eddie as her own son, but just two years earlier, during the run of *Last of the Hogans*, she had lost her daughter Emily.

Harrigan endured playing *The Major* for another week, then closed the theatre. He was convinced that actor-managers were an obsolete breed, that only speculative, hardheaded business managers could now succeed. His views did not, however, deter him from leasing the "daintiest and prettiest theatre in the city"[11] to another actor-manager, Richard Mansfield. Mansfield had been appearing in Shaw's *Arms and the Man* at the nearby Herald Square Theatre (Harrigan's Park). Unfortunately Harrigan had failed to negotiate the name of the theatre into the lease. Mansfield discovered that by substituting *G* for *H* and altering the final three letters, he could open *Arms and the Man* on April 23 (Shakespeare's birthday) in the "Garrick" Theatre. Harrigan and the press were incensed at Mansfield's insensitivity, attaching an English name to America's most distinguished playhouse.

The spring's sadness did not pass easily. In the summer, Harrigan and Dave Braham, Jr., went to Europe, their first trip abroad. In London they took bed-and-breakfast rooms in Craven Street, and Harrigan roamed the streets day and night digging about in the city's low life. If he had done for New York what Dickens had done for London, as some reporters claimed, he wanted to see for himself. In Paris he practiced his French, stopping to ask directions even when he knew or didn't want to know them, and found his French met the challenge. In Ireland he discovered a multitude of Harrigans and Mulligans. They looked familiar, but he did not trouble them. He settled for a bit of Ireland to take back home with him: a corduroy suit tailored in Dublin with huge patch pockets on the coat (the big one in the rear meant for pheasants) and breeches that fastened at the knee with buckles. When he came down the plank from the Cunard liner in September, Annie asked if he was proposing to revive *The Lorgaire*.[12]

They were all glad to be back together in New York. The family summer at Schroon had not been happy. It couldn't be, without Ned, and it was the first summer without Eddie. Annie had even omitted her visit to the Saratoga dentist.

As the joy of reunion erased the memories of a sad summer, it also helped to soften the blow of moving to a new location. Annie had found less expensive quarters for them farther uptown, at 122 West One Hundred Thirteenth Street, just off Lenox Avenue. Ned accepted the change philosophically. As always, he trusted Annie's judgment about such matters.

Their stay in Harlem did not last long. Within a year Annie discovered that they could live better in Brooklyn and for less money. She found a four-story house at 310 Park Place that was sturdy and pleasant. It had floors, cabinets, and mantels of yellow oak, and shiny marble fireplaces. Best of all it was in a quiet and respectable neighborhood, just off Vanderbilt Street and two short blocks from Prospect Park, Brooklyn's challenge to Central Park.[13] And the journey to the city was not difficult: the trolley from Park Place to City Hall Park for the Ninth Avenue El to the West Side, or changing at the Brooklyn Bridge for the Third Avenue El to the East Side.

Harrigan's next season in the theatre (1895–1896) was the slowest since he had begun at the Olympic in San Francisco. He had only a few weeks of *Old Lavender* in Philadelphia, Boston, and Brooklyn before he retreated to Schroon. The evenings were loneliest. His long, steady routine of going to a theatre somewhere almost every night of his life was difficult to break. As he once said, the accumulation of money had never driven him to the theatre. He simply had to be onstage: "I love it. I love the dressing room, the shop talk with old associates. I'm only happy when I face the public."[14]

He continued to write constantly, as he always had, though with less assurance that the characters would ever mount the stage. Four plays of the nineties—*The Blue Ribbon* (1894), *My Son Dan* (1895), *Low Life* (1897), and *An Old New Yorker* (1899) —were copyrighted, but only *My Son Dan* was ever played and that for only a few nights in Brooklyn in the spring of 1896.[15]

Harrigan spent the summer of 1896 working on "The Memoirs of Mulligan," later to be published as *The Mulligans,* and on a play that would reach the stage, though not in his theatre. He would never perform in his own theatre again, but the Harrigans depended on rent from the Garrick for a substantial part of their income.

Marty Malone—the manuscript is dedicated to his daughter Adelaide—opened at the Bijou Theatre (Thirty-First and Broadway) on August 31, 1896, and held on for only a month, a low point in the Harrigan record. Hanley tried to stir up interest with an "affadavit" declaring that "Harrigan and his company are still alive and well, even if not in their own theatre."[16] Harrigan rehearsed the play as if anticipating a hit. In mid-August a visitor said that he had never seen more spirited rehearsals: "Harrigan is a painstaking stage manager, working every day of the week from eleven till four, and often spending an hour over the smallest detail."[17] Later Harrigan admitted that he produced the play against Annie's advice: "It was a mistake. When I have listened to my wife, I have always done the right thing. This time I didn't listen."[18]

Marty Malone, a hearty old salt who has deserted the sea, befriends a homeless waif who makes a hit as a music hall singer and then turns out to be an heiress and marries a lord. The subplot tracks Marty from Sally Jordan's Sailors' Lodging House to Marie Pinto's handsome apartment on Riverside Drive and to her country house and grounds at Whitestone, Long Island. Marie is the leader of the Cuban cause in New York, but it is her exotic beauty rather than her political charisma that has charmed Marty.[19]

The critics were not kind to *Marty*. Many thought that Harrigan had lost much of his "huge animal spirits of comicality."[20] Only a few bits deserved the laughs they provoked: The sanitation man who cleans statues and falls off Columbus's neck, "de Italian that found America and left it to his relations." Marty's boast of his Irish luck: "I was cast away on a Friday and fish don't eat meat on that day." In the final days of the run, the newspapers announced that Harrigan would not be seen in the city for some time, and at the last performance, as if to assure him that the waterfront crowd would not forget him, the New York Pilot's Association bought out all the main-floor seats.

Harrigan did not have a new play or a regular Broadway engagement for the next six years, though he was not sunning himself in Prospect Park. He was racing across the country, filling more short engagements and one-nighters than in his early barnstorming days and only occasionally returning for a breather at home and a week or two playing in Brooklyn or Williamsburgh and for limited engagements in New York, at the Murray Hill, People's, and Third Avenue theatres.

During the first road season (1896–1897), with Dave Braham, Jr., replacing Hanley as manager—Hanley had joined Robert Mantell's Shakespeare company—he concentrated on New England, upstate New York, New Jersey, and Pennsylvania, playing in such unlikely spots as Torrington, Turner's Falls, Lewiston, Ogensburgh, and Allentown. He began with *Marty Malone,* then quickly shifted to his old standby *Old Lavender.*

Someone had suggested that Harrigan move along with the times and try the new vaudeville that was doing so well at Oscar Hammerstein's Manhattan Opera House and at Koster and Bial's, though Koster's had recently augmented its programs with that latest eye-straining novelty, the moving pictures. His response to that suggestion appeared in the *New York Dramatic Mirror*: "No vaudeville for Harrigan—It's all guff. When the hunt began, I was in at the birth. Some will remember my early plays were often called Harrigan vaudevilles. I don't propose to be in at the death."[21]

In the spring he had changed his tune. The *Dramatic Mirror* now announced: "The latest and perhaps the most important capture for vaudeville ranks is Edward Harrigan whom Robert Grau has induced to play a season of eight weeks in a sketch of his own with music by Dave Braham."[22] The engagement began on May 3, 1897, at Proctor's Twenty-Third Street Theatre (just off Sixth Avenue), with Harrigan as the headliner in the twelfth and final act. The program began at noon and continued until 11:00 P.M.: "Come at any time. Remain as long as you please."

Harrigan must have felt that he had come full circle, even if the new artists with whom he shared the stage paled in comparison with his first associates at the old Comique. Only three acts could have qualified for Josh Hart's bill: The "Great American Female Baritone, Emilie Edwards." Henry Lee and his living statues, "Great Men Past and Present," thirteen of them, including Shakespeare, Bismarck, and General Grant. And Heath and Silbor with their burlesque sword combats and gun drills. They were feeble imitators of the Mulligan Guard.[23]

Ordinarily big names were thought not to effect the vaudeville box office. Grau gambled that Harrigan's name would and risked $750 a week on his star, an unheard-of salary for a vaudevillian. Grau was right. Harrigan's army of followers had such a "warm place in their hearts for the man who has done so much to lighten their cares and make them forget their troubles"[24] that they crowded the house at every performance at Proctor's, at Koster's, at Gilmore's in Philadelphia, at Tony Pastor's both in July and again in September, when he shared the Pastor program with the "new and highly interesting views by Lumiere's Cinematographe."[25]

Harrigan's vaudeville sketch *Sergeant Hickey,* featuring Dave

Braham, Jr., his sister Rose Braham, and Harry Fisher, was a condensed version of *The Grip,* with Harrigan playing an Irishman and a German. His old routine.

Harrigan wrote three other vaudeville sketches, which were never produced: *The New Butler,* about a husband who loves target shooting and a wife who's entranced by an effeminate interior decorator. *Darcy McGlone* and *The Compact,* different versions of the same sketch, satirized vaudeville: Garrick Montravers writes dramas while you wait, loves stage realism, real money, real suppers. He once played in *The Black Crook* with real crooks. He's condensed *Hamlet* to twenty minutes for a G.A.R. benefit, built a tank for a celebrated actor to dive into and remain under water, and he's dismayed with his partner, a monkey who can talk but won't. The monkey's afraid that they'll put a shovel in his hands and put him to work on the subway. Another sketch, *Larry Logan,* in which Harrigan appeared for two weeks at Proctor's in mid-February 1899, has not survived. It apparently included the *Romeo and Juliet* burlesque, though without Yeamans.

After fulfilling his contract with Grau, Harrigan persuaded Yeamans to rejoin him in *The Grip,* the long version, and after a week at the Third Avenue Theatre (just above Thirtieth), they took it on the road, to Pittsburgh, Johnstown, Lancaster, and Harrisburg, but without arousing enough enthusiasm to sustain them. Harrigan canceled the tour, compressed *Old Lavender* so that it could be played by twelve actors, without Yeamans, and after Christmas headed west through New York, Pennsylvania, and Ohio to Chicago and then to San Francisco. It was like the early years of touring with Hart when they were building their reputation. Now, more than twenty years later, he was back where he had begun. And though the press cheered him as they always had, too often now they found it necessary to defend him: No one would guess that he was nearing fifty-five. His hoarseness was merely a temporary affliction; he had caught a cold.

In Chicago in March, Harrigan received word that his old friend Johnny Wild had died at Troy, that Annie had sent white roses and attended the funeral at the Little Church around the Corner. None of the old crowd were with him on the road. Gray, Bradley, Hart, and now Wild would never be again. He was in Tacoma when he got a report about a benefit for Wild's widow. Annie Yeamans and Harry Fisher had appeared in a scene from *Cordelia's Aspirations* and Ada Lewis had done the tough-girl bit from *Reilly*. He was comforted to know that Harrigan had been represented at the tribute to Johnny Wild. He had found little comfort in the Northwest Territory. From Victoria, he wrote to Annie: "We squeezed out of Tacoma flat broke."[26] He was glad to abandon the road and return to Schroon.

He now found more pleasure in the summers than in earlier years, when he had never escaped the enlarging shadow of the fall's opening night. Every morning he walked to the village. It was his duty to check that all the houses were still there. He spent long days in his boat pretending to fish, killed an occasional deer "by proxy," never trimmed trees or mowed grass. He was "a philanthropist in his farming," reserving such tasks for friends and neighbors.[27] One summer Billy Burke, Annie's sister Adelaide's husband, attacked the trees with a vengeance, felling one monster near the house that crashed through the kitchen. When Annie asked Ned what he was going to say to Billy, he replied, "Nothing! What can one say to a man who's smashed half your house?"[28]

In the fall of 1898 he was on the road again, this time back to *The Mulligan Guard Ball,* and for almost a month in San Francisco. To augment the Skidmores' swift descent through the ceiling, he introduced a three-round boxing exhibition between the world's champion Robert Fitzsimmons and his sparring partner Yank Kenn. And to forestall the enormous excitement that he knew would be generated by the pugilists, the program cautioned the audience that "cat calls, whistling and stamping of feet are positively prohibited."[29] He had resurrected *The Ball* to alert the public to his book *The Mulligans,* which was about to appear. Of the two-million-plus words he had written, these were the only Harrigan words to get into print.

The Mulligans, published in 1901 and "Dedicated to the Memory of Tony Hart," divided the Mulligan adventures into three "books" (451 pages, fifty-four chapters), with illustrations by L. F. A. Lorenz: Skidmores dropping through the ceiling at the Harp and Shamrock; Cordelia passing out on the floor while Rebecca examines the bottle.[30] The three books, roughly approximating the contents of *The Mulligan Guard Ball, Cordelia's*

Aspirations, and *Dan's Tribulations* with episodes from other plays interjected here and there, were aimed at both old friends of the Mulligans and Broadway newcomers who had only heard the Mulligan name. Some Mulligan family details were pinpointed as if Harrigan were sharing inside information: Mulligan's Alley was really at the Five Points. Cordelia has been in America for twenty years. Walsingham McSweeney was the first man Dan met in New York. The Harp and Shamrock, on Bleecker Street near Minetta Lane, housed Snuff McIntosh's Last Call Beanery on the ground floor. And in the final pages Harrigan brought the Mulligans up to date. Tommy and Kitty have returned with a "baker's dozen of children" and moved into Cordelia's Madison Avenue house, and Dan and Cordelia have retired to a country cottage somewhere above the Harlem River and on Sundays take the trolley to the city to visit their grandchildren.

In the turn-of-the-century years Harrigan took another turn at vaudeville with *Larry Logan* and an abbreviated *McSorley's Inflation,* a few New England performances of *Old Lavender,* an Elks benefit in Boston, and he talked briefly about taking *Old Lavender* to London. In December 1901, he put on his "Uncle Pete" burnt cork and replaced Wilton Lackaye as Uncle Tom (Yeamans played Aunt Ophelia) at the Grand Opera House in a one-week revival of the spectacular William A. Brady production of *Uncle Tom's Cabin.* Harrigan was not entirely off the mark when he told friends that he had been forgotten around Broadway. The *Times* could muster no more Harrigan copy than: "He's a feature of special interest."[31]

In the spring he returned to San Francisco for six weeks at the Grand Opera House with *Old Lavender, Reilly,* and *Waddy Googan.* San Francisco remembered and welcomed him with an ovation and sweet words in the press. Ashton Stevens wrote: "He brings back memories of a world that seems a century old—tears for the ne'er-do-well whether called Rip or Old Lavender. The house was ready to share the boozy emotions of this warm-hearted old reprobate, as if whiskey were the milk of human kindness."[32] In the 1890s San Francisco saw more of Harrigan than did New York.

The next year he was back on Broadway and again in an unfamiliar role, in a play written by someone else.[33] This time he was reassured that he had not been forgotten. He appropriated almost all the favorable notices while Clyde Fitch, then Broadway's hottest playwright, gathered only a few crumbs. *Bird in the Cage* was declared an impossible play, weighted with false sentiment, cheap claptrap, hideous pathos. *"Bertha the Sewing Machine Girl* was a model transcript from life in comparison."[34] At the Boston Museum tryout Harrigan was greeted with wild rejoicing, and in New York at the Bijou on January 12, 1903, the audience applauded his entrance for five minutes in spite of the ushers' attempts to subdue them. He appeared as Michael O'Brien, a congenial labor agitator who loves whiskey and conversation. "Harrigan arrived in the first act just in time to stop the yawning and after he departed in the third, the audience should have departed. He knows how to live on the stage; he is as virile, spontaneous, and free of stage tricks as ever, and his soft oily brogue has lost none of its sweet music."[35] The critics were unanimous in their "Hurrah for Harrigan." Max Beerbohm, who came one night with Fitch, remembered Harrigan's walk, "as if threading his way among broken bits of glass, don't you know—at once comic and extraordinarily graceful."[36]

When Fitch's play closed, Harrigan had a play of his own in the works, and on April 8, he signed a contract with the producers Theodore A. Liebler and George C. Tyler. He was to approve all actors; manage the stage; have his name starred on all announcements; receive $150 per week starting with rehearsals plus 50 percent of the net profits. Some press stories intimated that the theatre would be renamed the Harrigan, but the Murray Hill (at Lexington and Forty-Second) retained its own name throughout the run.[37]

Under Cover, called "Bird in Hand" in an early draft, ranged over an expansive panorama. Harrigan had not subdued his generosity. There were five New York locales. It took thirty-five actors, six supers, and just under three hours to perform and included an old-fashioned Harrigan melee. A packed trolley car rolls to center stage, stops with a jerk, and pitches the female straphangers into a mound. The seats were all occupied by men. (Mark Twain once said that, if a man gave his place to a lady, "the act betrayed, like spoken words, that he was from the provinces.")[38]

Harrigan, looking like another Reilly in tight trousers, a double-breasted frock coat, auburn wig, and high black hat, played Owney Gilmartin. Gilmartin is a pool hall proprietor and political boss of his "Tower of Babel" district, where the Irish flag floats from the top of the flagpole and dead men retain the right to vote. Yeamans, equally elegant in a blue and white gown, appears as Owney's partner and sweetheart, Dixie Merryall. She manipulates the racing crowd and in one scene plays on their weakness for religion and pretty girls. She appears as a Salvation Army lass, an emissary from the Hope Mission. Dixie is trying to acquire five acres at Willow Run to expand her racetrack, but she has strong opposition. The Native Sons of Manhattan desperately need the land for their cemetery. Their Brudder Bullhead froze to death in July in a cold-storage warehouse and is threatening to thaw.

Under Cover sported a rich collection of fresh types: an English dude with a monocle, a white-haired bluegrass horseman from Lexington, and a "Black swell" in patent leather and diamonds at the track. (For the first time Harrigan referred to Negroes as blacks.) And the New Waldorf Astoria Lodging House, not to be confused with the original—"a room at de new Waldorf is ten cents a night, and de old Waldorf costs you ten dollars a minute, and dat's de difference between capital and labor"—accommodated a brotherhood of derelicts: A long-haired anarchist in a slouch hat with papers bulging from his pockets, presumably modeled on Herr Johann Most, the German-American anarchist who had been jailed for rejoicing at the assassination of McKinley. A fat, little man with sagging suspenders. A consumptive in a red wig. An effeminate young man who chases an imaginary bird. A Chinaman who plucks an Oriental harp. This sad crew is kept in line by the posters on the hotel lobby's wall:

> Use the Cuspadores [*sic*]
> Ice Water 2 Cents Extra
> Keep Boots Off Beds
> Pillows 5 Cents Extra
> Don't Blow Out The Gas

And their "Lower-Depths," "Iceman-Cometh" tedium is relieved only once when Boozie Susie (Jennie Yeamans), "a type of fallen woman with her face showing traces of beauty," sings "The Fringe of Society." As with Kitty in *Reilly,* Harrigan restricted Susie to a single scene, a parsimonious trick he said he had learned from Shakespeare. Why had Shakespeare disposed of Mercutio so early? Simply because Romeo could not compete with that flamboyant swashbuckler![39]

The critics praised Harrigan for flashing sunbeams on this gloomy, sordid place. Again he had shown that no one "even in the most advanced school of realism possesses his lambent cunning in raising the crude canvas of the low-life world to the dignity of a genre painting."[40] Only Alan Dale complained about the sordidness: The theatre demanded "intelligible people speaking in a nice intelligible way, for the sake of the nice, intelligent people who go to the theatre in their best bibs and tuckers."[41] Harrigan did not subscribe to such refinements. To be sure, "human life in all its pathos cannot be placed within the painted wings naked and shivering, but a sympathetic dramatist sure of his art can, by dextrous means, present the partial and pleasant views and retain the truth of sweet reasonableness."[42] That was his aim.

Under Cover was a comfortable family affair with Annie Yeamans and her daughter Jennie, Joe Sparks, Dan Collyer, Harry Fisher, George L. Stout, two of Wild's children and two of Braham's—Ida in the cast and George composing the music and directing the orchestra. George Braham later succeeded his father at Wallack's Theatre, became David Belasco's musical director, and though his career did not match his father's, he never got the theatre out of his blood. When Joshua Logan produced *Mister Roberts* in 1948, George and his sister Rose were invited to a special preview. They came, and George continued to come. Years later the Logans learned that George had taken the subway from Harlem to Times Square every night for four years, just to watch the *Mister Roberts* crowds.[43]

When *Under Cover* opened on September 14, 1903, after tryouts in Bridgeport and Boston, Harrigan knew that he was not forgotten. The *New York Times* reporter wrote that he had never heard such applause: "forte, with all loud pedals working; such a continuous love feast we thought the play would never get started."[44] Although Harrigan had announced that the theatre had been leased for the season and optioned for the next, when business began to fade, he scheduled the souvenir program night at the fiftieth performance mark—he could not risk waiting for the hundredth—and the next week supplemented *Under Cover* with Vesta Tilley, "London's Idol," a male impersonator whose repertoire of cutaway coats and hunting jackets attracted more attention than her singing. One reporter hoped that Harrigan's run "would be prolonged under cover of Miss Tilley's London costumes."[45] It was prolonged until November 28, when the curtain rang down on Harrigan's thirty-third and final play to reach the stage.

On December 5, an unidentified newspaper item reported that Harrigan had contracted with James Reardon to manage the theatre at the St. Louis Exposition and star in a season of Irish plays, opening with *The Lorgaire*.[46] Nothing more was heard of this project.

21

"Goodbye, Ned, and Good Luck"

During the next few seasons Harrigan scattered his engagements between suburban and second-class New York theatres: New Rochelle, Yorkville, the American (Eighth Avenue at Forty-Second), and the Metropolis (One Hundred Forty-Second and Third Avenue), where orchestra seats went for twenty-five cents and the balcony for fifteen cents. He launched occasional forays into New England and upstate New York, playing *Old Lavender,* sometimes *Waddy Googan* and *Squatter Sovereignty,* and at least twice, a new sketch, *The Simple Life* (also called *The Village*), extolling the virtues of country living.[1] These spasmodic and unrewarding engagements did not boost his spirits. Nor did the intimations of mortality that struck rapidly in 1905. He lost his two most valued friends. When contemporaries begin to go, the road ahead never looks bright.

For years he had spent most of his waking hours with David Braham or with Martin Hanley. Braham died in April, Hanley in September, and both funerals were held at the Braham home, 75 West One Hundred Thirty-First. Braham's ceremony was the more impressive. His old musician friends, augmented by the orchestra from Wallack's Theatre, where he had been conducting, and fifteen brass players from the Arschenbroedel Verein, directed by his xylophonist Edward King, played Chopin's *Funeral March* as they led the Braham procession to the All Saints Roman Catholic Church at One Hundred Twenty-Ninth and Madison.[2]

If Harrigan was tempted to stay in Brooklyn and guard his remaining years by being careful, he resisted that temptation. He took *Old Lavender* on the road and, because Dave Braham, Jr., had deserted him in favor of a Broadway engagement, he took his son William out of the military academy at Cornwall and enlisted him as Dick the Rat (Hart's role). Years later, near the close of his own career in the theatre, William said that he wished he'd rebelled and stayed in school. If he had, he might now have a dollar left in his pocket.

William had tried the theatre earlier under his father's tutelage. He made his debut in *Dan's Tribulations* and when he was only five appeared in *Reilly,* sporting long, golden curls, racing after a ball he rolled on stage, and inquiring if Reilly had seen it. On his first night the applause stopped him in his tracks, and when his father muttered, "Bow, you damned fool! Don't freeze, you so and so,"[3] the playwright's lines evaporated and William was obliged to invent his own speech. "I waited in the wings," Bill recalled later, "for Papa to come over and kick me in the buttside which he always did when I made a mistake. Instead he turned to Mrs. Yeamans and said, 'What do you think of the little mug, ad libbing at five!' "[4]

His father's lessons in acting were never forgotten. Harrigan once told his son to go to Wallack's to watch a particular actor, to "study everything he does." When William returned and assured his tutor that he'd catalogued every moment, every inflection, his father told him, "Remember all those things and never do any of them."[5] Better to learn from a bad example than to struggle for a second-rate imitation of a good one.

When the *Old Lavender* tour began, the negotiations between the new partners were handled with great solemnity. Harrigan addressed his son as "Mr. Harrigan" and after outlining his duties informed him that his weekly salary would be ten dollars. A month later, while they were still circling the outlying theatres around Manhattan, Charles Frohman offered William fifteen dollars to appear in a new Broadway play. Bill conveyed the news to his father, informing him that if young Mr. Harrigan were to remain with *Old Lavender* he would have to have a salary that matched Frohman's offer. Harrigan contemplated his decision for an unbearable five minutes and then exclaimed, "Who put you up to this?" The question came too quickly. Bill was unprepared. He blurted out, "Mama!"[6] Harrigan gave him the raise and the next year advanced his weekly stipend to thirty dollars.

Ned Harrigan would have been proud to know that other managers later rewarded his son more handsomely. William remained in the theatre and motion pictures until his death in 1966. He played the title role in O'Neill's *Great God Brown* at the Garrick (formerly Harrigan!). Later he was in Joshua Logan's *Mister Roberts,* and when he played Bothwell in Maxwell Anderson's *Mary of Scotland,* one critic wrote: "He cannot make the slightest movement on stage without creating an effect of significance and emotional power."[7]

One evening shortly before his death, his sister Nedda caught him in a singing mood and spun her tape recorder. Bill knew the rhythmic swing of his father's songs—he'd sung along with him too many times to ever forget—and hearing the tape now, one cannot miss the magic of the Harrigan-Braham songs, the magic that brought them such incredible popularity. The lyrics and music simply hang in the ear until one begins to sing, or whistle, or at least hum.

William cherished the memory of his father, was delighted to be told that he had his old man's mannerisms. He once said, "There was nothing connected with the theatre my father didn't know, nothing he wasn't capable of doing."[8] But in 1906, yanked out of school and not certain he really wanted to be an actor, he regarded his taskmaster less kindly: "All through that time he'd never give you a good word; he'd say, 'Keep your hands out of your pockets' or 'stand still, don't mug,' always criticizing you during performances."[9] At other times William was simply embarrassed. In Geneva, New York, at Christmastime, they had gone for a walk after the matinee and stopped to admire a Christmas tree glowing in a bay window. Ignoring Bill's protests, Ned knocked at the door and announced, "We've been looking at your tree, my boy and me. We're lonesome and homesick on Christmas." According to Bill, "the man recognized Pop and invited us in for dinner."[10]

Three or four times during the tour, Harrigan had laryngitis and

William went on for him as Old Lavender while the property man took over Bill's role as Dick, with Bill feeding him the lines under his breath. For the first time Harrigan managed to suppress his aversion to using a wig and makeup on a young actor to transform him into an old man. William was not quite twenty.

Back in New York in the spring of 1907, the company settled in for a twelve-week farewell at the Lincoln Square Theatre. A pathetically small audience greeted them during the first week, with practically no one in the orchestra seats and only a few lonely souls camping here and there in the balcony. It looked as if the troupe had already taken its farewell. Still Harrigan persisted. He needed money for the Garrick mortgage and taxes, and when he was too ill to make the journey from Brooklyn to Manhattan, he insisted that Bill go on for him: "Listen—you're a goddamn good actor. Go over and play it." Those words were engraved on Bill's memory: "It was the first time in a year-and-a-half he'd ever said I was all right. I played the part for two weeks, never lost a dollar. It was the only time I can remember any praise, and then it was because he needed that dough so desperately."[11]

The Garrick Theatre achieved considerable glory for itself but gave the Harrigans more headaches than profits. The mortgage seemed to increase as the rentals diminished, an economic perversion that even Annie, with "her Jewish instinct for business" (a Chicago businessman's phrase),[12] could not fathom, and it later became almost unbearable when she had to carry the burden alone.

For a few years after 1909, when Annie received an unexpected windfall, the Harrigan economy brightened. Her mother's sister left her $50,000. One reporter commented that it was good that the estate had been shared with others: "If all had been left to Mrs. Harrigan she would spend every cent of the legacy to have her husband again before the public."[13] She spent none of the money to bring Ned to the public, though she did dispense most of it supporting Philip and Nolan at Princeton and keeping up the payments on their house and theatre.

Ned Harrigan, unlike so many actors who thrive for years on farewell tours, stuck to his word. After the 1907 stand at the Lincoln Square Theatre, he never again appeared in one of his own plays. He had not, however, given up writing. Two plays were filed for copyright: *In the North Woods* (July 5, 1907) and *The Lord Mayor of Dublin* (December 14, 1908). Neither really sounded like Harrigan. Neither reached the stage.

In the North Woods was overloaded with catastrophe: A lightning bolt fells a giant tree on the hero, transforming him into a deranged wanderer. He's pursued by a villain who pleasures himself with blackmail, poaching, and arson until he's caught in a bear trap and gored to death by a buck deer. Harrigan had found peace and quiet in the Adirondacks during his summers at Schroon. His characters did not.

The Lord Mayor of Dublin was reworked more than any other Harrigan play. The first draft was titled "Barney Brogan," the second "The Irish Cousin," and the third began as "The Lord Mayor of London" but then became *The Lord Mayor of Dublin.* The manuscripts supply a rich catalogue of what was on Harrigan's mind from 1906 to 1908.

Barney Brogan has deserted theatre management for playwriting. His latest opus, called "The Bride of a Minute," requires six loads of scenery, a huge derrick with a large hammer to fall on the bride, a tank of real water in which to drown her, a red-hot furnace for roasting her, and a tunnel under the East River that will fall on her. Brogan has another play in his head, "The Blond and the Serpent." The Serpent murders the blond's aged father, abducts her in a red automobile, and takes her to a furnished flat in the Tenderloin district. She spurns his advances, runs to the roof of the Flatiron Building with the Serpent in hot pursuit. A mob of spectators on Broadway looks up at the struggle as he throws her over the ledge. A gigantic airship floats above the villain, lowers a rope, and the Serpent escapes. In the next scene, just as the blond and a farmer boy are about to be married in an immense glass hothouse, the Serpent drops from the airship, crashes through the glass and is killed.

The final version was filled with assorted fresh slants on contemporary New York. An update on the Irish: "Freedom's electric spark flashes from this grand Republic, the Dynamo of Liberty, and is carried on the currents of the ocean to our little green isle where every bird that flies the sky warbles his song of love for

'Columbia, the Land of the Free!'. . . It's no joke for the poor Irish immigrant to fight his way from poverty to riches, and oh the thousands who have!" And in a lighter vein: "Never corrupt Irish stew with Dutch noodles."

Cruel landlords who cry, "No children wanted here, no smiling dimpled dears." Theatre managers losing out to the moving pictures. Architects studying the castles on the Rhine so they can build mansions for Pittsburgh millionaires. Rich American girls stalking husbands in Europe—"Ten thousand francs did Mary pay / When she wed the noble Count Frappé." Negroes discovering that a "college education gets you on the floor [when] ig'rant colored people can't look in the door." Marguerite Culpepper, a quadroon Virginia Culpepper descended from Pocahontas who has been traveling the "Orphan Circuit" singing "It's It":

> You must be graduated
> From de College Tuskgagee
> If you wish to be a leader
> In swell society.

In the fall of 1908, the Harrigans moved back to Manhattan to be nearer the theatres—he had a part in a play—and to provide their son with an office. Anthony had just received his M.D. from Columbia's College of Physicians and Surgeons. "Dr." Anthony took over the bow-windowed front room on the ground floor while the family occupied the three upper floors of a stone house at 249 West One Hundred and Second Street, just west of Broadway. It was a good location for Anthony, handier than Brooklyn for Ned, and brought Annie close to Mother Braham on One Hundred Thirty-First Street.

Anthony already looked like the successful doctor he was to become, over six feet tall and with a head like a Greek god. He became a distinguished surgeon, was on the staff of three hospitals —St. Vincent's, St. Francis, and Fordham—and throughout his life found daily pleasure and relaxation in playing the piano. He kept Schroon in the family by buying out his brothers and sisters and began to assemble his father's manuscripts.

Annie and Ned could—and did—take pride in their children. Like so many Irish-Americans, they enhanced the life of the city through their progeny. The children stuck together and each of them was "whole-souled, just like Ned"—Annie Yeamans's description.[14] When Philip and Nolan attended Germantown Academy in Philadelphia—among the first sons of Ireland to invade that Germanic stronghold—they lived with their sister Adelaide. They both attended Princeton, then like their two brothers served their country in World War I; they went on to solid careers in finance and business: Nolan as a senior vice-president of the Irving Trust Company and Philip as president of the Sunrise Coal Company.

Harrigan was rejuvenated by his return to Manhattan and to Broadway, proud to be appearing with his son William, though he held little hope for the play, *His Wife's Family* by George Egerton.[15] At the opening (October 6, 1908) Ned received a hearty welcome, and the critics declared that only in his one short scene was the Irish dialect recognizable and comprehensible. The play closed after fifteen performances.

The pre-Broadway tour of *Cameo Kirby*, by Booth Tarkington and Henry Leon Wilson, turned out equally disastrous, a pitiful finale to Harrigan's career as an actor. His part, a lazy, low-comedy Negro valet with a broken-record line, "I'se a very sick man," offered less opportunity than his first roles at the Bella Union and little grist for the critics. One wrote, "Mr. Harrigan had little chance to do anything and did it."[16] After less than a week in Philadelphia, the play was withdrawn.

Even with this inauspicious return to the stage, the press was at his door assuring him that he was not forgotten and requesting his updated views on Broadway.[17] He willingly obliged. Although the theatre had changed, he was encouraged that some actors, like the screamingly funny Weber and Fields, still believed in making an audience laugh. (Perhaps that team got off on the right track when they donned short breeches, pretended to be Irishmen, and imitated Harrigan and Hart singing "The Market on Saturday Night" from *McSorley's Inflation*.)

There were, according to Harrigan, still a few people—God bless—who wanted happiness in the theatre. Not everyone was obsessed with lobster. He himself had never had to fight the lobster crowd. For him, "Mike and Jerry," whether jammed into the gallery or luxuriating in the parquet, kept themselves glued to the play until the final curtain. Only then did they think of food, and even while they munched a dozen oysters at the corner stand, they tested their voices on the newest Harrigan-Braham tunes. In many theatres now—some said most—the play itself was merely an annoying interruption in the evening's festivities. The orchestra seats were filled with impatient patrons waiting to get on to their lobster suppers. And it seemed that there were other patrons who had become so refined that they thought it improper, even vulgar, to be reminded of those old-fashioned, hardworking New Yorkers that we all sprang from: "Now we must have our Salomes and our dance poems and our, what I call, four-cornered plays—you know, a husband and a wife and a mistress and a lover."[18] The new kind of play was not his meat: "A man may be a success in the delicatessen business and a failure at dry goods; I'll never attempt to sell dry goods."[19]

Harrigan regretted that his favorite section of New York had changed. Now the East Side had become Russianized, overcrowded with sad souls who had had the humor crushed out of them by poverty and oppression. In his time there was just as much poverty and oppression, but no shamrock-true Irishman allowed such inconveniences to foreclose on fun in the parlor at the end of the day. Evenings were meant for joshing, for singing and dancing. He remembered that when he was working up a play he could simply wait on his stoop. His neighbors would bring him all the jokes he needed, sometimes even supply a bit of plot, a contribution he always welcomed.[20]

In the spring of 1909, Harrigan again returned to the stage, unexpectedly. His son William, who had agreed to appear in the annual Lambs Club Gambols, was unable to join the festivities when he got a part in a play, and he asked his father to substitute for him. Ned agreed. After being hastily initiated into the club and christened a "Lamb," he drilled a half-dozen actors in a Harrigan march and the entire company in singing "The Mulligan Guard," "Paddy Duffy's Cart," and "Little Widow Dunn." He must have overdone the marching. At the final dress rehearsal he collapsed and was taken home. Anthony called in a Dr. Le Fèvre, and they agreed that Harrigan had probably had a mild heart attack. They also agreed that the audience at the Metropolitan Opera House offered good medicine.

On May 24, Harrigan joined DeWolf Hopper, Weber and Fields, David Belasco, and the other "twenty-eight stars" in a gigantic minstrel show. He appeared as an endman, as captain for his marchers, in a sketch called *Tuesday, a Comedy of Errors,* and with the entire company in the finale. (In the *Tuesday* sketch, David Belasco was lowered from the clouds—"thunder and the roar of guns"—a tribute to his own spectacular stage effects!) The $40,000 house at the Metropolitan had not forgotten Harrigan. The next day the *Morning Telegraph* editorialized: "I'd rather hear Ned Harrigan sing one verse of 'The Mulligan Guard' than Caruso warble his entire repertoire."[21] But when the Lambs company boarded a special train for a week-long party and performances in Boston, Philadelphia, Washington, Baltimore, Pittsburgh, Cleveland, and Chicago, Harrigan was not along. Anthony had sent him to Atlantic City for a rest.

After recuperating in Atlantic City, he went to Schroon for the summer and in the fall to Philadelphia for a visit with his daughter Adelaide, now Mrs. Louis Loughran. Adelaide had been married for three years, and Harrigan had yet to see the house in Germantown that her husband's father had given them as a wedding present. Forty-five years later Adelaide recalled his visit in a letter to her sister Nedda.[22] Every morning they walked together just as they had in Greenwich Village when she was a child, and "as we walked we would play a game. Papa would be an American patriot and I a Germantown miss on her way to the market. Only those who knew Papa can appreciate the poetical grace with which he brought back that far older and dramatic scene—even to making me believe that I was dressed in a quilted frock and bonnet. He was a magnificently entertaining companion."

Harrigan loved his children, may even have loved his two girls more than the boys. The girls resembled their mother: Adelaide with her smooth white skin and cheeks touched with natural rouge, and Nedda with her sparkling dark eyes and abundant dark brown hair. Nedda (née Grace) was called their "little miracle." She had appeared long after Ned and Annie had given up "expecting" and most awkwardly when Annie was visiting in Rumson, New Jersey, and only two hours after William had been rescued from drowning. William had climbed up on the rail of a bridge and had fallen off. Perhaps Grace's spur-of-the-moment arrival was meant to forecast her later behavior. Annie often declared that Grace had an extraordinary command over her destiny, and she more than any of the other children could twist Ned around her finger. Nedda now recalls that she did adopt a daily routine of climbing on his knee and twisting his hair into such a tight braid that she later wondered how he ever got it out. One time her father arrived home when she had been naughty, and her mother announced that the young lady must be spanked. He accepted his paternal duty, marched her upstairs, closed the door, gave her five dollars, and whispered, "Now yell!" (In a song called "Hello Baby" in *Investigation,* Harrigan had advocated gumdrops in place of the birch for recalcitrant children.)

On another occasion her father visited her at Mount St. Vincent. He knew that she dreaded the school, dreaded all those frightening hours when the pupils were not allowed to talk. When he appeared, she developed a nosebleed. Unwilling to see her suffer, he bundled her in the car and took her home. Annie Harrigan quickly cured the nosebleed, and the next day Grace was transported back to Mount St. Vincent. It was a good recess, if too brief. Riding into town and back up the Hudson in the family's Lozier was an exciting event. Her mother had bought the car—Philip and Nolan later converted it into a racer—and it was normally used only for drives around Central Park with a hired chauffeur, a journey that Ned said he didn't give a damn about but usually tolerated.

Harrigan would have been as proud of Nedda as he was of the others if he had lived to follow her career. After Mount St. Vincent, she attended the National Park Seminary in Washington, where Adelaide encouraged her to try acting. It was when she saw Nedda as Rosalind that Adelaide was convinced that her sister belonged in the theatre. With her sister's encouragement, Nedda, at age sixteen, joined Arnold Daly's company, and from then until 1941 she appeared in over a dozen Broadway plays. She is now best remembered for her Donna Lucia D'Alvadorez in the famous *Charley's Aunt* production in 1940, directed by Joshua Logan and starring José Ferrer. One reviewer said, "With the honest tradition of Harrigan and Hart behind her, she knows how to relish a farce."[23]

Ned Harrigan's last public appearance was on March 16, 1910, as guest of honor at a Friends of Ireland dinner at Shanley's Restaurant. After the orchestra ran through a Harrigan-Braham medley and the audience cheered, Ned rose to respond. His voice failed him. He settled for a bow, and his friends covered his embarrassment with a lusty "H A double R I G A N spells HARRIGAN."[24]

That summer, when Dr. Anthony thought the trip to Schroon might be too exhausting, Grandma Braham, Nedda, and a nurse went with Ned to a hotel at Long Beach, Long Island, to test the seaside. W. H. Reynolds's new hotel—he later built the Chrysler Building—boasted luxury and efficiency. Harrigan was unimpressed, and Nedda was frightened by the perverse elevator that always touched base at the top floor before risking any other stops. They soon gave up on the shore and returned to Schroon. Even though the Adirondack comforts and pleasures for Harrigan had now been radically reduced, he still felt at home there. He was not allowed to row the boat, and the family took most of their meals at the Taylor House. Anthony even insisted that his father ride in the cart to Taylor's, though it was only a short walk from their house.

The following New York winter seemed long and cold. It seemed as if it would never end. Harrigan was rarely out of the house, though he was seldom alone. Visitors appeared daily to hear him sing, listen to stories they had heard before, to bring him fresh reports of the friends who had asked about him, and every week Professor LeMaire came for the family French lesson.

Late in March, when spring appeared thwarted, Anthony ordered a domestic reorganization. The Harrigan bedroom was shifted down to the second-floor library to shorten the journey for the nurses, now in almost constant attendance, and to rejuvenate everyone by a change of scene. Annie Yeamans, the most regular visitor, came on Sundays. She was still on the stage although she was a half-dozen years older than Harrigan. She recalled that she and Ned repeated one dialogue so often that the routine invariably ended in a laugh. "He would say, 'Annie, here I am only sixty-six years old and I'm forgotten already.' And I would say, 'Ned, that's ridiculous. Look at me, I'm seventy-five, and they haven't forgotten me!' "[25] In early June, Yeamans told a reporter that her visits had begun to lose their jollity: "I could not realize that the trembling old man with his head sunk on his breast and his thin hands playing idly with bedclothes was the hero of the gallery gods a generation ago."[26]

Annie Harrigan recalled another day in June when he asked for a pen and for one of his playscripts and feebly scribbled on the title page: "My Dear Annie, my ambition is satisfied. We own a beautiful theatre, a fine home for ourselves, and we're blessed with wonderful children.—Ned." When he handed the script back to her, he whispered, "Annie, the last curtain is about to ring down."[27]

Harrigan died on Tuesday, June 6, 1911, of heart disease. His wife and six children were at his bedside, and the sidewalk in front of the house was crowded with friends, many of whom had known him only across the footlights.

For the next week, newspapers across the country reported his death to Butte, Vincennes, Boise, Paducah, Portland, Fall River. He was known everywhere because he had played everywhere, and also because a visit to New York always meant a visit to Harrigan's Comique or to Harrigan's. All the French- and German-language newspapers carried obituaries. The *Providence Journal* urged his heirs to publish a series of volumes of his plays: "Nowhere else is there so faithful a portrayal of an epoch of New York life that is now as dead as a dinosaurus and which was of such great importance in the social and political destiny of the city."[28] In Richmond a reporter recalled that on Decoration Day last he had heard a company of cadets singing "The Charleston Blues." The *New York Times* recounted his entire career and on the editorial page concluded: "He was a man of kindly nature, well informed and thrifty, and he will be remembered as one who served his era well and helped to lighten the cares of life. His death has ended an epoch, an era of good fellowship. Though present-day prosperity and expansion may be good, it is sad that the seventies and eighties have been forgotten, that they're now almost as foreign as Hongkong, that time when Harrigan's characters were his neighbors and friends. There was never a better man living than Ned Harrigan."[29] Annie Yeamans shared these sentiments. She told a reporter: "It would be a better world if all men were like him."[30]

The day before the funeral, mourners streamed through the library. Nedda still remembers the crowd, the overpowering odor from the mountains of flowers, the monumental piece spelling "Our Idol," which seemed so sacrilegious and which sent her to her bedroom weeping.

On Friday, June 9, services were held at the house, then at the Church of Ascension on One Hundred Seventh, where over a thousand heard the solemn requiem high mass read by Father Michael J. Tighe. Among the mourners were his old-time associates Harry Fisher, Annie Mack, Dan Collyer, and Joe Sparks. Annie Yeamans was too stricken to attend. A blind man from Yonkers, led by an old woman—every newspaper carried the story—wanted to touch the coffin. Before he went blind, he had seen every Harrigan play.

As the cortege moved toward Woodlawn Cemetery, it passed a firehouse where the men at the window and at the front door called, "Goodbye Ned, goodbye—and good luck."[31] Perhaps they knew that he had run with "Old Tiger."

Postscript

In her remaining years, Annie was glad that Ned was spared the final, futile struggle to keep up the mortgage payments on the Garrick, on the One Hundred Second Street house, that he had not lived to see their beloved theatre occupied by second-class attractions. There were repeated attempts to sell the theatre after Charles Frohman had taken over the lease from Mansfield. In 1914, an Edward Margolis proposed to trade some apartments on West Sixty-Third Street for the Garrick. When that prospect evaporated, Annie invited some forty Broadway managers to make her an offer. None responded. The Frohman lease expired in May 1915.[1] In June, the press reported that the theatre had been sold, that Mrs. Harrigan would receive a $300,000 equity in another piece of real estate. When that deal collapsed, Annie again leased the theatre, first to Arnold Daly for a Shaw season, then to the Joyland Girls burlesque troupe—they were arrested for performing an immoral show—and then to an entrepreneur who used the Garrick as New York's first all-night motion picture house. Finally, in May 1916, it was sold at public auction for $224,000 to satisfy the mortgage and taxes, and the next year Otto Kahn rescued the building from the wreckers, turned it over to Jacques Copeau's French company and then to the Theatre Guild.[2] In 1917, a year before her death, Annie also lost their house on One Hundred Second Street and moved in with her son Anthony at 391 West End Avenue.

The Garrick Theatre, née Harrigan, had an illustrious history, if not for Annie and Edward Harrigan. Under Frohman's banner it housed William Gillette's *Secret Service,* Ethel Barrymore in *Captain Jinks of the Horse Marines,* Maude Adams in *The Little*

Minister, and after it was taken over by the Theatre Guild, the famous *John Ferguson* production that monopolized Broadway while Actor's Equity struck the other theatres, and finally George Bernard Shaw's *Heartbreak House* and *St. Joan* before it was abandoned and torn down in 1932.

Notes and Sources

Abbreviations

Annie's Ltrs.	Annie Braham Harrigan Letters, Th. Col. L. C.
A's Mems.	Adelaide Harrigan's Memoirs, N. H's Col.
H. Scrap.	Edward Harrigan's Scrapbooks, N. H's Col.
Hart's Scrap.	Tony Hart's Scrapbook, N. H's Col.
Harv. Th. Col.	Harvard Theatre Collection.
Locke Scrap.	Robinson Locke Scrapbooks, Th. Col. L. C.
Ms. NYPL	Manuscript Collection, New York Public Library.
N. H's Col.	Nedda Harrigan's Collection.
Players	Library at the Players Club on Gramercy Park, New York.
Rose ms.	Sidney Rose, "Edward Harrigan and His Plays," Th. Col. L. C.
Spirit	*New York Spirit of the Times.*
Th. Col. L.C.	Museum of the Performing Arts, Theatre Collection, New York Public Library at Lincoln Center.
Th. Col. Mus. City N.Y.	Theatre Collection, Museum of the City of New York.
Walsh Scrap.	Townsend Walsh Scrapbooks, Th. Col. L. C.
W's Scrap.	William Harrigan's Scrapbook, N. H's Col.
W's Tape	William Harrigan's Tape Recording of his Memoirs, N. H's Col.

Chapter 1

1. Information about the Harrigan Club meetings from souvenir programs and scrapbooks, N. H's Col. and from unidentified clippings, July 14, 1910, N. H's Col.; *New York Times,* March 27, 1914; *New York Herald,* Sept. 10, 1914; *New York Telegraph,* Nov. 28, 1914; *New York Telegraph,* Sept. 14, 1914; unidentified clippings,

Dec. 15, 1915, N. H's Col.; *New York Tribune*, Dec. 16, 1915; *New York Telegram*, Oct. 6, 1926.

2. See *Al Smith, Hero of the Cities*, by Matthew and Hannah Josephson (Boston: Houghton Mifflin Co., 1909); *Al Smith, Up to Now: An Autobiography* (New York: Viking Press, 1929); *The First Hurrah, A Biography of Alfred E. Smith*, by Richard O'Connor (New York: Putnam, 1970).

3. *History of the Society of the Friendly Sons of Saint Patrick*, by Richard C. Murphy (New York: J. C. Dillon Co. 1962), p. 466.

4. On December 14, 1915, Dr. Anthony Hart Harrigan (Harrigan's son) arrived late at the festivities after saving a life at Fordham Hospital, but in time to hear Harry Fisher sing Harrigan's "Babies on Our Block" and Dan Collyer rendering "Maggie Murphy's Home." Fisher and Collyer had been in Harrigan's company.

5. *Variety*, June 13, 1927, p. 25. William had scored the year before as William Brown in the original production of *The Great God Brown*, although Alexander Woollcott noted that he worked under a handicap. "His father taught him to act without his hands and now the poor boy has to act without his face" (*New York Times*, Jan. 25, 1926). O'Neill's characters wore masks. William also gave a solo concert of his father's songs at the Hippodrome on New Year's Eve 1916, with an orchestra conducted by George Braham (William's uncle).

There were other celebrations and reminders of Harrigan. On January 29, 1917, "The Mulligan Guards of Greenwich Village, James P. Geagan, Captain" staged a dinner and cabaret at the Amsterdam Opera House. On St. Patrick's Day, 1922, the New York Lodge, No. 1 of the B.P.O. Elks presented a "Harrigan and Hart and Ye Old New York Night" under the direction of Brother Joe Humphreys.

On June 1, 1916, the *New York Telegraph* announced the formation of a Harrigan Film Corporation. It proposed to produce films of all the plays, directed by George Marion and with William appearing in all of his father's roles. The project never advanced beyond the announcement.

Except for a production of *The Mulligan Guard Ball* at the American Theatre in New York on January 20, 1977, none of Harrigan's plays has been produced since his death, and only one, *The Mulligan Guard Ball*, has ever appeared in print and that not until 1966 in *Dramas from the American Theatre, 1762–1909* by Richard Moody (Cleveland and New York: World Publishing Co., 1966; Boston and New York: Houghton Mifflin Co., 1968.

Public reminders, though less frequent, did not disappear in the 1920s and 1930s. On June 14, 1931, WJZ's "Theatrical Scrapbook" radio series presented an imaginary half-hour interview with Harrigan, with short excerpts from his *Squatter Sovereignty* and *Cordelia's Aspirations.* A misguided advertising copywriter took account of the occasion, proclaiming that "A.P.W. Satin Tissue was the finest when Harrigan and Hart were headliners. Today it's still the finest."

6. Lyrics to "Harrigan" copyright: George M. Cohan Music Publishing Co., Inc. Used by permission. The verses:

> Who is the man who will spend or will even lend?
> Har-ri-gan that's me!
> For I'm just as proud of my name you see,
> As an Emperor, Czar, or a King could be
> Who is the man helps a man ev'ry time he can?
> Har-ri-gan, that's me!
>
> Who is the man never stood for a gad about?
> Har-ri-gan, that's me!
> Who is the man that the town's simply mad about?
> Har-ri-gan, that's me!
> The ladies and babies are fond of me;
> I'm fond of them, too, in return, you see.
> Who is the gent that's deserving a monument?
> Har-ri-gan, that's me!

An Irish librarian in the Music Collection at Lincoln Center remembers it from their family songfests. Oliver Jensen, former editor of *American Heritage,* regularly tests his baritone against his cylinder recording. Sam Leve, the Broadway scene designer, still renders the parody he learned in camp:

> LO double-L Y P O P spells Lollypop, Lollypop.
> The man who made it was a dandy,
> Never made a better piece of candy.
> L O double-L Y P O P you see
> It's a lick on a stick,
> Guaranteed to make you sick,
> Lollypop for me.

Cohan's earlier "M A double-R I E D" never matched the popularity of "Harrigan."

7. Harrigan had been Cohan's idol. When Cohan first got a trial spot on a benefit program in the 1890s, he recalled that he followed Harrigan from one side of the stage to the other. Years later he confessed that he had tried repeatedly to execute two "taps" on the proscenium arch in imitation of Eddie Harrigan, Jr. (*Twenty Years on*

Broadway by George M. Cohan [New York: Harper & Bros., 1924], p. 81.) Harrigan's son, the love of his life, was only seventeen when he died in 1895.

At a Ned Harrigan Club meeting at the Teutonia Assembly Rooms on December 10, 1914, Cohan proclaimed his debt:

> Edward Harrigan was a fine artist, a great writer of human comedies and one of the grandest men it has ever been my pleasure to meet. Harrigan inspired me when I applauded him from a gallery seat. Harrigan encouraged me when I met him in after years and told him of my ambitions. I live in hopes that some day my name may mean half as much to the coming generation of American playwrights as Harrigan's name has meant to me. (Souvenir program, N. H's Col.)

8. Joshua Logan told me this story.

9. The first disc (1911) featured Billy Murray and the Haydn Quartette.

10. "A Talk with Edward Harrigan," *New York Daily News*, Dec. 4, 1904.

11. Interview with Harrigan, *New York Telegraph*, June 22, 1911.

12. Unless otherwise noted, details about the plays and sketches are from Ms. NYPL.

13. *Harper's*, July, 1886, pp. 315–17.

14. Undated clipping, H's Scrap.

Chapter 2

1. Biographical details about Harrigan, and particularly about his early years, are largely derived from numerous conversations with his daughter Nedda Harrigan Logan from 1973 to 1978, from her collection of scrapbooks and memorabilia, from her sister Adelaide's memoirs, and from a tape of her brother William's recollections of his father. Shortly before Adelaide's death in 1960, Nedda sent her a tape recorder and asked her to "talk in" all her memories of the family. The transcription of Adelaide's memoirs, running to over three hundred typed pages, preserves details about the family that no one else could know. In July 1962, four years before his death, William taped his recollections and also recorded his renderings of the Braham-Harrigan songs. Listening to that tape, and another one with all the brothers singing, one can understand the incredible popularity of the songs.

The memories of these three also drew on the recollections of the other children who had survived Harrigan: Anthony, Nolan, and Philip. All of them dearly loved their father and shared their memories of him with each other. Dr. Anthony had been particularly diligent in collecting Harrigan manuscripts and memorabilia. He regularly dispatched inquiries from his office on Fifty-Third Street, just east of Fifth Avenue, to photographers and dealers who were rumored to have Harrigan material. At his death in 1932 his collection was passed to Nedda Harrigan (now the only living survivor), and she in turn gave most of the play manuscripts to the New York Public Library.

On several occasions in magazine articles and interviews, Harrigan himself revealed details about his life: Letter to Dexter Smith, Esq., printed in *Dexter Smith's* (a Boston newspaper), Aug. 8, 1874, Locke Scrap.; "Harrigan and His Plays," *New York Times,* Sept. 29, 1887; "Edward Harrigan at Home," *New York World,* March 15, 1891; "Hunting Types in Slums with Edward Harrigan," *New York Herald,* July 12, 1891; Edward Harrigan, "How I Became an Actor and Author," *San Francisco Call,* April 17, 1898; Alan Dale, "A Chat with Harrigan," *New York Dramatic Mirror and Journal,* Jan. 25, 1903; Edward Harrigan, "Holding the Mirror Up to Nature," *Pearson's Magazine,* Nov., 1903; "The Playwright's Art, Harrigan's Views Concerning the Making of Dramatic Pieces," unidentified clipping, Players.

2. Letter, N. H's Col.

3. In the 1830s, when William Harrigan turned to caulking, some fourteen shipyards operated on the Hook, employing over four hundred men, with carpenters and caulkers earning two dollars for a ten-hour day and apprentices fifty to sixty-four cents. Until 1841, when the first steamship was built, the yards of Christian Bergh, Thom and Williams, Carpenter and Bishops, James Morgan & Son, and Enden and Lawrence concentrated on clipper ships. They apparently accomplished the shift to steam without breaking stride. By 1850 they had slipped thirty-eight steam vessels into the East River.

Information about Corlear's Hook from: *The Iconography of Manhattan,* by I. N. Phelps Stokes (New York; R. H. Dodd, 1915–28); "Corlear's Hook District," *East Side Chamber News,* May, 1935; *History of New York Ship Yards,* by John H. Morrison (New York: Smetz & Co., 1909); *Appleton's Dictionary of New York* (New York: D. Appleton & Co., 1879); "Edward Harrigan and His Plays," by Sidney Rose, ms. Th. Col. L. C.

4. Stokes, *Aug. 22, 1818.*

5. Stokes, *June 24, 1824.*

6. These volunteers, who protected New York as late as 1865, when the population had reached nearly a million, developed as much skill in fighting each other as in fighting fires. Harrigan remembered many bitter and bloody battles when the Americus was challenged by Old Stag, Number 41, at the head of East Broadway and Chatham Street, where they invariably crossed paths.

7. Harrigan obituary, *New York Evening Post,* June 6, 1911.

8. A's Mems.

9. H. Scrap.
10. *New York World,* Mar. 15, 1891.
11. Ibid.
12. Ibid.
13. Harrigan never spoke of his parents' divorce. In later years when his own happy home life was well known, he sometimes told reporters that he had undertaken his adventures to New Orleans and San Francisco after the death of his mother.
14. H. Scrap.
15. New York State Historical Society.
16. A's Mems.
17. W's Tape.
18. N. H's Col. Also in Locke Scrap.
19. Preceding details from A's Mems. and W's Tape.
20. Unidentified clipping, H. Scrap.

Chapter 3

1. A brief account of the journey is in Harrigan's "Holding the Mirror up to Nature."
2. Coal tar waste from the gas company blackened the sand.
3. In the sixties many believed that Vallejo might well outdistance San Francisco as the leading city. It is thirty miles closer to Sacramento, thirty miles nearer the East Coast.
4. Harrigan interview, *San Francisco Call,* Apr. 17, 1898.
5. For more details on melodeons, see *San Francisco Theatre Research* (Works Progress Administration, Project 10677), in Th. Col. L. C. and Bancroft Library, University of California, Berkeley.
6. *San Francisco Dramatic Chronicle,* Dec. 11, 1867.
7. *Daily Alta California,* Aug. 12, 1870.
8. *San Francisco Daily Dramatic Chronicle,* Oct. 19, 1867. Unless otherwise noted, the record of Harrigan in San Francisco is from the Bella Union programs, Harv. Th. Col., and from the following newspapers in the Bancroft Library, University of California, Berkeley: *Daily Dramatic Chronicle; Daily Morning Call; San Francisco Bulletin; Police Gazette; Golden City.*
9. Program, Harv. Th. Col.
10. *Daily Morning Call,* Oct. 20, 1867.
11. *San Francisco Call,* April 17, 1898.
12. Harrigan apparently drew a strong representation of Irishmen from the waterfront and from the mines. They chose the Olympic over the more serious Fenian meetings announced in one newspaper: "Amusement and Pleasure Guide. Tuesday, Association for the Prevention of Yankee Immigration and Protection of the Superior Race; Wednesday, United Brotherhood for the Propagation of the Superior

Race and Down Wid the Saxons; Thursday, the Tipperary Circle of Fenian Red Fire; and Friday, Stockholders of the House for Inebriated Hod Carriers." (Unidentified clipping, H. Scrap.)

13. *Dramatic Chronicle,* Oct. 26, 1867.

14. *Virginia City Daily Safeguard,* Dec. 28, 1868.

15. Gertrude Streeter Vrooman, "A Brief Survey of the Musical History of Western Nevada," *Nevada Historical Society Papers, 1921–1922;* Bancroft Library, University of California, Berkeley.

16. W's Tape.

17. Pauline Jacobson, *City of the Golden Fifties* (Berkeley and Los Angeles: University of California Press, 1941), p. 67.

18. For more details on the Bella Union, see "Bella Union," by Idwal Jones, *Westways,* Sept. 1940, pp. 16–17; "Early San Francisco Theatres," *Collector's Guide,* Dec. 1940, pp. 3–6; "Some Shadows of the San Francisco Stage," by James Madison, *California Historical Society Quarterly* 4 (1924): 59–63.

19. The conversion from gambling was made by Sam Tetlow, a mechanic from Manchester, England, who arrived in the early fifties, became fascinated by the gaming tables, and soon was known as a heavy plunger. Some said he won the Bella Union at its own tables.

20. Jacobson, *City of the Golden Fifties,* p. 281.

21. The directories carry another tantalizing Harrigan entry in these years: "William H., calker, Natoma in the 'Valley.' " His brother?

22. The Tetlows' Bella stretched along forty-eight feet of Kearny, and the rear of the structure butted against the back of the old theatre. The stage was thirty feet deep, sheer extravagance for those days. The audience was distributed in a parquet, dress circle, and gallery, the gallery being divided into twenty-three private boxes, "after the European style and where one can meet friends without the inconvenience of intruders." For such privacy one paid $3.00; next to the proscenium, $5.00. For an ordinary seat, Madame Tetlow was satisfied with fifty cents.

23. Bret Harte, "The Plaza," *Stories and Poems and Other Uncollected Writings* (Boston and New York: Houghton Mifflin Co., 1914), p. 332. Originally published in *The Californian,* Oct. 8, 1864.

24. On November 1, 1868, the *Police Gazette* called for a grand jury investigation of the other melodeons, those "Low Places of Amusement," that are infested with smutty, indecent talk and vulgar actions and where women of loose character are employed to prey on innocent young men and boys.

25. On the new transcontinental rails they could have reached New York in eleven days, with an investment of $250. With their resources limited to talent and time, they resisted that temptation. A patient cattle train met their requirements.

26. A's Mems.

Chapter 4

1. Information about Chicago theatre from programs at the Chicago Historical Society, the Chicago Public Library, the University of Chicago Library. From Chicago newspapers: *Weekly Journal, Tribune, Evening Journal, Times, Interocean.* And from Robert L. Sherman, *Chicago Stage* (Chicago: privately printed, 1947); J. H. McVicker, "Theatre, Its Early Days in Chicago," *Chicago Historical Society Publications,* Feb. 19, 1884; Lyman B. Glover, *The Story of a Theatre* (no pub., n.d.)—all in Newberry Library.

2. Harrigan, "Holding the Mirror up to Nature," p. 3.

3. *Mark Twain's Travels with Mr. Brown, Being Heretofore Uncollected Sketches Written by Mark Twain* (New York: Russell & Russell, 1940), p. 177.

4. Details on other attractions, here and later, from *Annals of the New York Stage,* by George C. D. Odell (New York: Columbia University Press, 1927, 1949).

5. Harrigan, "Holding the Mirror up to Nature," p. 3.

6. *Twain's Travels with Mr. Brown,* pp. 85–86.

7. J. W. Buel, *Metropolitan Life Unveiled, or, the Mysteries and Miseries of America's Great Cities* (St. Louis: Historical Publishing Co., 1882), p. 41.
The girls in these establishments, dressed in abbreviated ballet costumes, performed triple duty. They served drinks, collecting a percentage; did occasional song-and-dance turns on the miniature stage; and lured customers into the closed apartments that circled the room. One reporter advised the out-of-town visitors to temper their expectations: "Beauty and freshness are rare articles." And, of course, these concert saloons, like the melodeons, carried on a running battle with the protectors of public morals. The customary sequence of events: "Immodesty throws off as it were the last fig leaf, and sensuality, stimulated by drink, celebrates a high revelry of demons. As soon as the evil reaches the terrible height, the press doles out its moral wailings; the police arrive; and for awhile the dresses get longer." (Gustav Lening, *The Dark Side of New York: Life and Its Criminal Classes from Fifth Avenue Down to the Five Points* [New York: F. Gerhard, 1873]).

8. Odell, *Annals,* vol. 9, p. 75; Joseph Jefferson, *Autobiography* (New York: The Century Co., 1889), pp. 338–40.

9. Biographical details from Pastor clippings, Th. Col. L. C., and from *Tony Pastor: Dean of the Vaudeville Stage,* by Parker Zellers (Ypsilanti: Eastern Michigan University Press, 1971).
Pastor became Harrigan's patron, his friend, and then his friendly rival in 1875, when Pastor's Theatre moved to 585 Broadway. The rivalry continued after 1881, when the theatre made its permanent

home in the Tammany Hall Building on East Fourteenth, where Pastor introduced the Four Cohans to New York.

10. Details about Hart's early years from Hart's Scrap.

11. Hart's Scrap.; M. B. Leavitt, *Fifty Years in Theatrical Management* (New York: Broadway Publishing Co., 1912), p. 309.

12. Ibid.

13. Harrigan described their meeting in "Holding the Mirror up to Nature," p. 3.

14. "Tony Hart and His Career," *New York Herald,* n.d., Hart's Scrap.

15. Harrigan, "Holding the Mirror up to Nature," pp. 3–4.

16. Ibid., p. 3.

17. A's Mems.

18. Nat C. Goodwin, *Nat Goodwin's Book* (Boston: R. G. Badger, 1914), p. 83.

Chapter 5

1. Material on Harrigan and Hart at the Howard Athenaeum from programs, Boston Public Library, Harv. Th. Col., Walsh Scrap.; also "Danforth Dramatic Reviews," *Daily Advertiser and Morning Journal,* Boston Public Library.

2. Harrigan, "Holding the Mirror up to Nature," p. 3.

3. Program, Boston Public Library.

4. A's Mems.

5. The Brahams were not descended from the famous English singer John Braham. David Braham was born in St. George's, Middlesex, in 1834 and according to the 1851 census his occupation was "Music. Brass Turner (Tuner?)." His father, Joseph John Braham, a watchmaker, was born in Rochester, Kent, in 1801. David's grandfather, a surgeon (apothecary), was, according to family legend, born in Frankfurt am Main in 1755 and migrated to England in the late eighteenth century. David's mother, Elizabeth Ann Mary Atkinson, a dressmaker, died in London in 1854 at age fifty-three.

I am indebted to Ann Connolly (Nedda Harrigan's daughter) for information about the Brahams. She has scoured all the London records, including those of the Water-works Planning Department at the Greater London Council, which she found particularly helpful in locating the Braham residences.

6. Before he committed himself almost exclusively to Harrigan, Braham had set the tune for Gregory Hyde's "You're the Idol of My Heart," thirty years before the song became more familiarly known as "Sweet Adeline."

7. *Syracuse Daily Standard,* Jan. 30, 1872, p. 4.

8. Harrigan notebook, Ms. NYPL.

Chapter 6

1. *Spirit*, March 2, 1875, p. 134.
2. *Spirit*, Nov. 14, 1874, p. 340.
3. Odell, *Annals*, vol. 9, p. 607.
4. *Spirit*, Nov. 7, 1874, p. 312.
5. Unidentified clipping, March 9, 1874, Walsh Scrap.
6. Odell, *Annals*, vol. 9, p. 602.
7. Rose ms., p. 19.
8. Ibid.
9. Ibid., p. 29.
10. Letter to Dexter Smith, Aug. 8, 1874.
11. Charles E. Wingate and F. E. McKay, eds., *Famous American Actors of Today* (New York: T. Y. Crowell & Co., 1896), p. 395.
12. Harrigan, "Miscellaneous Plays and Songs," Th. Col. L. C.
13. Ibid.
14. Augustine F. Costello, *Our Firemen* (New York: A. E. Costello, 1887), p. 190; William J. McKenna, "They All Loved a Parade," *Jersey Journal*, March 18, 1942.
15. W. S. Ludlow, "Old Target Companies and Firemen," *Valentine's Manual* 4 (1920): 180.
16. Lady Emmeline Stuart Wortley, *Travels in the United States During 1849 and 1850* (New York: Harper & Bros., 1851), p. 155.
17. Costello, *Our Firemen*, p. 190.
18. Ibid.
19. Charles Dickens, *All the Year Around: A Weekly Journal Conducted by Charles Dickens*, March 16, 1861, pp. 537–38.
20. Ludlow, "Old Target Companies," p. 180.
21. Costello, *Our Firemen*, p. 191.
22. Throughout the seventies Harrigan and Hart stumbled through the manual of arms, discovering new misadventures for sword and rifle and on one occasion concocting a new set of words for a "Second Annual Parade," the last verse of which ran:

> Whin we fall in to return home
> Wid the target shot away
> A drum and fife and a German band
> The soup house sweetly play
> We fine the men that's sober
> And the drunken men who fall
> We put thim you see on the committee
> To lead the Mulligan Ball

Nedda Harrigan and the Lilly Library at Indiana University have the most complete collections of Harrigan and Braham sheet music. Copies are also available in the music collections at the Library of

Congress and in the music section of the New York Public Library at Lincoln Center.

23. *The Illustrated History of the Mulligan Guard* (New York: Collin & Small, 1874), 31 pp., Rare Book Room, Library of Congress.

24. *The Ten Little Mulligan Guards* (New York: McLoughlin Bros., 1874). Copy in Th. Col. L. C. inscribed, "Townsend Walsh from Auntie, Dec. 25, 1875." Another copy, University of Chicago Library.

25. Sketches in Ms. NYPL.

26. Thomas DeWitt Talmadge, the popular Presbyterian clergyman.

27. Harrigan notebook, Ms. NYPL.

There were other sketches. In *The Absent-minded Couple* Dan shoves his pants in the stove, substitutes a pot for his hat, and when his wife puts his umbrella in the crib and hands him the baby, he sails the baby through the window.

The Editor's Troubles combined observations on shyster newspaper editors and politicians.

April Fool might be subtitled "Fun at a Christening." To enliven the ceremony Dan Malone (Harrigan) hides his own baby under the table and offers Mrs. Snow's black baby as the christening candidate. When the screams of astonishment subside, he produces baby Malone, pitches the impostor across the room, and shouts "April Fool."

No Irish Wanted Here; or, Out on Strike took a serious turn. While Barney Farrell has "sacrificed himself for the workingman," his child has died of hunger. As he roams the town pleading for a job, all he hears is "No Irish Wanted Here":

> For God in Heaven made the world
> Wid lots of room for all
> Let's stretch our hands across the sea
> To the green ould Isle so dear
> And give the Irish Boys and Girls
> A glad welcome over here.

The Porter's Trouble traced a wild night in a small Fifth Avenue hotel. Dan Dunphey (Harrigan), the hotel clerk, is besieged by eccentric lodgers. Among them, Christopher Skein, alias Junius Brutus Tupper Edmund Kęan Brown. He wants "a room near the bride's chamber in the tower of the castle, 'neath the belfry above," and reappears throughout the night, spouting Shakespeare.

Harrigan covered a wide territory in these sketches, as other titles will suggest: *New York by Night; Who Got de Flo; or, Scenes from the South Carolina Legislature; Lightning; or, Scenes at the Long Branch Races; Ireland vs. Italy; Lo, the Poor Ingine.*

28. *Spirit*, Jan. 30, 1875, to June 12, 1875.

29. If Harrigan had a hand in the writing he never took nor was given credit. No playwright's name appears on the program. When

manager Hart copyrighted the play, he did not indicate who wrote it. With G. L. Stout in the cast, it seems likely that the credit, or part of the credit, belongs to him.

30. *Spirit*, June 5, 1875, p. 438.

Chapter 7

1. "Martin W. Hanley," *New York Dramatic Mirror*, June 27, 1896, p. 15; also unidentified clippings in H's Scrap. .

2. "Hanley," *New York Dramatic Mirror*, June 27, 1896, p. 15.

3. Two copies, Ms. NYPL.

4. Details of tour and quotations from Harrigan's letters to Annie Braham, 86 Carmine Street, Annie Braham Harrigan's letters, Th. Col. L. C.

5. On March 12, 1975, *Variety*, reporting on the evening of tributes to Joshua Logan at the Imperial Theatre in New York, noted that Nedda "Harrington" Logan had appeared in a scene from *Charley's Aunt*.

6. *Indianapolis Journal*, Dec. 13, 1875, p. 5.

7. Clipping, H's Scrap.

8. Ibid.

9. It was Harry who married Lillian Russell.

10. When the brothers who have been fighting against each other return home in the final scene, the family reunion is climaxed with a patriotic flourish:

> BARNEY: Dan, we are two fools, trying to break up a family that's lived one hundred years! There's Washington, Putnam, Daniel O'Connell and all our great grandfathers. If they lived today, 'twould break their hearts to see us making jackasses of ourselves. Let us shake hands across the chasm. Let us have peace! (*Shaking hands vigorously.*)
>
> DAN: And when we are molested by any foreign power (*raises flag*) under this flag, you and I will march in Blue and Grey.
>
> *Song and march:*
>> We only have one country
>> Columbia my darling
>> We sing most cheerfully
>> Your troubles now are ended.
>>
>> . . . . .
>>
>> If foreign power insult us,
>> Hand in hand with Dixie's land
>> We'd march in blue and grey.

11. Clipping, Auburn, N. Y., n.d., H. Scrap.
12. *Spirit*, June 10, 1876, p. 462.
13. *Spirit*, July 15, 1876, p. 603.

Chapter 8

1. Harrrigan, "Holding the Mirror up to Nature," p. 4; *Spirit*, Aug. 9, 1879, p. 16.
2. *Spirit*, Nov. 11, 1876, p. 364.
3. Daniel Crilly, "Irish Landlordism," *Irish American Almanac* (1888), p. 82, Library of Congress.
4. Unidentified clipping, Dec. 9, 1876, N. H's Col.; also A's Mems.
5. The family name may originally have been Abraham or Brahms, the preference of David's musician friends. David's father, Joseph, apparently retained some Jewish traditions. Annie Harrigan once recalled that when Joseph visited them, he had a heavy beard, wore a skull cap, and rejected the bacon that was prepared for him. (Interview with Nedda Harrigan.)
6. Just a few months earlier the Brahams had moved around the corner from their Carmine Street place. Harrigan had either lived with them before the wedding or used their address. The manuscript of *Iascaire*, dated Sept. 13, 1876, gives the Varick number.
7. A's Mems.
8. Details on Grand Duke Opera House, *Spirit*, March 31, 1877, p. 204; and from *Julius the Street Boy* by Horatio Alger (New York: A. L. Burt, 1904), chapter 2, "The Grand Duke's Opera House."
9. Alger, "The Grand Duke's Opera House."
10. Body snatchers did a thriving business in the nineteenth century. They stripped the corpse of valuables, removed gold teeth, and then sold the corpse to a doctor or a medical school.
11. In two scenes, multiple locales were on view simultaneously, a staging practice that was to become common for Harrigan. In the opening scene: the reverend's parlor, the porch, the cemetery, and the exterior of the church. In the rookery (tenements resembled birdhouses): Caroline's flat and another room in which the heroine is held captive.
12. Harrigan's father apparently was again with the company, as advance man and talent scout. From Bridgeport on June 11, 1877, he wrote: "Ed, I have just seen the boys at the shooting business and they beat the Austin Brothers bad. They're seventeen and eighteen, can live at home as long as they like, but they want to go with you. There is money in them and I say take them if you had to let somebody go." Harrigan didn't take them. (Annie's Ltrs.)

Chapter 9

1. Programs, H's Scrap.
2. Ibid.
3. *Twain's Travels with Mr. Brown*, p. 221.
4. The music for "College Days," the only song in the initial version of the play, was not composed by Braham but by G. W. H. Griffin. Griffin also acted the part of Pop Jones and a year later briefly replaced Hanley as Harrigan's manager.
5. Harrigan, "Holding the Mirror up to Nature," p. 5.
6. Harrigan interview, *New York Herald*, July 12, 1891. Walsh Scrap. Boucicault's *Qui Vive* had been at Wallack's earlier in the season.
7. *New York Dramatic News*, Nov. 24, 1877.
8. H. Scrap.
9. *Spirit*, Sept. 6, 1879, p. 130.
10. Harrigan often recalled his visit to Mormon country on this tour. Family platoons marched into the theatre, each headed by a dignified, bearded man who was followed by an assortment of wives and children. When all were seated, each pater familias stood up and ran his eyes over the lot as if calling roll. *Eminent Actors in Their Homes*, by Margherita Arlina Hamm (New York: J. Pott & Co., 1902), p. 101.
11. *New York Dramatic News*, July 20, 1878.
12. More details on these sketches and others:
My Wife's Mother. Arabella Pinch, back from England with her valet, Corilanion Muggs, and a cannibalistic parrot, is in pursuit of her disobedient daughter who has married a pusillanimous Englishman. "You are in America," she explains to Muggs, "where the star-spangled banner is shot off from the top of Bunker Hill and where we women have the first right. My daughter shall have a divorce, and I shall be borne triumphant from the courthouse by the women of this land." Pursuers and pursued chase through adjoining hotel rooms, tumble over beds, climb through transoms, then continue their hide-and-seek at Coney Island, where the lung tester, the weight guesser, and the photographer become unwilling participants and where Muggs's and Arabella's clothes are stolen while they're swimming and Muggs, for no apparent reason, is rolled along the beach in a barrel.
The Rising Star. Other behind-the-scenes episodes: A shyster theatrical agent auditioning singers, jiggers, and gymnasts. A tintype studio where a budding actress squirms into a pose that will look good in cigar-store windows. A private dramatic lesson with a coach who boasts that when he played Romeo in Hackensack, he bankrupted the management "buying mops to mop tears," and who recites Hamlet's ad-

vice to the players, suiting action to word: "Trippingly on the tongue" requires a drink; "mouthe it," a bit of a sandwich.

Coloured Baby Show. To prepare for the contest, Harrigan's motley assembly of quasi mothers roams the streets snatching likely winners from their prams.

The Lady of Lions. Derived from Edward Bulwer-Lytton's play, this entertainment was filled with fearful puns: "lying," "alliance," "loan." Hart appeared as Pauline and Harrigan as Claude Meddlenotte, "on the spot where good oysters are got."

A Celebrated Hard Case. This lampoon of *A Celebrated Case* by Eugene Cormon and Adolphe Phillipe Dennery (better known as the authors of *The Two Orphans*) featured Harrigan as John Rainhard, "a bold militia boy who never fought at Fontnoy," and Hart as his daughter Adri-Anna Rainhard "the little Martha Washington who never told a lie for fear of a libel suit." The story of jewel robbery, murder, false imprisonment, and happy reunion is told in rhymed couplets of dubious quality:

> Feather me, scald me with tar
> Don't make the child condemn her papa.
>
> . . . .
> No, No, my child, it is not your fault
> The piece wasn't translated by Boucicault.

The Italian Junkman gave Harrigan an Italian role, Marcello Corelli, and a trial run for what was later to be *Waddy Googan.* Corelli's junk shop adjoins DeArcy McGlone's (Hart's) saloon, a hangout for thieves and other unsavory waterfront characters, where a captain can acquire a crew for his vessel by sliding drunks through a trapdoor and into a secret passage to the water's edge. (Such facilities, though then inoperative, could still be seen on Corlear's Hook when Harrigan was a boy.)

Chapter 10

1. Quotes from Harrigan obituary, *New York Times,* June 7, 1911, p. 8.
2. William V. Shannon, *The American Irish* (New York: Macmillan Co., 1966), p. 146.
3. *Detroit Free Press,* June 11, 1911, H. Scrap.
4. *New York World,* June 3, 1894, Walsh Scrap.
5. Edward Harrigan, "The Play's the Thing," unidentified clipping, Harv. Th. Col.
6. One reporter detected a marked similarity between the clerical

postures assumed by Billy Gray in his impersonation of Puter and those of the Brooklyn preacher Henry Ward Beecher. Another remarked that as farce-comedy the play was only challenged by the Talmadge Trial at the South Presbyterian Church in Brooklyn, where "one De-Witt Talmadge, a comedian of the lowest and broadest type, accused of being a liar and perjurer, was being tried by a male chorus of thirty-three Presbyters." On second thought, the real-life proceedings in Brooklyn are much too profane to be compared with Harrigan's play, and "if later performances of the Talmadge drama are not better managed, they must be catalogued with 'The Female Bathers' and other disreputable entertainments." (*New York Dramatic News,* April 26, 1879).

7. Montrose J. Moses, "Edward Harrigan," *Theatre Arts Monthly,* March, 1926, p. 177.

8. *Boston Traveller,* March 24, 1894.

9. Harrigan once said that "Gaelic was the prevailing language around Cherry Hill, and every Irish woman had freckles enough on her face to hold a day's rain." ("The Playwright's Art," unidentified clipping, Players.)

10. *Spirit,* March 22, 1879.

11. *Spirit,* May 24, 1879, p. 385.

12. *New York Dramatic News,* Feb. 1, 1879.

13. *Spirit,* March 22, 1879, p. 158.

14. Full coverage of walking matches in *Spirit,* March 8 to Sept. 27, 1879.

15. *Spirit,* Sept. 27, 1879, p. 202.

16. *Spirit,* March 22, 1879, p. 156.

17. Program, Locke Scrap.

18. *New York World,* June 3, 1894, Walsh Scrap.

19. Dale, "A Chat with Harrigan."

20. *New York Times,* Nov. 20, 1902, p. 9.

21. "Yeamans," unidentified clipping, Th. Col. L. C.

22. Ibid.

23. Biographical details from "Annie Yeaman's Career," *New York Times,* Oct. 8, 1899, p. 16; "Mrs. Annie Yeamans," *The Theatre,* Dec. 5, 1887, p. 395; both in H. Scrap.

24. Richard Harding Davis, "Edward Harrigan and the Eastside," *Harper's Weekly,* March 21, 1891, p. 210.

25. Biographical details from "Annie Mack" clippings, Th. Col. L. C.

26. *New York Dramatic Mirror,* April 7, 1888, p. 6.

27. "Echoes of the Week," March 5, 1891, H. Scrap.

28. Davis, "Edward Harrigan and the Eastside," p. 210.

29. Unidentified clipping, Feb. 14, 1898, H. Scrap.

Chapter 11

1. *Spirit,* Aug. 9, 1879, p. 14.
2. See "Charles W. Witham: Scenic Artist to the Nineteenth-Century American Stage," by Thomas F. Marshall, in *Anatomy of an Illusion: Studies in Nineteenth-Century Scenic Design,* Lectures of the Fourth International Congress on Theatre Research, Amsterdam, 1965 (Amsterdam: Scheltema and Holkema, 1969), pp. 26–30, 78, 79. Many of Witham's sketches are in the Th. Col. Mus. City N. Y.
3. Al Smith remembered attending a monster chowder breakfast at Sulzer's Harlem River Park at One hundred Twenty-Seventh Street and the East River, when over five thousand men, women, and children turned out. (Matthew and Hannah Josephson, *Al Smith,* p. 55.)
4. John Francis Maguire, *The Irish in America* (New York: D. & J. Sadlier, 1867), p. 227.
5. Nathan Glazer and Daniel Patrick Moynihan, *Beyond the Melting Pot* (Cambridge, Mass.: M. I. T. Press, 1963), p. 242.
6. Calamity also struck the company during the run of *Nominee.* "Just before the curtain rose last Saturday night, information was brought to the theatre that the little child of Mr. Harrigan [Annie, aged ten months] and the baby of Mr. Fisher had died. Everybody behind the scenes knew of this double loss except the poor fathers, from whom the intelligence was carefully concealed. For three hours they went on with their fun and jollity, their little darlings dead at home, their wives weeping over the empty cradles, the whole company scarcely able to restrain their tears as they looked upon the unconscious fathers, who, as usual, were the life and soul of the piece. What situation can equal this for simple pathos?" (*Spirit,* Feb. 12, 1881, p. 34).
7. Although New York sheltered few "Heathen Chinee," they apparently did smoke opium, did underprice the Irish washerwomen, and because of a scarcity of Oriental women, did treasure an alliance with an Irish lass.
8. Unidentified clipping, H. Scrap.
9. Odell, *Annals,* vol. 11, p. 313.
10. Undated clipping, H. Scrap.

Chapter 12

1. The only known copies are in the Library of Congress.
2. Although the tabloid displayed Harrigan and Hart on the masthead and many of the feature articles were credited to them, the partners had simply lent their names to the publishers, A. J. Dick and J. H. Stecher.
3. On Five Points and tenements, see *A History of New York*

City, by Benson J. Lossing (New York: G. E. Perine, 1884), vol. 2; *On the Town in New York,* by Michael and Ariane Batterberry (New York: Charles Scribner's Sons, 1973), p. 106; *Iconography,* by Stokes *Jan. 30, 1846; Lights and Shadows of New York Life,* by James D. McCabe (Philadelphia: National Publishing Co., 1872), p. 402; *Mark Twain's Travels with Mr. Brown,* passim; *The Irish in America,* by John Maguire; *The Dark Side of New York: Life and Its Criminal Classes from Fifth Avenue Down to the Five Points,* by Gustav Lening (New York: F. Gerhard, 1873); *Forty Years at the Five Points,* by William F. Barnard (New York: Five Points House of Industry, 1893); *Old Bowery Days,* by Alvin F. Harlow (New York: D. Appleton & Co., 1931), pp. 179ff; *Nooks and Corners of Old New York,* by Charles Hemstreet (New York: Charles Scribner's Sons, 1899); *Tenement Tales of New York,* by James W. Sullivan (New York: H. Holt & Co., 1895.)

4. Daniel J. Boorstin, *The Americans: The Democratic Experience* (New York: Random House, 1973), p. 248. On immigration, see *Irish in America,* by Maguire; *Tenement Tales,* by Sullivan; *Irish-American Almanac for 1888; The American Irish,* by Shannon; *Ireland and Irish Immigration to the New World from 1815 to the Famine,* by William Forbes Adams (New Haven, Conn.: Yale University Press, 1932); *Immigrant Life in New York City, 1825-1863,* by Robert Ernst (New York: King's Crown Press, 1849); *Al Smith,* by Matthew and Hannah Josephson; *We Who Built America,* by Carl Wittke (New York: Prentice-Hall, 1939); *The Irish in America,* by Carl Wittke (Baton Rouge: Louisiana State University Press, 1956); *Irish American Historical Miscellany,* by John D. Crimmins (New York: Published by the author, 1905); *St. Patrick's Day: Its Celebration in New York and Other Places, 1737–1845,* by John D. Crimmins (New York: Published by the author, 1902); *The Age of Energy,* by H. M. Jones (New York: Viking Press, 1970); *A History of American Immigration, 1820–1924,* by George Stephenson (New York: Ginn & Co., 1926); *Ireland and the American Emigration, 1850-1900,* by Arnold Schrier (New York: Russell & Russell, 1958).

5. Jacob Riis, *How the Other Half Lives* (New York: Charles Scribner's Sons, 1890). Quoted in *Mirror for Gotham,* by Byard Still (New York: New York University Press, 1956), p. 245.

6. "The Impress of Nationalities on the City of New York."

7. Lossing, *History of New York City,* vol. 2, p. 626; Michael and Ariane Batterberry, *On the Town,* p. 106.

8. The Ladies Home Missionary Society of the Methodist Episcopal Church had bought the old brewery in 1852 and turned it into the House of Industry mission, and in 1871 the mission had conducted a census of the neighborhood. The immediate vicinity housed some

23,000: 3,500 Irish families; 416 Italian; and 393 German. Over 1,500 persons lived in cellars and some 4,800 in garrets.

9. *Spirit*, March 31, 1877, p. 204.

10. Maguire, *Irish in America*, p. 224.

11. Allan Nevins and Milton Halsey Thomas, eds., *The Diary of George Templeton Strong* (New York: Macmillan Co., 1952), vol. 4, p. 295.

12. Finley Peter Dunne, *Observations by Mr. Dooley* (New York: R. H. Russell, 1902), pp. 83–84.

13. Charles Darnton, "Edward Harrigan Touches on the Irish Harp," unidentified clipping, Dec. 1908, Th. Col. L. C.

14. Adams, *Ireland and Irish Immigration*, p. 31.

15. Quoted in Glazer and Moynihan, *Beyond the Melting Pot*, p. 238.

16. Shannon, *American Irish*, p. 12.

17. Glazer and Moynihan, *Beyond the Melting Pot*, p. 246. Also see Maguire, *Irish in America*, pp. 282–85.

18. Glazer and Moynihan, *Beyond the Melting Pot*, p. 257.

19. Maguire, *Irish in America*, p. 285.

20. Arthur M. Schlesinger, Jr., *The Age of Jackson* (Boston: Little, Brown, 1945), p. 408. On Irish in politics, see *On the Town*, by Michael and Ariane Batterberry; *The Democratic Experience*, by Boorstin; *American Irish*, by Shannon; *Beyond the Melting Pot*, by Glazer and Moynihan; *Memorial History of the City of New York*, by James Wilson (New York: New York History Co., 1892–1893), p. 541; *Boss Tweed*, by Dennis T. Lynch (New York: Boni & Liveright, 1927); *The Wild Seventies*, by Dennis T. Lynch (New York: D. Appleton-Century, 1941); *The Attitude of the New York Irish Toward State and National Affairs, 1842–1892*, by Florence F. Gibson (New York: Columbia University Press, 1951); *The American Irish and Their Influence on Irish Politics*, by Philip H. Bagenal (London: Kegan Paul, Trench & Co., 1882); *Foreign Influences in American Life, Essays and Critical Bibliographies*, edited by David F. Bowers (Princeton, N. J.: Princeton University Press, 1944).

21. Glazer and Moynihan, *Beyond the Melting Pot*, p. 223.

22. William H. Russell, *My Diary North and South* (New York: O. S. Felt, 1863). Quoted in Still, p. 195.

23. Jim Farley, "What I Believe," *Atlantic Monthly*, June 1959, p. 36.

24. Glazer and Moynihan, *Beyond the Melting Pot*, pp. 228, 264.

25. The Irish first attempted to join the society on April 24, 1817, when, two hundred strong, they marched on Tammany Hall to persuade the braves to nominate Thomas A. Emmet for Congress. In spite of the avalanche of bricks and chairs that supported their

petition, the Sachems denied their request and, as if to underline this rejection, passed a resolution denouncing foreigners and urging the public to buy only articles made in America by Americans.

Michael Walsh was the first Irish political leader to make a mark in New York City. In 1840 he organized his Spartan Band, a group of young Irishmen who followed him around as bodyguards and cheerleaders. One contemporary account said that Walsh was fond of whiskey and carousing, that his speeches were "slangy, raucous, and sarcastic" and, though drawled out, convulsed the audience with their wit and ridicule. In 1842 he founded a political weekly called *The Subterranean* which boasted that it was "Independent in Everything —Neutral in Nothing." In 1846 Walsh was nominated for the state assembly and in 1850 went to Congress, where he served until his death in 1859.

26. Shannon, *American Irish,* p. 67.
27. Ibid., p. 70.

Chapter 13

1. Details on theatre: *New York Times,* Aug. 5, 1881, p. 8; Aug. 30, 1881, p. 4; "An Account of the Different Theatres Managed by Harrigan and Hart in New York City, Illustrated with Playbills, Portraits and Scenes Collected and Arranged by Charles C. Moreau," New York, 1894 (Ms., Players).
2. *New York Herald,* July 12, 1891, Walsh Scrap.
3. Unidentified clipping, Hart Scrap.
4. Souvenir program, Th. Col. L. C.
5. *Spirit,* Sept. 3, 1881, p. 144.
6. Allen Churchill review of *Merry Partners,* in *Saturday Review,* July 30, 1955, p. 11.
7. Jan. 20, 1882. Quoted in A's Mems.
8. See *Recollections of an Old New Yorker* by Frederick Van Wyck (New York: Liveright, 1932), p. 53.
9. Harrigan said he got the idea for the astronomer one night in Chicago. "I was walking along one rainy night on my way to the theatre and I came across an old man with a big telescope standing at a street corner and patiently awaiting the arrival of customers who would pay him a dime for a peep through his spyglass. There was something so comical to me in the idea of the old man trying to sell a peep at the moon on a pouring wet night, when the sky was as black as ink, that I stopped and spoke to him." ("Edward Harrigan's Plays," *Boston Herald,* March 24, 1889, Harv. Th. Col.).
10. Unidentified clipping, Locke Scrap.
11. Annie's Ltrs.
12. Ibid.
13. Ibid.

14. From Nedda Harrigan; Annie's Ltrs.
15. Annie's Ltrs.
16. Details about life at Schroon, A's Mems.
17. Hamm, *Eminent Actors*, p. 99.
18. Annie's Ltrs.

Chapter 14

1. *The Critic*, Sept. 9, 1882, p. 246.
2. *Spirit*, Nov. 4, 1882, p. 404.
3. W's Tape.
4. *Spirit*, Dec. 2, 1882, p. 500.
5. *Spirit*, April 7, 1883, p. 264.
6. Boston program, Th. Col. L. C. On March 23, 1880, Harrigan wrote a Mr. Classman: "I don't allow anyone to play my pieces. I wrote the plays for myself, my company, and my theatre. I cannot conceive of anyone else doing them. They are not just plays but complete productions that have our own special stamp on them beginning to end." (H. Scrap.)
Reportedly, when Harrigan heard that Charles Hoyt, who had been invading Harrigan's territory with contemporary plays of the New York scene, wanted to engage Emma Pollock after she had made such a hit in Harrigan's *Reilly*, he said: "Tell Mr. Hoyt he's taken enough material out of my plays without taking my actresses too." (*New York Evening Sun*, Feb. 23, 1894.)
7. H. Scrap.
8. *New York Mirror*, Aug. 11, 1883, quoted in *Theatre U.S.A.*, by Bernard Hewitt (New York: McGraw-Hill, 1959), p. 246.
9. Odell, *Annals*, vol. 12, p. 300.
10. A family joke? Annie Harrigan's Madison Avenue house was in her name.
11. "American Playwrights on American Drama—Edward Harrigan Speaks," *Harper's Weekly*, Feb. 2, 1889, p. 98.
12. Nym Crinkle (Andrew Carpenter Wheeler, critic on the *New York World*), quoted in Rose ms., p. 55.
13. Quoted in Isaac Goldberg, "Harrigan, and Hart, and Braham," *American Mercury*, Feb. 1929, p. 209.

Chapter 15

1. Detailed accounts of fire: *New York Times*, Dec. 24, 1884, p. 1; *New York Herald*, Dec. 23, 1884, p. 1.
2. Fire engines with steam-operated pumps.
3. *New York Herald*, Dec. 23, 1884, p. 1.
4. Ibid.
5. *New York Times*, Dec. 24, 1884, p. 1.

6. *New York Herald*, Dec. 23, 1884, p. 1.

7. *New York Times*, Dec. 24, 1884. p. 1.

8. Judge Hilton did not construct a new theatre on the site. After clearing the rubble, he moved in some boothlike structures, placed them against the old church walls and renamed the place "Old London Street, a quaint representation of a picturesque past." It featured marionettes, midgets, giants, seals, and buskers. (Odell, *Annals,* vol. 13, p. 352.)

9. *New York Times*, Dec. 22, 1881, p. 6.

10. *New York Times*, March 3, 1885, p. 4.

11. *New York Times*, Jan. 6, 1885, p. 5.

12. *New York Times*, Jan. 24, 1885, p. 4.

13. *New York Times*, Jan. 22, 1885, p. 3.

14. *New York Times*, Jan. 6, 1885, p. 5.

15. *New York Times*, April 30, 1885, p. 2.

16. *New York Times*, May 5, 1885, p. 5.

17. *New York Times*, May 7, 1885, p. 3.

18. *New York Times*, May 10, 1885, p. 2.

19. Ibid.

20. *Are You Insured?* was a farce about two ambitious insurance agents, two husband-hungry spinsters, and two seedy actors who are stranded in the wilderness and dreaming of Union Square. George Braham, David's son, wrote the music, and Dan Collyer, who was to become Hart's replacement, was in the cast.

21. *New York Times*, May 10, 1885.

22. *Chicago Herald*, Jan. 17, 1887, Hart's Scrap.

23. *New York Times*, Aug. 7, 1887, p. 12.

24. A's Mems.

25. Ibid.

26. Unidentified clipping, Locke Scrap.

27. Details on home from Hart's Scrap.

28. Scrapbook, "Newspaper Tributes to the Memory of Edward Harrigan," Th. Col. L. C.

29. *New York Times*, May 5, 1885, p. 5.

Chapter 16

1. *The Theatre*, May 3, 1886, p. 193.

2. Unidentified clipping, March 11, 1887, Boston Public Library.

3. Details and quotations about Braham's composing from "Hunting Types in the Slums with Harrigan," *New York Herald*, July 12, 1891.

4. *New York Times*, Dec. 21, 1885, p. 5. Harrigan had once lent properties and costumes to the Seventh's Musical and Dramatic Association.

Harrigan's Seventh Regiment friends apparently missed *The O'Reagans*, but they did "let loose" at *McNooney's Visit* on Feb. 14, 1887.
Another group, the Brotherhood of Locomotive Engineers, bought out
the house for *The O'Reagans* one night in mid-October 1886.

5. *Spirit*, Feb. 20, 1886, p. 110.
6. Unidentified clipping, Harv. Th. Col.
7. For more on policy, see *Sucker's Progress: An Informal History
of Gambling in America from the Colonies to Canfield*, by Herbert
Asbury (New York: Dodd Mead and Co., 1938), chap. 6; *Dark Side
of New York*, by Lening, pp. 490–94; *The Nether Side of New
York*, by Edward Crapsey (New York: Sheldon, 1872), p. 107; *Lights
and Shadows*, by McCabe, p. 728; "The Rogues and Rogueries of New
York" (New York: Haney & Co., 1865), p. 12.
8. Rose ms.
9. *New York Times*, n.d., Hart Scrap.
10. *The Theatre*, Aug. 23, 1886, p. 518.
11. *The Theatre*, Dec. 20, 1886, p. 268.

Chapter 17

1. "Our Gallery of Players—Edward Harrigan," *Illustrated American*, Feb. 25, 1893, p. 242.
2. "Editor's Study," *Harper's*, July, 1886, pp. 315–17.
3. George Edgar Montgomery, "American Playwriters: III, Edward Harrigan," *The Theatre*, July 5, 1886, p. 397.
4. Ibid.
5. Richard Harding Davis, "Edward Harrigan and the East Side,"
Harper's Weekly, March 21, 1891, p. 210.
6. Unidentified clipping, H. Scrap.
7. "Edward Harrigan at Home," *New York World*, March 15,
1891.
8. *Harper's Weekly*, Feb. 2, 1889, p. 98.
9. Ibid.
10. *New York Morning Telegraph*, June 21, 1903, Locke Scrap.
11. "Echoes of the Week," March 5, 1891, H. Scrap.
12. "The Play's the Thing," unidentified clipping, Players.
13. *Harper's Weekly*, Feb. 2, 1889, p. 97.
14. Ibid.
15. Unidentified clipping, Harv. Th. Col.
16. Harrigan frequently made his point with a story about a
pathetic Southern Negro he had once encountered straddling a rail
fence, wearing a ragged straw hat, his old pants held up by a single
suspender that was about to break. When Harrigan asked what the
man was doing there, the Negro explained: "See dose woods away
over yandah. Well, sah, I walked fum way oer dah this mawning, and

252 / Notes and Sources

I'se been sitting hyah ev'y sence." He paused to let that much sink in, then continued: "See dat tootcyah out on de railroad. Over dah. I'se been waitin' all day to see whether day cyah was going dis way or whether it was agoin' dat way. Ken you tell me?" That Negro would have been lost in New York. ("Edward Harrigan at Home," *New York World*, March 15, 1891.)

17. Unidentified clipping, Locke Scrap.
18. Unidentified clipping, Players.
19. "Echoes of the Week," H. Scrap.
20. *New York Herald*, July 12, 1891. He was right. His handwriting in his later years is difficult to decipher.
21. *Harper's Weekly*, Feb. 2, 1889, p. 98; "The Play's the Thing," *New York Herald*, July 12, 1891.
22. "The Playwright's Art," unidentified clipping, Players.
23. Unidentified clipping, Dec. 13, 1891, Harv. Th. Col.
24. Unidentified clipping, Harv. Th. Col.
25. "The Eloquence of Rags," *New York World*, Nov. 18, 1888.
26. Unidentified clipping, Players.
27. Ibid.
28. Ibid.
29. Interview, *New York Herald*, March 25, 1888, Walsh Scrap.
30. "Harrigan and His Plays," *New York Times*, Sept. 29, 1887, p. 8.
31. *New York Times*, Feb. 24, 1888, p. 2.

Chapter 18

1. *New York Times*, Sept. 29, 1887, p. 8.
2. Unidentified clipping, Th. Col. Mus. City N.Y.
3. Harrigan was among the twenty-one original members of the Players Club along with Booth, Drew, and Jefferson. He attended the formal ceremonies on Jan. 12, 1889, when Edwin Booth bequested his Gramercy Park home to the Players. Harrigan valued his membership. Once in 1902 he sent in his delinquent dues of $40 requesting reinstatement, explaining that he had been "out to the coast when the notice came."
4. "Echoes of the Week," H. Scrap.
5. *The Theatre*, Dec., 1887, p. 443.
6. Unidentified clipping, H. Scrap.
7. The big blizzard, March 11–14, 1888. The happy run of *Pete* was marred by the death of Michael Bradley on March 28, after he had been playing for three weeks with a ruptured appendix. A replacement could easily be found for "Sunset Freckles," his part in *Pete*. No one could substitute for his rendering of Walsingham Mc-

Sweeney in the Mulligan plays; no one for him in the Harrigan family.

8. Hart Scrap.

9. *New York Times,* Sept. 12, 1887, p. 5.

10. *New York Herald,* Dec. 15, 1887, Walsh Scrap.

11. Unidentified clipping, Dec. 24, 1887, signed "The Giddy Gusher," Harv. Th. Col. Also see "The Giddy Gusher Papers," by Harrison Gray Fiske, "American Fiction Series," vol. 3, reel F 12, no. 1877, Chicago Public Library.

12. *New York Times,* Feb. 19, 1888, p. 9.

13. *New York Times,* March 9, 1888, p. 9.

14. Brutus .... William H. Crane
Marc Antony .... Nat C. Goodwin
Flavius .... Francis Wilson
Casca .... Frank Mayo
Metellus .... Steele MacKaye

15. *New York Herald,* n.d., Hart Scrap.

16. *New York Times,* June 25, 1888.

17. Unidentified clipping, "The Giddy Gusher," Dec. 1, 1888, Hart Scrap.

18. At her funeral on Feb. 5, 1889, her friend Robert Ingersoll delivered the memorial tribute to the "Queen of Bohemia," as he called her. (Hart Scrap.)

19. *The Theatre,* April 10, 1889, p. 257.

20. *New York Dramatic Mirror,* March 22, 1890, p. 7.

21. *New York Times,* May 27, 1890, p. 8.

22. *New York Times,* June 5, 1890, p. 8; Nov. 11, 1890, p. 8.

23. "Backstage with James Lee," *Worcester Gazette,* Aug. 25, 1955, N. H's Col.

24. *Worcester Gazette,* Nov. 6, 1891; *New York Times,* Nov. 7, 1891, p. 5.

25. No club was formed to honor Hart's memory, though he occasionally shared attention at Harrigan Club meetings. At one gathering Victor Moore told the deathbed story of his father, who looked up one day and saw a new doctor at his side. He stared at him for a moment, told him, "I know you're a bum doctor, but you look like Tony Hart," and then settled back with a trusting smile on his face. (*New York Times,* March 27, 1914, p. 11.)

26. *New York Times,* Aug. 21, 1888, p. 8.

27. *New York Times,* May 5, 1888, p. 2.

28. *New York Times,* Sept. 4, 1888, p. 5.

29. Nedda Harrigan was to attend this Catholic girls' school. The school, which is still operating, occupies the site of Edwin Forrest's former Hudson River estate. Forrest's Fonthill Castle has been transformed into the school's library.

30. A's Mems. Harrigan and his children were being tutored in French by Prof. Edward Le Maire. According to Adelaide, he wore pince-nez, a rose in his buttonhole, and a large silk handkerchief that smelled of perfume.

31. *New York Times,* Oct. 27, 1888, p. 4.

32. The pitcher now rests on the coffee table in the Logans' living room.

33. "A Letter from 'Frisco, Aug. 12, '89," *The Theatre,* Aug. 24, 1889, p. 433.

34. Scrapbook of Eddie Harrigan, Jr., Th. Col. L. C.

35. Unidentified clipping, Players.

36. Unidentified clipping, Aug. 27, 1889, Harv. Th. Col.

Chapter 19

1. Interview with Hanley, *New York Times,* Feb. 23, 1889, p. 5; also W's Tape.

2. *New York Times,* Feb. 23, 1889, p. 5.

3. *The Theatre,* April 10, 1889, p. 257.

4. John Golden and Viola Brothers Shore, *Stage-Struck John Golden* (New York: Samuel French, 1930), pp 9–11.

5. *New York Times,* Dec. 5, 1890, p. 3; *The Theatre,* Nov. 10, 1890, p. 91.

6. *New York Times,* Dec. 19, 1890, p. 8.

7. *Spirit,* Dec. 3, 1892. Harrigan acknowledged only one superstition. He knew that the letter "M" was his lucky letter.

8. Unidentified clipping, H. Scrap. Also see *New York Times,* Dec. 30, 1890, p. 5.

9. *Theatre Magazine,* March 7, 1891, p. 31.

10. Since the first Delmonico brothers had arrived from Switzerland in 1827 and opened their restaurant at 17 William Street, the name Delmonico had become synonymous with elegant dining. Gastronomical and social status were assured whether one visited their establishment on Broad Street, at the Irving House on Broadway, at Fourteenth and Fifth Avenue, or on Twenty-Sixth Street. (*Spirit,* April 7, 1877.)

11. Ward McAllister, *Society as I Have Found It* (New York: Cassell Publishing Co., 1890), p. 118. Two years earlier Charley Jay Taylor's picture book *In the 400 and Out* (New York: Keppler & Schwarzmann, 1889) had shown society at play in Newport and in New York.

12. W's Tape.

13. Not unlike the crowds at *Hair* who came to view the "Hippies" without danger of contamination.

14. *The Theatre*, Jan. 3, 1891, p. 207.
15. Shannon, *American Irish*, p. 143.
16. *New York Morning Telegraph*, June 21, 1903, Locke Scrap; and W's Tape.
17. W's Tape.
18. Unidenified clipping, Dec. 13, 1891, Harv. Th. Col.
19. *New York Herald*, July 12, 1891.
20. Ibid.
21. *New York Dramatic Mirror*, March 7, 1891.
22. Ibid.
23. A's Mems.
24. Such barge collisions apparently were not uncommon. In 1885, *Valentine's Manual* (vol. 10, p. 130) reported that two rival pleasure-loving societies—four hundred of the roughest characters found in the city—set off from Clinton Street on the East River (a block from where Harrigan was born) for an excursion up the North River to Spring Hill Grove. Off Spuyten Duyvil, a "slight man with light hair and mustache and in the uniform of the Eleventh Regiment had too much beer" and jumped overboard. In battling over the rescue the barges rammed together, the crews struggled with fists and knives, while the two bands blared at each other trying to subdue the combatants with music.
25. *New York Evening Sun*, Aug. 28, 1893.
26. Ibid.
27. *Spirit*, Sept. 9, 1893. Also see *Memorial History of New York*, by Wilson, p. 536.

Chapter 20

1. A's Mems.
2. Ibid.
3. Ibid; Annie's Ltrs.
4. A's Mems; and "Edward Harrigan at Home," *New York World*, March 15, 1891, Walsh Scrap.
5. *New York World*, March 15, 1891, Walsh Scrap.
6. Annie's Ltrs.
7. *New York Times*, Dec. 11, 1894, p. 5.
8. Unidentified clipping, Th. Col. L. C.
9. See *Hetty Green: A Woman Who Loved Money*, by Boyden Sparkes (New York: Doubleday, Doran and Co., 1930); and "The Witch of Wall Street," in *Twelve Daughters of Democracy*, by E. M. Sickles (New York: Viking Press, 1941), pp. 33–50.
10. A's Mems; also, Nedda Harrigan.
11. Unidentified clipping, Th. Col. Mus. City N. Y.
12. A's Mems.

13. Ibid. The house is still standing.

14. Dale, "A Chat with Harrigan."

15. None of these plays is extant. A few years ago lack of space forced the Library of Congress to destroy all play manuscripts antedating 1901! They simply retained the title pages.

16. Unidentified clipping, Locke Scrap.

17. *New York Dramatic Mirror*, Aug. 15, 1896, Walsh Scrap.

18. Dale, "A Chat with Harrigan."

19. In this manuscript, Harrigan's handwriting is almost impossible to decipher.

20. Rose ms.

21. *New York Dramatic Mirror*, Oct. 24, 1896.

22. *New York Dramatic Mirror*, April 24, 1897, p. 17.

23. Program, Walsh Scrap.

24. *New York Dramatic Mirror*, May 15, 1897.

25. *New York Dramatic Mirror*, Oct. 2, 1897.

26. Victoria, B. C., May 2, 1898, Annie's Ltrs.

27. Hamm, *Eminent Actors*, p. 99.

28. Philip Harrigan's daughter, Mrs. Sheedy Stuart, told me this story.

29. Program, Walsh Scrap.

30. Edward Harrigan, *The Mulligans* (New York: G. W. Dillingham & Co., 1901). Copies in Library of Congress and Yale University Library.

31. *New York Times*, Dec. 3, 1901, p. 9.

32. *San Francisco Examiner*, April 29, 1902.

33. Like George M. Cohan appearing in Eugene O'Neill's *Ah Wilderness* in the 1930s.

34. *The Theatre*, Feb., 1903, p. 30.

35. Unidentified clipping, Locke Scrap; *Newark Telegraph*, Jan. 18, 1903.

36. S. N. Behrman, *Portrait of Max* (New York: Random House, 1960), p. 59.

37. H. Scrap.

38. *Twain's Travels with Mr. Brown*, p. 226.

39. *New York Sun*, May 3, 1903.

40. Rose ms., p. 153.

41. Alan Dale, *"Under Cover* Review," *New York American*, Sept. 18, 1903.

42. Unidentified clipping, Boston Public Library.

43. Nedda and Josh Logan told me this story.

44. *New York Times*, Sept. 15, 1903.

45. Ibid.

46. Unidentified clipping, Dec. 5, 1903, Th. Col. L. C.

Chapter 21

1. Harrigan has one of his characters say, "Lincoln never saw the city until he was president."

2. Details from *New York Dramatic Mirror*, April 22, 1905, p. 13.

3. W's Tape.

4. Ibid.

5. Ibid.

6. W's Scrap.

7. Ibid.

8. W's Tape.

9. Ibid.

10. Ibid.

11. Ibid.

12. Letter, Samuel Mayer, Monadnock Building, Chicago, to Townsend Walsh, n.d., Walsh Scrap.

13. Unidentified clipping, Locke Scrap.

14. *New York Times,* June 6, 1911, p. 9.

15. A pseudonym for the English novelist Mrs. R. Golding Bright.

16. *Philadelphia Enquirer,* Dec. 15, 1908.

17. Harrigan repeatedly bemoaned the short memory of theatregoers. At one point in *The Lord Mayor of Dublin,* a lady declares that she can't remember that Barney Brogan once played Uncle Tom, whereupon Barney turns to the audience with a depressing aside: "That's what they all say."

18. Frank C. Drake, interview with Harrigan, *New York World,* n.d., H. Scrap.

19. Charles Darnton, "Edward Harrigan Touches on the Irish Harp," unidentified clipping, Dec., 1908, Th. Col. L. C.

20. Ibid.

21. *New York Morning Telegraph,* n.d.,, H. Scrap.

22. Letters, Nov. 4, 1954, N. H's Col.

23. *New York Times,* Oct. 18, 1940, p. 24.
During World War II, Nedda Harrigan was one of the six actors in the first Camp Show troupe sent to military installations in Europe to perform an abbreviated version of *Personal Appearance.* After she married the actor Walter Connolly in 1923, she spent a good share of her time in Hollywood and for a brief period operated an antique shop on Beverly Drive. Connolly died in 1940, and she then returned to the New York stage. Only once did Nedda try to emulate her father as a writer. While she was in Hollywood she wrote a bit of verse on old-fashioned names:

> The good old-fashioned names of Ann and Jane
> Have gone by the wayside as much too plain.
> Neither Pearl nor Ruby, Opal or Mae
> Do we see in the pictures of today,
> But Isa and Osa, Olympe and Iona,
> Ilka, Tala, Una, and Ona
> Lya, and Greer, Ara and Hedda.
> But they can't top me, my name is Nedda.
>
>   (Unidentified clipping, Th. Col. L. C.)

24. Unidentified clipping, H. Scrap.
25. *New York Times,* June 6, 1911, p. 9.
26. *New York Mail,* June 9, 1911.
27. Scrapbook, "Newspaper Tributes to the Memory of Edward Harrigan," Th. Col. L. C.
28. *Providence Journal,* June 9, 1911.
29. *New York Times,* June 11, 1911, p. 3.
30. *New York Times,* June 6, 1911, p. 9.
31. A's Mems.

Postscript

1. Nolan wrote her a comforting letter from Princeton where he was about to be graduated: "I hope the theatre turns out all right but anyway, Mom, don't be all cast down. You still have old Schroon and 249 which will give you a little income and don't forget the plays will bring in a few thousand that will help a lot." (N. H's Col.)

2. Details about leases and sale of the Garrick: interviews with Nedda Harrigan; W's Scrap; Annie Harrigan's account book (N. H's Col.); Ann Connolly's notes.

Harrigan's Plays and Sketches

Date indicates first performance, or copyright date if not produced.

The Blue Ribbon. 1894.

Christmas Joys and Sorrows. Jan. 1, 1877.

Cordelia's Aspirations. Nov. 5, 1883.

Dan's Tribulations. Apr. 7, 1884.
    (Also called *Tribulations.*)

The Donovans. May 31, 1875.
    (May have collaborated on this.)

The Doyle Brothers. May 17, 1875.
    (With John Woodard.)

Eureka. 1874.
    (With John Woodard.)

The Grip. Nov. 30, 1885.

Iascaire. Nov. 20, 1876.

In the North Woods. 1907.

Investigation. Sept. 1, 1884.

The Last of the Hogans. Dec. 22, 1891.

The Leather Patch. Feb. 15, 1886.

The Lord Mayor of Dublin. 1908.
    (Also called *Barney Brogan; The Irish Cousin; The Lord Mayor
    of London.*)

The Lorgaire. Feb. 18, 1878.

Low Life. 1897.

McAllister's Legacy. Jan. 5, 1885.

McNooney's Visit. Jan. 31, 1887.
    (Also called *4-11-44.*)

McSorley's Inflation. Nov. 27, 1882.
    (Also called *Inflation; McSorley's.*)

The Major. Aug. 29, 1881.

Marty Malone. Aug. 31, 1896.

Mordecai Lyons. Oct. 26, 1882.

The Muddy Day. Apr. 2, 1883.
    (Also called *Bunch o' Berries.*)

The Mulligan Guard Ball. Jan. 13, 1879.

The Mulligan Guard Chowder. Aug. 11, 1879.
The Mulligan Guard Nominee. Nov. 22, 1880.
The Mulligan Guard Picnic. Sept. 23, 1878.
The Mulligan Guards' Christmas. Nov. 17, 1879.
The Mulligan Guards' Surprise. Feb. 16, 1880.
The Mulligans' Silver Wedding. Feb. 21, 1881.
My Son Dan. 1895.
Notoriety. Dec. 10, 1894.
Old Lavender. Sept. 3, 1877.
　　　(Originally *Old Lavender Water, or, Around the Docks.*)
An Old New Yorker. 1899.
The O'Reagans. Oct. 11, 1886.
Our Cranks. 1881.
　　　(With G. L. Stout.)
Pete. Nov. 20, 1887.
Reilly and the Four Hundred. Dec. 29, 1890.
Squatter Sovereignty. Jan. 9, 1882.
Under Cover. Sept. 14, 1903.
Waddy Googan. Sept. 3, 1888.
The Woollen Stocking. Oct. 9, 1893.

Principal Sketches

The Absent-minded Couple. Sept. 22, 1873.
April Fool. Apr. 12, 1875.
Are You Insured? May 11, 1885.
Bar Ber Ous. Nov. 6, 1876.
The Big and Little of It. Apr. (?), 1871.
The Blue and the Grey. Aug. 16, 1875.
The Bold Hibernian Boys. Oct. 23, 1876.
The Bradys. Dec. 25, 1876.
Callahan, the Detective. Jan. 15, 1877.
A Celebrated Hard Case. Mar. 18, 1878.
Coloured Baby Show. Feb. 11, 1878.
The Day We Went West. Apr. (?), 1871.
Down Broadway. Apr. 19, 1875.
Down in Dixie. Aug. 28, 1876.
An Editor's Troubles. Dec. 8, 1873.
Fee-Gee. Jan. (?), 1875.
The German Emigrants. May (?), 1871.
The Grand Duke's Opera House. Feb. 5, 1877.
The Great In-Toe-Natural Walking Match. Mar. 25, 1879.
Innocence at Home. Apr. (?), 1875.
Ireland vs. Italy. Dec. 16, 1872.
　　　(Also called *Who Owns the Line?*)

The Irish Emigrant. May (?), 1871.
The Italian Junkman. Jan. 28, 1878.
The Lady of Lions. Jan. 11, 1878.
The Little Fraud. Apr. (?), 1871
Love vs. Insurance. Jan. 21, 1878.
Malone's Night Off. Oct. 9, 1876.
Matrimonial Ads. Feb. 19, 1877.
The Mixed Couple. Feb. 17, 1873.
The Mulcahey Twins. Apr. (?), 1870.
Muldoon, the Solid Man. Jan. (?), 1874.
The Mulligan Guard. May (?), 1873.
My Wife's Mother. Oct. (?), 1878.
No Irish Wanted Here. Apr. (?), 1875.
O'Brien, Counselor-at-Law. Jan. 6, 1879.
Our Irish Cousins. May 7, 1877.
Our Law Makers. Oct. 28, 1878.
The Pillsbury Muddle. Dec. 17, 1877.
The Porter's Troubles. Apr. 12, 1875.
    (Also called *Fifth Avenue Hotel.*)
The Raffle for Mrs. Hennessey's Clock. Nov. 23, 1874.
The Regular Army, O! Oct. 19, 1874.
The Rising Star. Oct. 22, 1877.
St. Patrick's Day Parade. Sept. 14, 1874.
    (Also called *The Day We Celebrate.*)
Sergeant Hickey. May (?), 1897.
Shamus O'Brien at Home. 1872.
Sing Sing. Dec. 16, 1872.
The Skidmores. Dec. 14, 1874.
Slavery Days. Mar. 22, 1875.
S.O.T. (Sons of Temperance). Aug. 28, 1876.
Sullivan's Christmas. Dec. 24, 1877.
The Telephone. Mar. 19, 1877.
A Terrible Example. Mar. 9, 1874.
Walkin' for Dat Cake. Oct. 2, 1876.
Who Stole the Monkey? Oct. 5, 1874.
You 'Spute Me. Apr. (?), 1871.

Bibliography

Books, Articles, and Unpublished Materials Relating to Harrigan and His Career

Alger, Horatio. "The Grand Duke's Opera House." Chapter 2, *Julius the Street Boy*. New York: A. L. Burt, 1904.

Baer, Warren. *The Duke of Sacramento*. San Francisco: Grabhorn Press, 1934. Includes "Sketch of Early San Francisco Stage by Jane Bissell."

Burns, W. T. "The Plays of Edward Green Harrigan: The Theatre of Intercultural Communication." Unpublished Ph.D. dissertation, Pennsylvania State University, 1969.

Chapman, John, and Sherwood, Garrison P., eds. *Best Plays 1894—1899*. New York: Dodd Mead & Co., 1955.

Cohan, George M. *Twenty Years on Broadway*. New York: Harper & Bros., 1924.

Dale, Alan. "A Chat with Harrigan." *New York American and Journal,* Jan. 25, 1903, Walsh Scrap.

Darnton, Charles. "Edward Harrigan Touches on the Irish Harp." Unidentified clipping., Dec. 1908, Th. Col. L. C.

Davis, Richard H. "Edward Harrigan and the East Side." *Harper's Weekly*, March 21, 1891, pp. 204–10.

"Early San Francisco Theatres." *Collector's Guide*, Dec. 1940, pp. 3–6.

"The Eloquence of Rags." *New York World*, Nov. 18, 1888, Harv. Th. Col.

Franklin, Eleanor. "How Edward Harrigan Finds His Types in Real Life." *Leslie's Weekly*, Oct. 22, 1903, Walsh Scrap.

Freedley, George. "Broadway Playhouses." Manuscript, Th. Col. L. C.

Glover, Lyman B. *The Story of a Theatre*. N. Pub., n.d.

Goldberg, Isaac. "Harrigan, and Hart, and Braham." *American Mercury,* Feb. 1929, pp. 201–10.

Goodwin, Nat. *Nat Goodwin's Book*. Boston: R. G. Badger, 1914.

Hamm, Margherita A. *Eminent Actors in Their Homes*. New York: J. Pott & Co., 1902.

Harrigan, Edward. "Holding the Mirror up to Nature." *Pearson's Magazine*, Nov. 1903, pp. 2–6.

Harrigan, Edward. "How I Became an Actor and Author." *San Francisco Call*, April 17, 1898. Th. Col. Mus. City N. Y.

Harrigan, Edward. *The Mulligans*. New York: G. W. Dillingham & Co., 1901.

Harrigan, Edward. "The Play's the Thing." Unidentified clipping. Harv. Th. Col.

Harrigan, Edward; Daly, Augustin; Howard, Bronson; and Gillette, William. "American Playwrights on the American Drama." *Harper's Weekly*, Feb. 2, 1889, pp. 97–99.

"Edward Harrigan." *The Biographer Illustrated*, May 1883, pp. 62–64.

"Edward Harrigan at Home." *New York World*, March 15, 1891. Walsh Scrap.

"Harrigan and His Plays—New Departure." *New York Times*, Sept. 29, 1887, p. 8.

"Harrigan's New Theatre." *The Theatre*, Nov. 10, 1890, p. 91.

Howells, W. D. "Edward Harrigan's Comedies." *Harper's Monthly*, July 1886, p. 132.

"Hunting Types in the Slums with Harrigan." *New York Herald*, July 12, 1891. Walsh Scrap.

Illustrated History of the Mulligan Guards. New York: Collin and Small, 1874.

Jones, Idwal. "Bella Union." *Westways*, Sept. 1940, pp. 16–17.

Kahn, E. J. *The Merry Partners*. New York: Random House, 1955.

Ker, Minnette A. "The History of the Theatre in California in the Nineteenth Century." Master's thesis, University of California, Berkeley, 1924.

Leavitt, Michael B. *Fifty Years in Theatrical Management*. New York: Broadway Publishing Co., 1912.

Leslie, Amy (Lillie Brown Buck). *Some Players*. New York: H. S. Stone & Co., 1899.

Madison, James. "Some Shadows of the San Francisco Stage." *California Historical Society Quarterly*, 1925, pp. 59–63.

Mantle, Burns, and Sherwood, Garrison P., eds. *Best Plays 1899–1909*. New York: Dodd Mead & Co., 1944.

Mark Twain's Travels with Mr. Brown, Being Heretofore Uncollected Sketches Written by Mark Twain. New York: Russell & Russell, 1940.

Marshall, Thomas F. "Charles W. Witham: Scenic Artist to the Nineteenth Century American Stage." *Anatomy of an Illusion: Studies in Nineteenth-century Scenic Design*. Lectures of the Fourth International Congress on Theatre Research, Amsterdam, 1965. Amsterdam: Scheltema & Halkema, 1969.

McCabe, John H. *Theatrical Journals.* Vol. 4, *1849–1882.* San Francisco: Sutro Library (California State Library). Typewritten manuscript deposited in 1917.

McVicker, J. H. *Theatre: Its Early Days in Chicago.* Chicago Historical Society Publications. Chicago: Chicago Historical Society, 1884.

Montgomery, G. E. "American Playwriters: III, Edward Harrigan." *The Theatre,* July 5, 1886, pp. 397–98.

Moody, Richard, ed. *Dramas from the American Theatre, 1762–1909.* Cleveland and New York: World Publishing Co., 1966; Boston and New York: Houghton Mifflin Co., 1968.

Moreau, Charles C. "Harrigan and Hart: An Account of the Different Theatres Managed by Them in New York City, Illustrated with Playbills, Portraits, and Scenes." New York: privately printed, 1894. Players Club Library.

Morehouse, Ward. *George M. Cohan.* New York: Lippincott Co., 1943.

Moses, Montrose J. "Edward Harrigan." *Theatre Arts Monthly,* March 1926, pp. 176–88.

Moses, Montrose J. "Harrigan, American." *Theatre Guild Magazine,* June 1930, pp. 24–29, 64.

"Newspaper Tributes to the Memory of Edward Harrigan." Scrapbook, Th. Col. L. C.

Odell, G. C. D. *Annals of the New York Stage.* Vols. 13, 14, 15. New York: Columbia University Press, 1927–49.

"Our Gallery of Players—Edward Harrigan." *Illustrated American,* Feb. 25, 1893, p. 242.

"The Playwright's Art, Harrigan's Views Concerning the Making of Dramatic Pieces." Unidentified clipping, Players Club Library.

Quinn, Arthur Hobson. "The Perennial Humor of the American Stage." *Yale Review,* 16 (April 1927), 553–66.

Rose, Sidney. "Edward Harrigan and His Plays." Manuscript, Th. Col. L. C. (Gift from Barrett H. Clark, June 24, 1940.)

San Francisco Theatre Research. Vols. 13, 14, 15, 17. Works Progress Administration, Project 10677.

Sherman, Robert L. *Chicago Stage.* Chicago: privately printed, 1947.

Simon, Louis M. *A History of the Actors' Fund of America.* New York: Theatre Arts Books, 1972.

Spillane, Daniel. "Looking Backward." *The Theatre,* July 13, 1889, p. 362.

"A Talk with E. Harrigan about the Good Old Days." *New York Daily News,* Dec. 4, 1904. Walsh Scrap.

Ten Eyck, Edward E. *The Mulligan's Boarding-House.* New York: Frank Tousey, 1883.

Ten Little Mulligan Guards. New York: McLoughlin Bros., 1874.

"Tony Hart and His Career." *New York Herald,* n.d. Hart Scrapbook.

Vrooman, Gertrude S. "A Brief Survey of the Musical History of Western Nevada." Nevada Historical Society Papers, 1921–22.

Wingate, Charles E., and McKay, F. E., eds. *Famous American Actors of Today.* New York: T. Y. Crowell & Co., 1896.

Zellers, Parker. *Tony Pastor, Dean of the Vaudeville Stage.* Ypsilanti: Eastern Michigan University Press, 1971.

Selected Books and Articles on Social and Political History

Adams, William Forbes. *Ireland and Irish Emigration to the New World from 1815 to the Famine.* New Haven, Conn.: Yale University Press, 1932.

Appleton's Dictionary of New York. New York: D. Appleton & Co., 1879.

Asbury, Herbert. *The Gangs of New York.* New York: A. A. Knopf, 1928.

Asbury, Herbert. *Sucker's Progress: An Informal History of Gambling in America from the Colonies to Canfield.* New York: Dodd Mead & Co., 1938.

Bagenal, Philip H. *The American Irish and Their Influence on Irish Politics.* London: Kegan Paul, Trench and Co., 1882.

Barnard, William F. *Forty Years at the Five Points.* New York: Five Points House of Industry, 1893.

Batterberry, Michael, and Batterberry, Ariane. *On the Town in New York.* New York: Charles Scribner's Sons, 1973.

Bode, Carl. *The Anatomy of American Popular Culture.* Berkeley and Los Angeles: University of California Press, 1959.

Boorstin, Daniel. *The Americans: The Democratic Experience.* New York: Random House, 1973.

Botkin, Benjamin A. *New York City Folklore.* New York: Random House, 1956.

Bowers, David F., ed. *Foreign Influences in American Life.* Princeton, N. J.: Princeton University Press, 1944.

Brown, Henry Collins. *Old New York, Yesterday and Today.* New York: Privately printed for Valentine's Manual, 1922.

Brown, Thomas N. *Irish-American Nationalism, 1870–1890.* New York: Lippincott, 1968.

Buel, J. W. *Metropolitan Life Unveiled, or, the Mysteries and Miseries of America's Great Cities.* St. Louis: Historical Publishing Co., 1882.

Carruth, Gordon, ed. *The Encyclopedia of American Facts and Dates.* New York: T. Y. Crowell & Co., 1966.

Commager, Henry Steele, ed. *Immigration and American History.* Minneapolis: University of Minnesota Press, 1961.

"Corlear's Hook District." *East Side Chamber News,* May 1935.

Costello, Augustine F. *Our Firemen*. New York: A. E. Costello, 1887.

Crapsey, Edward. *The Nether Side of New York*. New York: Sheldon, 1872.

Crilly, Daniel. "Irish Landlordism." *Irish American Almanac for 1888*. (Library of Congress.)

Crimmins, John D. *Irish-American Historical Miscellany*. New York: Published by the author, 1905.

Crimmins, John D. *St. Patrick's Day: Its Celebration in New York and Other American Places, 1737–1845*. New York: Published by the author, 1902.

Ernst, Robert. *Immigrant Life in New York City, 1825–1863*. New York: King's Crown Press, 1949.

Gerard, James, "The Impress of Nationalism upon the City of New York." A paper read before the New York Historical Society, May 1883.

Gibson, Florence E. *The Attitude of the New York Irish towards State and National Affairs, 1848–1892*. New York: Columbia University Press, 1951.

Glazer, Nathan, and Moynihan, Daniel Patrick. *Beyond the Melting Pot*. Cambridge, Mass.: M.I.T. Press, 1963.

Handlin, Oscar. *Immigration as a Factor in American History*. Englewood Cliffs, N. J.: Prentice-Hall, 1959.

Handlin, Oscar. *The Uprooted*. Boston: Little, Brown, 1951.

Hansen, Marcus Lee. *The Atlantic Migration, 1607–1939*. Cambridge, Mass.: Harvard University Press, 1940.

Hansen, Marcus Lee. *The Immigrant in American History*. Cambridge, Mass.: Harvard University Press, 1940.

Harlow, Alvin F. *Old Bowery Days*. New York: D. Appleton & Co., 1931.

Harris, Charles T. *Memories of Manhattan in the Sixties and Seventies*. New York: The Derrydale Press, 1928.

Hemstreet, Charles. *Nooks and Corners of Old New York*. New York: Charles Scribner's Sons, 1899.

Jacobson, Pauline. *City of the Golden Fifties*. Berkeley and Los Angeles: University of California Press, 1941.

Jenkins, Stephen. *The Greatest Street in the World*. New York: G. P. Putnam's Sons, 1911.

Jones, Howard M. *The Age of Energy*. New York: Viking Press, 1970.

Jones, Howard M. *Ideas in America*. Cambridge, Mass.: Harvard University Press, 1944.

Jones, Howard M. *Violence and Reason*. New York: Atheneum, 1969.

Josephson, Matthew, and Josephson, Hannah. *Al Smith, Hero of the Cities*. Boston: Houghton Mifflin, 1969.

Kilroe, E. P. *Saint Tammany and the Origin of the Society of Tammany*. New York: Columbia University Press, 1913.

Klein, Alexander, ed. *The Empire City*. New York: Rinehart, 1955.

Lening, Gustav. *The Dark Side of New York Life and Its Criminal Classes from Fifth Avenue Down to the Five Points.* New York: F. Gerhard, 1873.

Leonard, John W. *History of the City of New York, 1609–1909.* New York: The Journal of Commerce and Commercial Bulletin, 1909.

Lossing, Benson J. *History of New York City.* New York: G. E. Perine, 1884.

Ludlow, W. S. "Old Target Companies and Firemen." *Valentine's Manual,* 1920, pp. 180–82.

Lynch, Dennis T. *Boss Tweed.* New York: Boni & Liveright, 1927.

Lynch, Dennis T. *The Wild Seventies.* New York: D. Appleton-Century, 1941.

McAllister, Ward. *Society as I Have Found It.* New York: Cassell Publishing Co., 1890.

McCabe, James D. *Lights and Shadows of New York Life.* Philadelphia: National Publishing Co., 1872.

McKenna, William J. "They All Loved a Parade." *Jersey Journal,* March 18, 1942.

Maguire, John Francis. *The Irish in America.* New York: D. & J. Sadlier, 1867; reprint: New York: Arno Press, 1969.

Marcuse, Maxwell F. *This Was New York.* New York: LIM Press, 1969.

Mark Twain's Travels with Mr. Brown, Being Heretofore Uncollected Sketches Written by Mark Twain. New York: Russell & Russell, 1940.

Morris, Lloyd. *Incredible New York.* New York: Random House, 1951.

Morrison, John H. *History of New York Shipyards.* New York: Smetz & Co., 1909.

Nevins, Allan, and Thomas, Milton H., eds. *The Diary of George Templeton Strong.* Vol. 4, *1865–75.* New York: Macmillan Co., 1952.

Novotny, Ann. *Strangers at the Door: Ellis Island, Castle Garden, and the Great Migration to America.* Riverside, Conn.: Chatham Press, 1971.

O'Connor, Richard. *The First Hurrah: A Biography of Alfred E. Smith.* New York: Putnam, 1970.

Phillips, Catherine. *Portsmouth Plaza.* San Francisco: J. H. Nash, 1932.

Riis, Jacob. *The Battle with the Slums.* New York: Macmillan, 1902.

Riis, Jacob. *The Children of the Poor.* New York: Charles Scribner's Sons, 1892.

Riis, Jacob. *Children of the Tenements.* New York: Macmillan, 1903.

Riis, Jacob. *How the Other Half Lives.* New York: Charles Scribner's Sons, 1890.

Riis, Jacob, *Making of an American.* New York: Macmillan, 1901.
Riis, Jacob. *Out of Mulberry Street.* New York: The Century Co., 1898.
The Rogues and Rogueries of New York. New York: Haney & Co., 1865.
Russell, William H. *My Diary North and South.* New York: O. S. Felt, 1863.
Schlesinger, Arthur M. *The Rise of the City, 1878–1898.* New York: Macmillan, 1933.
Schlesinger, Arthur M., Jr. *The Age of Jackson.* Boston: Little, Brown, 1945.
Schrier, Arnold. *Ireland and the American Emigration, 1850–1900.* New York: Russell & Russell, 1958.
Severn, Bill. *Ellis Island: The Immigrant Years.* New York: J. Messner, 1971.
Shannon, William V. *The Amercan Irish.* New York: Macmillan, 1966.
Smith, Alfred E. *Up to Now: An Autobiography.* New York: Viking Press, 1929.
Smith, Matthew Hale. *Sunshine and Shadow in New York.* Hartford, Conn.: J. B. Burr, 1869.
Smith, William Carlson. *Americans in the Making.* New York: Arno Press, 1970.
Solomon, Barbara Miller. *Ancestors and Immigrants.* Cambridge, Mass.: Harvard University Press, 1956.
Stephenson, George. *A History of American Immigrations, 1820–1924.* New York: Ginn & Co., 1926.
Still, Byard. *Mirror for Gotham.* New York: New York University Press, 1956.
Stokes, I. N. Phelps. *The Iconography of Manhattan Island.* New York: R. H. Dodd, 1915–28.
Sullivan, James W. *Tenement Tales of New York.* New York: H. Holt & Co., 1895.
Van Karlstein, Henrich Oscar. *Gotham and the Gothamites.* Chicago: Laird and Lee, 1886.
Van Pelt, Daniel. *Leslie's History of Greater New York.* New York: Arkell Publishing Co., 1898.
Van Wyck, Frederick. *Recollections of an Old New Yorker.* New York: Liveright, 1932.
Wilson, James Grant. *The Memorial History of the City of New York.* New York: New York History Co., 1893.
Wittke, Carl. *In the Trek of the Immigrants.* Rock Island, Ill.: Augustana Book Concern, 1964.
Wittke, Carl. *The Irish in America.* Baton Rouge: Louisiana State University Press, 1956.

Wittke, Carl. *We Who Built America: The Saga of the Immigrant.* New York: Prentice-Hall, 1939.

Wortley, Emmeline Stuart, Lady. *Travels in the United States During 1849 and 1850.* New York: Harper & Bros., 1851.

Index

First ward, near the dock, Where Ireland's rep-re-sent-ed By the Ba-bies on ou[r]
noise would stop a clock! Oh there's no perambula-to-ry With the Ba-bies on ou[r]
sol-id as a rock, The en-vy of the neighbors'boys A-liv-ing off ou[r]

Block. There's the Pha-lens and the Wha-lens From the sweet Dun-och-a-dee, They ar[e]
Block. There's the Clea-rys and the Lea-rys From the sweet Black wa-ter side, They ar[e]
Block. There's the Bran-nons and the Gan-nons, Far-down and Connaught men, Quite

sit-ting on the rail-ings With their chil-dren on their knee, All gos-sip-ing an[d]
lay-ing on the Bat-t'ry And they're gaz-ing at the tide; All roy-al blood an[d]
ea-sy with the shov-el And so han-dy with the pen; All neigh-bor-ly an[d]

talk-ing With their neigh-bors in a flock, Singing " Lit-tle Sal-ly Waters," With
no-ble, All of Dan O'Con-nell's stock, Singing " Grav-el, Green-y Grav-el," With
friend-ly, With re-la-tions by the flock, Singing " Lit-tle Sal-ly Waters," With